Jenny Coogan (Ed.)

PRACTICING DANCE:
A SOMATIC ORIENTATION

LOGOS VERLAG BERLIN
λογος

PALUCCA HOCHSCHULE FÜR TANZ DRESDEN

SPONSORED BY THE
Federal Ministry of Education and Research

This publication is part of the research project *InnoLernenTanz*, which was carried out at the Palucca University of Dance Dresden. The project was funded by the Federal Ministry of Education and Research (BMBF) in the framework of the Quality Pact for Teaching, a joint program of the German Federal Government and States (*Länder*) to improve study conditions and the quality of teaching in higher education (under the project number 01 PL 11093).
Responsibility for the contents of this publication rests with the editor.
www.palucca.eu

Bibliographic information published by the Deutsche Nationalbibliothek
The Deutsche Nationalbibliothek lists this publication in the Deutsche Nationalbibliografie; detailed bibliographic data is available on the Internet at http://www.dnb.de/EN

ISBN 978-3-8325-4213-9

This book is also published in German under the title:
Tanz praktizieren – ein somatisch orientierter Ansatz

Cover illustration: Tina Warmuth
Layout and typesetting: Sophie Weckeßer
Graphic design of the images: Tina Warmuth, Jürgen van Buer, Maria Katherina Franz
Photographs: Jürgen van Buer, Karin Matko, Katharine Schwarzer
Dancers featured in Chapter 3: First-year students in the Bachelor of Arts program in Dance at the Palucca University of Dance Dresden, 2014/15
Dancer featured in Chapter 9: Franziska Kusebauch
English translations: Jake Schneider, Petra Novak-Walsh, Jenny Coogan

Logos Verlag Berlin GmbH
Comeniushof, Gubener Str. 47
10243 Berlin
Tel.: +49 (0)30 42 85 10 90
Fax: +49 (0)30 42 85 10 92
INTERNET: http://www.logos-verlag.de

in the spirit of the Palucca students and
for all those people with whom I have shared the
passion for dance

CONTENTS

Acknowledgments 06
Preface *Jason Beechey* 07
Introduction *Jenny Coogan* 09

1. FRAMING THE FIELD OF STUDY *Jenny Coogan* 13

2. THE FELDENKRAIS METHOD *Jenny Coogan* 29

EXPERIENCE IN DANCE ART:
REFLECTIONS IN THE PALUCCA COMMUNITY
In conversation with Matthias Markstein 43

3. SOMATIC APPROACHES IN CONTEMPORARY DANCE CLASS:
A Case Study *Jenny Coogan* 47

4. STUDENTS' PERCEPTIONS AND ACCEPTANCE
OF SOMATIC INSTRUCTIONAL OPPORTUNITIES:
An Analysis from a Psychological Perspective
Susanne Narciss and Karin Matko 83

5. KITCHEN-TABLE TALK:
Students and Alumni in Discussion
Moderated by Jenny Coogan and Fanny Barz 95

INTERMEZZO: REFLECTIONS OF DANCE EDUCATORS

To Be Connected / To Stay Connected
Karin Munters Jameson 104

The Body: A Work in Progress
Jan Burkhardt 108

6. ATTRIBUTES OF SUCCESSFUL TEACHING:
New Findings from Research on Teaching and Learning
Jürgen van Buer 111

INTERMEZZO: REFLECTIONS OF DANCE EDUCATORS

Moving Between First-Person and Third-Person Bodies in Dance Teaching *Jennifer Roche* 123

Somatic Acquaintanceship *Libby Farr and Jacob Storer* 127

7. SYNAESTHETIC SEEING: **Perspectives on the Body in Dance** & EXPERIENCING DIFFERENCE: **Practices of Attention and Repetition in Dance** *Nina Patricia Hänel* 131

8. REFLECTIONS OF CHOREOGRAPHERS 141

The Echo of a Movement *Shumpei Nemoto* 142

How the Pursuit of Accessing the Individual Led Me to Stream-Flow *Heidi Vierthaler* 146

The Virtuosity of Being *Yuval Pick* 150

Visions of Physicality *Georg Reischl* 154

9. APPLIED FELDENKRAIS IN CONTEMPORARY DANCE PRACTICE: **Three Examples** *Jenny Coogan and Nina Patricia Hänel* 157

10. STATEMENTS OF PROGRAM DIRECTORS 175

Dance Somatics as Radical Pedagogy: Reflections on Somatic Practice within UK Higher Education and Training in Dance *Sara Reed* 176

Dancing from the Inside Out: Researching the Integration of Somatic Practices in Dance Training *Jason Beechey* 181

11. A LOOK INTO THE FUTURE 185

Daring to Create Gaps *Gabriele Wittmann* 186

Closing Words *Jenny Coogan and Jürgen van Buer* 189

References 191

Contributors 208

ACKNOWLEDGEMENTS

The efforts of many people and institutions have brought this volume to fruition. I am deeply appreciative of all who have contributed to this undertaking. I thank, in particular, Jason Beechey, rector of the Palucca University of Dance Dresden, for his support during the five-year life span of the *InnoLernenTanz* project. I also wish to thank the German Federal Ministry of Education and Research (BMBF) for the grant that powered the project out of which this publication grew.

I express my thanks to the members of the research team—Anja Balzer, Fanny Barz, Nina Patricia Hänel, Franziska Kusebauch, and Karin Matko—for their generous, committed, and skillful input throughout the development of the book, and for the challenging and thought-provoking exchanges we have shared. In addition, I would like to thank the consultants Jürgen van Buer and Susanne Narciss for the invaluable expert advice they provided throughout, and Gabriele Wittmann and Andrea Wolter for offering editorial encouragement.

I would like to greatly thank all the contributing authors—Jason Beechey, Jürgen van Buer, Libby Farr, Nina Patricia Hänel, Karin Jameson, Matthias Markstein, Karin Matko, Susanne Narciss, Shumpei Nemoto, Yuval Pick, Sara Reed, Georg Reischl, Jennifer Roche, Jacob Storer, Heidi Vierthaler, and Gabriele Wittmann—for so graciously sharing the outlooks and methods of their practice, both artistic and academic. In addition, I'm most grateful to current students and alumni—Alexei Bernard, Valeria Danhauser, Luke Hayward, Nadja Güsewell, Swane Küpper, and Lars Reinschmidt—for their openness in discussing their experiences with somatic investigations, and to all the dancers who participated in the case study for their willingness to contribute to the research.

I especially thank my sister, Christa Coogan, who continually invites me to pursue self-questioning, and express gratitude to my daughter, Hannah for her boundless patience and understanding.

PREFACE

There are two primary research ideas at the core of the *InnoLernenTanz* project: somatically oriented pedagogy and individual coaching. Both ideas share the common desire to see if new and innovative methods can be developed in the teaching of dance. The research was anchored in contemporary dance and followed students during the duration of their three-year BA Dance degree course at the Palucca University of Dance Dresden. The aim of the research was then to see if such new methods could be transferred to other dance disciplines. The exploration of the inclusion of a somatically oriented pedagogy in contemporary dance training was led by Jenny Coogan, a long-time teacher of the Feldenkrais Method and a professor of contemporary dance. The intention was to see how the integration of the Feldenkrais Method into the contemporary dance training might impact the environment in ways that support dancers' self-regulatory and self-reflective learning processes. Somatic practices are becoming more commonplace in dance education curricula, as well as playing an ever-growing role in choreographic processes. The focus of this research was to investigate the extent to which dance practice could be synergized with the Feldenkrais Method at the onset of the Bachelor of Arts program in Dance.

In parallel to this, José Biondi, a fellow professor of contemporary dance, set out to explore whether a new method of directing the attention of the teacher solely to one student could be applied on a rotating basis within group dance classes. Thus, the newly minted coaching model (called "iCiF": "individual Coaching and interactive Feedback") employs this rotating system. The research involved the establishment of a specific feedback culture and demanded a shift of focus from both teacher and students, as the method differed greatly from standard practice in dance education.

To undertake such a research project required a great pooling and stretch of resources for a small university of our size. However, as the university leadership wished to support both research ideas, a common project was drawn up, in which the resources would be shared equally between the two research areas. It was thought that this could provide opportunities for multiple forms of exchange, and would be of benefit for both branches of research. The two publications that resulted from this common project are now also appearing in print simultaneously.

As the first such research project to have taken place in our university, it has been a learning curve that presented challenges along the way. I hope not only that the results of the research prove of benefit, provoke ideas, and inspire others, but also that much can be learned from the process itself as a sustainable best practice model for systematic empirically based innovation. Conducting practice-based research in dance remains a relatively new and little-explored field in Germany, and this factor alone provided its own series of challenges and necessitated the establishment of a support system and framework.

In conclusion, we want to express our sincerest gratitude for the support of the Federal Ministry of Education and Research (BMBF), under the auspices of the Quality Pact for Teaching *(Qualitätspakt Lehre)* program, for enabling this research project to take place. I hope truly that the research undertaken by *InnoLernenTanz* will provide new motivation, tools, and ideas for continuing to evolve the future study of the art form of dance.

Prof. Jason Beechey
Rector of the Palucca University of Dance Dresden

INTRODUCTION

Jenny Coogan

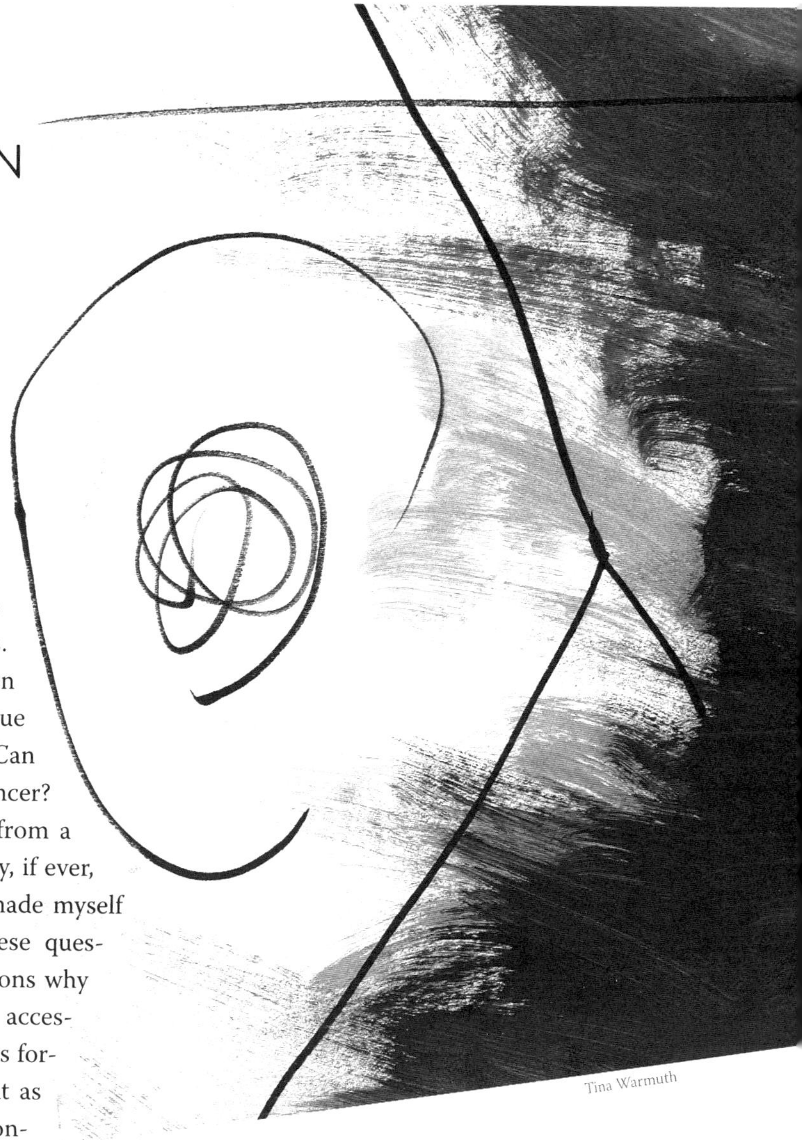

Tina Warmuth

"Who made you a dancer?" I often hear this question echo through the hallways and studios in exchanges of experience between first-semester students. Over the years, I started to listen more carefully. What is this issue concerning "making" a dancer? Can you "produce" dance—or a dancer? Why is this question addressed from a second-person perspective? Rarely, if ever, did I hear a student answer: "I made myself a dancer." My reflections on these questions led me to consider the reasons why personal agency is not so readily accessible for many students during this formative stage of their development as performing artists. I began to wonder: How are the parameters that are crucial to the understanding of contemporary dance, such as personal agency, actually embodied? How does our German conservatory educational system foster such parameters? And how could we more effectively encourage young dancers to experience their education from a first-person perspective of empowered, embodied, and somatic authority?

Throughout the field, the literature focusing on these questions suggests that somatically informed body awareness is a means for change, one that supports improved functioning, a sense of self, and the capacity to relate to others in an ethical and integral manner (Rouhiainen 2008; Shustermann 2004; Fortin 2009). In addressing these questions, I began to conduct pilot studies in contemporary dance classes with the groups of students with whom I was working that incorporated principles and strategies from the Feldenkrais Method of somatic movement education, such as "creative self-questioning" and "reflection in action." These investigations brought subjective questions of perception into our practice. They sought out ways to help the young dancers experience a somatic sensibility as both an artistic asset and a skill for taking greater command of their own decision-making and decision-taking processes. The findings of these studies contributed to the conception of the research domain in somatically informed pedagogical practices, a part of the project *InnoLernenTanz* (ILT). This practice-based research project was carried out at the Palucca University of Dance Dresden in Germany. ILT ran from 2012 to 2016, and was financed through a grant from the Federal Ministry of Education and Research (BMBF) under the auspices of the program, Quality Pact for Teaching *(Qualitätspakt Lehre)*.

Over the course of the past four years, the research conducted examined teaching and learning conditions that focused on supporting the parallel development of young dancers' physical competencies and self-regulative processes, in their preparation to meet the twenty-first century challenges of the profession. Strategies were explored through which students might learn more effectively to locate themselves within the interplay of contextualization, self-reflection, and specific work structures in which they themselves actively co-create. A primary aim was to facilitate the reframing of individual learning from external direction to internal steering.

The research draws on the teaching and strategies of somatic movement philosophies, most specifically the Feldenkrais Method. This method helps the practitioner to "know" more clearly the function and perceived organization of learned movement. The practice of the method makes the nervous system's ability for lifelong learning explicit, as it reveals its flexibility in creating new neural patterns (Feldenkrais 1981; Rywerant 1983). The Feldenkrais Method can direct the practitioner toward greater awareness of the multi-directionality and polycentric nature of movement, analogous to the multifarious choices one has for action (Langer 1997; Feldenkrais 2010).

As a response to the fluid and transformative nature of the dance profession, *Practicing Dance: A Somatic Orientation* argues for the efficacy of somatically oriented teaching and learning approaches in the conservatory landscape of dance in German higher education. The volume is intended for a broad audience, for all those who are inspired by dance, and who are curious to learn even more about the ways in which artists weave their individual fabrics of dance and somatics. It is written using the artistic, educational, and theoretical lenses of practicing dance artists and scholars. The authors' voices are all situated in their own worlds of experience. *Practicing Dance: A Somatic Orientation* is intentionally nonlinear and discursive in form. Its format includes interviews, a moderated discussion, artistic, educational, and culturally relevant reflections, essays and reports, as well as a practical outline, which demonstrates the synergy between contemporary dance and the Feldenkrais Method.

The volume begins with chapters by members of the research team. The first chapter delineates the core concepts and terminology used in this volume; the second offers an outline of the principles and strategies of the Feldenkrais Method. Following these is a personal account from Palucca graduate and teacher, Matthias Markstein. The third section documents and interprets a case study recently completed with students in the Bachelor of Arts program in Dance at Palucca University. Susanne Narciss and Karin Matko continue with a chapter that illuminates this case study from a psychologist's viewpoint, which is followed by students' and alumni's reflections on their encounters with somatics as part of the ILT project. Jürgen van Buer's contribution goes on to highlight the principal results of successful teaching and learning as reported in contemporary empirical studies. After this, Nina Patricia Hänel's two essays offer reflections on the concepts of kinaesthetic seeing and repetition in contemporary dance practice.

Presented as intermezzi scattered throughout the volume, five dance artists share their approaches for weaving a specific somatic method into their teaching/facilitating practices. In the first intermezzo, Karin Munters Jameson recounts the influence of the Klein Technique™ on her pedagogy, and Jan Burkhardt reflects on the interaction of Body-Mind Centering® and Laban/Bartenieff Movement Studies within his facilitating practice. In the second intermezzo, Jennifer Roche shares her insights about a practice that employs somatic methods, particularly Hanna Somatics and the Feldenkrais Method, with students in first-year tertiary dance education. This is followed by Libby Farr and Jacob Storer's dialogue about the somatic experience in dance practice and performance, with particular emphasis on the Alexander Technique and Gyrokinesis.

In a section devoted to interviews with choreographers, Shumpei Nemoto muses on the echo of movements; Heidi Vierthaler shares her own Stream-Flow Method; Yuval Pick posits a virtuosity of being; and Georg Reischl writes on play and pleasure in the context of artistic collaborations with students in conservatory settings. A chapter of practical applications provides examples that demonstrate the synergy of contemporary dance and the Feldenkrais Method in a way that makes them easily transferable to individual contexts.

In statements from program leaders, Sara Reed and Jason Beechey, director of Coventry University's Performing Arts Department and rector of the Palucca University of Dance Dresden respectively, discuss the professional profile of a dance artist working today. A look into the future closes the volume. Dance journalist, somatic practitioner, and researcher, Gabriele Wittmann muses on the political and sociocultural dimensions of somatics and self-efficacy. Jürgen van Buer and I consider the roles of students and teachers in relation to both institutional and individual development.

As I outline in chapter 1, which is also expressed in the personal experiences of the contributing authors provided throughout this book, curricular integration of dance and somatic practices in the Anglosphere has a rich history. In the German landscape of federally subsidized dance in higher education, this integration is at an earlier stage of development. Therefore, it is not surprising that the cross-fertilization of dance and somatic practice is met with diverse and often contrasting forms of appraisal, evaluation, or appreciation, which is a natural part of institutional discourses that invites open and argumentative modes of communication. Many of the chapters in *Practicing Dance: A Somatic Orientation* critically reflect upon the structure and content of institutionalized dance education and consider somatic methods as a possible means to more fully support young dance artists in navigating the unpredictable and ever-changing professional field with enhanced agency, kinaesthetic sensitivity, and social consciousness. That this approach can carry weight is in part due to the fact that the study of somatically oriented pedagogical practices in dance in German higher education is a new and innovative field of (published) research. The financing we received for the ILT project from the BMBF enabled research in this field to be conducted for the first time at the Palucca University of Dance Dresden. As a result, this publication makes a timely contribution to practice-based research in the field of dance in German higher education.

Maria Katherina Franz

1. FRAMING THE FIELD OF STUDY

Jenny Coogan

This publication argues for the efficacy of somatically oriented learning and teaching approaches in conservatory environments as a means to help prepare young dance artists to meet the twenty-first century challenges of the profession. As the scope of the profession becomes ever more diversified, such challenges increasingly demand skills in the areas of critical thinking, problem-solving, collaboration, self-direction and self-articulation, the aptitudes of adaptability and entrepreneurship, alongside artistry, curiosity, initiative, and the forming of a highly differentiated physical practice (DeLahunta, Hoerster 2007: 224; Sieben 2011: 145). How are dance artists who emerge from conservatory environments equipped to navigate an expanding professional field? How might socially somatic[1] approaches to learning and teaching in conservatory-based dance within higher education settings support dancers in building their professional careers?

In the Anglosphere, particularly, dance and somatics have entered the mainstream of tertiary education. Despite Germany's rich cultural heritage of non-dualistic thought, and the fact that numerous somatic systems originated in this country, somatic studies has been slow to take hold as an integral part of university dance programs. This fact was a primary factor in creating a line of research through the *InnoLernenTanz* project, which addresses opportunities for somatically oriented learning and teaching through dance within a conservatory setting. This practice-based research project was conducted with first-year students in the Bachelor of Arts Dance program at the Palucca University of Dance Dresden, and sought out ways to awaken a socially somatic sensibility in these young adults as a means of stimulating their individual learning processes and encouraging their growth as ethically conscious and self-determined human beings. Specifically, the methods and strategies of the Feldenkrais Method for somatic movement education were woven into the contemporary dance practice of this group of students in a way that offered a comprehensive approach to learning. The somatic intervention did not serve as an adjunct to dance training, but rather as a means to support individuals in cultivating their own learning strategy.

The pedagogical value of a somatic approach is widely accepted as helping students to establish an ideal foundation from which they can develop "technique" (as defined in the following subchapter), performance skills, and the ability to attune oneself to the deep "self-logic" of the nervous system's balancing and self-regulating processes (Johnson 1995). By drawing attention to self-regulation, and by placing emphasis on the consciousness of choice and its consequences, somatically oriented dance education has demonstrated that this approach can lead to improvement not only in artistic performance, but also in personal agency and self-reliance (Reed 2015; Dragon 2015; Green 2002b; Fortin 2003; Eddy 2015).

This chapter outlines the core concepts of somatics and somatic movement education as they are understood in this publication. The Feldenkrais Method provides the framework for identifying and delineating these concepts. In addition, the relationship of a professional dance artist's career profile to somatic movement dance practice is addressed. Figuring into this equation, the notion of "technique" is (re)considered. As the empirical research in this book was situated in a conservatory environment in Germany, this chapter begins by sketching out the regulatory and institutional framework of publically funded tertiary dance education in this country.

The professional conservatory model in Germany

Tertiary dance education in Germany takes place in art and music colleges (conservatories) called *Kunst-* and/or *Musikhochschulen.* Traditionally, academic scholarship has been carried out in universities. In response to recent educational reforms, however, *Kunst-* and *Musikhochschulen* have gained equivalent status to universities and are no longer identified as "colleges" of art and music, but are now called universities of applied sciences. The Palucca University is singular in Germany in that it is devoted exclusively to the study of dance. Typically, a single university of "art and music" will house a combination of departments in the performing, musical, and/or visual arts. Currently, ten such facilities offer a variety of bachelor's (BA) and/or master's (MA) degree programs in dance.[2]

The focus of this publication is on Bachelor of Arts programs in dance performance. These programs are structured according to the conservatory, or vocational, model; the curricula incorporate rigorous daily physical practice, supported by academic courses in related subjects. The profiles for these programs are all distinctive, but most have grown out of the styles of European concert dance. This tradition prioritizes the transmission of and critical reflection on idioms of ballet, improvisation, and modern and contemporary dance. A number of these dance departments, such as the Palucca University of Dance Dresden, the Folkwang University of the Arts in Essen, and the University for Music and Performing Arts in Frankfurt am Main, were established in the early part of the twentieth century by seminal figures from Germany's *Ausdruckstanz, Tanztheater,* and neoclassical heritage. In recent years, new profiles for Bachelor of Arts programs have grown out of current discourse revolving around issues of artistic research and scholarship (for example, at the Inter-University Centre for Dance in Berlin and the Center for Contemporary Dance at the University of Music and Dance in Cologne). These programs aim to strike a balance between theory and practice-based inquiry.

The inter-European Bologna Process[3] and the Tanzplan Deutschland[4] initiative have brought significant change to the practice of dance in higher education in

Germany. The Bologna Process fueled the restructuring of course curricula into integrative modular units with the aim of creating greater coherence and transparency within and between the programs. It particularly sought to ensure and simplify inter-university mobility and exchange. In addition, the reforms altered the regulatory framework of study, replacing diploma degrees (comprising eight to ten semesters of study) with Bachelor and Master of Arts degrees (comprising six and four semesters respectively). The duration of study in BA dance programs at most German universities, with the exception of the programs in Frankfurt, Cologne, and Essen, has thus been reduced from eight to six semesters.

University dance departments are networked with a variety of publically funded institutions that support the production, performance, and appreciation of the performing arts. For example, dance artists can find work in resident dance companies within Germany's extensive system of federal and state theaters *(Stadt- und Staatstheater)*, as well as state and local cultural institutions, and venues that offer alternative formats for the creation, production, and dissemination of dance. This climate enables dance artists to launch and sustain their professional careers. The prospects of employment in Germany, tuition-free education, and low enrollment levels have increased the internationalism and competitiveness of the programs in these institutions. The brevity of study time, and the fact that candidates in dance programs can matriculate upon completion of secondary school at the tenth-grade level (rather than the twelve years required as a prerequisite for academic study), means that graduates are entering into a professional field of mounting competition at younger ages. Yet, emerging dance artists are required to have a skill set of advanced physical, cognitive, and affective competencies. Therefore, education today must support the development of agency, independent thinking, and decision-making skills in dancers from the very beginning of study to enable students to navigate and negotiate a field that demands critically reflective and self-directing artists.

Technique/s for current professional profiles

Dancers are asked to confront and engage with the materials of creation in manifold situations and settings. In other words, the dancer must foster a profile that is emergently responsive to the hybrid environments in which their work is embedded. Today's dancer is tasked with being much more than an interpreter of the choreographic signatures of others, as dance artists are now expected to be at once a performer, collaborator, educator, curator, entrepreneur, and lobbyist. The professional landscape is now increasingly defined by fluctuations in social dynamics and work structures; it is characterized by interdisciplinary, multifarious choreographic signatures and physical eclecticism. Globalization and internationalism have impacted the field of dance in ways that affect educational institutions, the professional landscape, and the career profile of the dance artist. As a result, institutionalized dance education now faces the challenge of becoming more flexible in both its regulatory structures and curricula frameworks.

The prevalent modes of creating and performing dance works today necessitate a continual reconsideration of the materials and methods of dance education and training, as well as the formats for transmission in their respective settings. The institutions, in turn, have been required to adapt and (re)form in response to the evolving set of professional competencies, skills, tools, and techniques from which dancers of today are expected to draw. As artists increasingly create their own lineage, technique has become more personal and can now be considered a means for supporting individual decision-making processes (Parviainen 2003: 162). Dance artist Wendell Beavers advanced the idea that "technique" has come to mean "the principles of organization which underlie mind/body response" (2008: 129). "Technique" is thus understood as the skills experienced in practice and inscribed into one's own world of understanding. Dance scholar Jaana Parviainen considers dance technique to be the skills and materials that create the actualities and potentialities that enable dancers to execute the tasks at hand (2003: 161). The discovery of what is possible creates invention out of necessity and leads to the spawning of new "techniques." In support of this idea, performance theorist Ben Spatz describes "technique" as both embodied practice and research that structures actions by offering a range of relatively reliable pathways through given situations. Rather that regarding "technique" as something that can be aesthetically mastered, served, and reproduced through the dancer's body, he posits that a "technique" of embodied practice and research permits individual artistic freedom and empowers the dance artist with the artistry to act with agency, reflection, and creativity (Spatz 2015: 26). This position aligns with somatic approaches to dance technique, which help artists harvest from an inner authority and trust their perceptions of the experienced and experiencing body, imbued with a consciousness that these processes unfold in ever-changing patterns of situated relationships.

A brief overview of somatics

Etymologically, the term "somatics" derives from the Greek word somatikos, defined as "that pertaining to the body, experienced and regulated from within, encompassing the dimensions of body, psyche, and spirit" (Fraleigh 2014: 251). In the 1970s, philosopher and Feldenkrais teacher Thomas Hanna, a key initiator of the somatic movement, described somatics as "a field of study dealing with somatic phenomena: i.e., the human being as experienced by himself from the inside" (1995: 343). This phenomenological first-person (or "experiential") viewpoint stands in contrast to a third-person (or more objectified) perspective. Elaborating on this, Hanna speaks of somatics as the interrelation between awareness, biological function, and the environment, experienced as a synergetic whole (1976: 31). A somatic perspective thus acknowledges that thoughts, emotions, feelings, and imagination are all manifestations of an indivisible totality found in each person's biological and neurological makeup (Joly 2004: 5).

The term somatics has a diverse and interdisciplinary history, as it is influenced by phenomenological, existential, and Eastern philosophy and thought, educational constructivism, martial arts practices, and yoga, as well as the advent of modern/expressionistic dance (Eddy 2009). The reintroduction of non-Cartesian thought and practice during the nineteenth century established the terrain from which body-based holistic (somatic) systems of inquiry, and methods for learning and self-care emerged (Mangione 1993: 27). Edmund Husserl speaks of the soma as *Leib*, or "the lived body," acknowledging the body's capacity to realize its inborn intelligence as an integrated whole (Husserl, quoted in Parviainen 2002: 20). In the early twentieth century, artists and educators, including Heinrich Jacoby, Elsa Gindler, Gerda Alexander, Rudolf von Laban, and Mary Wigman, among others, were instrumental in fostering a *leibliche* (corporeal) encounter with dance in Germany. They shared a vision of embodiment that supported individual expressiveness and the return to "a hidden sense of the wise, imaginative, and creative body" (Johnson 1995: xv), which reveals its life-forms from the soma outward.

These pioneers proposed that kinaesthetic consciousness is central to creative expression. Their practice was quiet, pragmatic, and subtle—as in "listening to the body" with antenna-like awareness and paying attention to the "self that moves" (Johnson 1994: 181). The resulting development of somatic movement practices and the field of somatic movement education drew on this tradition.

Learning somatically

Somatic learning links body and mind by paying attention to sensory phenomena that often result from movement, whether executed or imagined. A hallmark of somatics is the method of learning to attend to sensory phenomena arising within a structured movement environment (Batson, Wilson 2014: 129). All human movement takes place through the interrelation of sensory stimuli, perceptual interpretation, and motor processing (Steinmüller, Schaefer, Fortwängler 2001: 108; Simmel 2014: 19). By learning somatically, one pays attention to these intimate relationships (Cohen 1993: 114).

The sensorimotor system functions as a closed-loop system: one cannot sense without acting nor act without sensing (Hanna 1995: 345). Sensorimotor processes involve the sensory input that informs the brain and how the brain integrates this information to give commands to the motor system in order to produce neuromuscular responses. These activities can be understood as the "recurrent feedback system between sensory input, perceptual interpretation, motor-planning, motor-response, sensory feedback, and perceptual interpretations" (Cohen 1993: 114). The nervous system controls and balances the muscle actions through both automatic reflexes and conscious deliberate movements (Sweigard 1974: 4; Simmel 2014: 21). It is responsible for coordination. The sensory readings play a key role in orienting, guiding, controlling, coordinating, and assessing movement (Steinmüller, Schaefer, Fortwängler 2001: 8). The perceptual interpretations of movement are dependent upon, and influenced by, one's previous repertoire of experiences. The reception of sensory stimuli is therefore filtered through preconceptions informed by one's past experiences (Cohen 1993: 115). Sensorimotor or perceptual-motor processes, as they are often referred to today in recognition of the role perception plays in one's engagement with the world (Batson, Wilson 2014: 128), are therefore responsible for the acquisition and assimilation of human movement.

Sensation is the first step in the moving body's experience of the world (Cohen 1993: 4). Sensing is embedded in the intelligence of the nervous system (Holdaway, Kovich, Simmonds 2002: 24). It involves the stimulation of the sensory receptors and sensory nerves (Cohen 1993: 114). In sensation, the physical stimulus, together with its physical properties, is registered by sensory organs and provides the necessary information to the brain to allow individuals to register reality as they experience it. Therefore, sensation alone must not be perceived as something that takes place automatically.

Perception refers to the occurrence when the brain processes information it obtains from the neural impulses, giving meaning to this information by means of emotions and memories. It engages in the process of translation and interpretation (Cohen 1993). Using past experiences and cultural predispositions as the baseline, everyone interprets sensory stimuli individually. Therefore, perception identifies and interprets sensory information, establishing its relation to oneself, as well as the relationship to one's environment, from what one is sensing (Cohen 1993: 114). Perception can be understood as the act that links the sensory and motor components of learning. Developmental studies demonstrate that perception is intermodal from the very beginning, and that it is not an intellectual accomplishment acquired after much practice, but an innate feature of embodied experience (Gallagher 2005: 170). Dance scholar and phenomenologist Sondra Fraleigh states that perception is a sensory precursor to affective-motivational and cognitive insight: "Perception is preverbal, global, and nonlinear" (Fraleigh 2014: 252). It is a willful act, resulting out of the recognition of sensation. Renowned for his research in enaction theory, phenomenologist Alva Noe writes:

> *The world makes itself available to the perceiver through physical movement and interaction. ... Perceptual experience acquires content thanks to our possession of bodily skills. What we perceive is determined by what we do; it is determined by what we are ready to do. ... To perceive is to understand, at least implicitly, the effects of movement on sensory stimulation.* (2004: 1-4)

Kinaesthesia and **proprioception** are neuromuscular processes that underlie all body orientation, postural control, and balance (Horak 2006: 91). The kinaesthetic or sixth sense, defined in 1888 by Charles Bell as muscular (Smith 2011), communicates between muscle and joint receptors, allowing the body to sense how it is moving in space. Kinaesthesia helps the body to refine sensitivity, response, and sense abilities essential to forming relationships between the interior self and the exterior world (van Manen 2007: 12). The kinaesthetic sense is continually providing feedback for the fine-tuning of intended actions initiated by the brain's motor cortex (Schmidt, Wrisberg 2001). The majority of responses made to kinaesthetic input proceed on an unconscious level, therefore it is sometimes best to "release" and get out of your own way, and trust the body's wisdom (Johnson 1995) to allow the central nervous system to choose the most efficient neuromuscular coordination for the movement's execution (Sweigard 1974: 6). Slowing down, taking time, and reducing muscular expenditure are vital for fine-tuning kinaesthetic awareness or "listening to the body," as Elsa Gindler and others describe (quoted in Johnson 1994: 181).

At the beginning of the twentieth century, leading British neuroscientist Charles Sherrington identified the feeling sense of proprioception. Proprioception thus replaced the term kinaesthesia as the preferred term for describing the "feeling state of muscles and related tissues associated with bodily positions and movements" (Batson, Wilson 2014: 91). Proprioception is the sensory mechanism that informs and localizes the muscular activity of the body according to where it is in space, its posture, and what relations the parts of the body have to one another. The speed of body movements, the forces these movements exert, and the relative timings of their various muscular contractions have been identified as the most relevant parameters for describing this phenomenon (McCloskey 1982: 14). The interrelation of kinaesthesia and proprioception is indisputable. It is has been hard to establish their distinction from one another, as these sensory phenomena are often used interchangeably, thus precluding a conclusive definition of either term (Batson, Wilson 2014: 91; Foster 2010). Together, these functions produce integrated and dynamically balanced movement, which is potentially responsive to change. The refinement of the movement senses of proprioception and kinaesthesia brings forth experience through the unity of sensing, perceiving, and moving in relation to one's environment (Batson, Wilson 2014: 90). All somatic practices rely on these processes, as they are necessary for learning or relearning movement patterns (Feldenkrais 1972; Hackney 1998; Eddy 2015).

A sketch of somatic movement education

Somatic learning highlights an innate capacity of the individual to continually grow and evolve, thereby creating more reliable neural connections in order to obtain more mature forms of self-regulation. Somatic movement education is an interdisciplinary field concerned with the "lived body" as it acquires awareness through movement within the environment (Joly 2004: 7). Approaches that emphasize "learning how to learn" in their methodology are referred to as "somatic education" systems (Holdaway, Kovich, Simmonds 2002: 20; Joly 2004: 6). These practices respect the integrative and embodied soma, and explore idiosyncratic experiences, body structure, and functional bodily organization (Ginot 2010; Eddy 2009). Commonalities of somatic practices include:

- Slowing down to feel and pay attention to bodily cues
- Releasing the body into gravity with breath support
- Reducing tension and discovering new patterns of coordination
- Becoming more aware of how to live and move in three-dimensional space (Eddy, Williamson, Weber 2014: 168)

In addition, somatic systems draw upon anatomical knowledge of structure and function in a manner that suits the methodologies particular to these systems. The efficient rendering of any movement or movements is dependent on the interaction of many complex factors—neuromuscular, biomechanical, psychosomatic, habitual, and environmental (Batson 2007: 147). The Feldenkrais Method, which is discussed in depth in the subsequent chapter, views the human skeleton as a blueprint for systematically exploring how the body can move along the lines of least biomechanical resistance and with the greatest mechanical efficiency. Trainer Carl Ginsberg describes a Feldenkrais lesson as "a direct connection of nervous system to nervous system through the medium of the skeleton" (1988: 13). In other words, direct contact through the skeleton arouses functioning that stimulates learning that in turn results in change to the self-image. Therefore thought, emotions, sensations, and imagination are experienced in the muscle structure, cardiac rhythm, breathing, and posture, as well as in how the body manifests movement through space (Damasio 1994). Somatic (re)education, as it is sometimes referred to (Eddy 2015), fosters a process of kinaesthetic inquiry that leads to the discovery of one's potential for learning, as well as one's heightened awareness of habitual movement and thinking habits and patterns that can result in improved efficiency and overall well-being (Batson 2007: 146; Hanna 1995: 348).

The rise of somatics in dance practice

In the 1940s, the pedagogue Margaret H'Doubler brought the study of dance into the university setting in the United States. She integrated Mabel Todd's somatic system of Ideokinesis and the constructivist pedagogies of John Dewey into the curriculum. The first conservatory-based dance department within higher education in the USA was established in 1951 by Martha Hill at the Juilliard School, and Ideokinesis was incorporated into the department's program. The American Dance Festival's director Martha Myers introduced somatic therapies[5] into the festival's program, and her seminal articles advocating for the reciprocity of dance and somatic practices triggered the adoption of somatic methods in the curricula of the American university dance programs that followed.

During the 1960s, the move into a postmodern era, where education and artistic practice were critically questioned, brought dance and somatics closer together. Sara Reed, one of the contributing authors to this volume, states that "dance and somatics have arisen out of a history of critique and practical deconstruction of formal and traditional dance practices" (2015: 192). Since this time, some new directions in dance have been shaped by the proprioceptive (or sensory-based) perceptions of body image. They use exploratory methods as a means to optimize neuromuscular functioning. These somatic-based approaches to movement research and processes of socialization include Judson Dance Theatre, contact improvisation, release techniques, and postmodern and contemporary dance. Their development extends from both the research of the early twentieth-century dance artists mentioned above (Eddy 2009; Bales, Nettl-Foil 2008; Batson, Wilson 2014), and the work of the somatic and educational pioneers Mabel Todd, LuLu Sweigard, Moshé Feldenkrais, Frederick M. Alexander, Gerda Alexander, and Margaret H'Doubler, among others. These lineages were, and continue to be, concerned with movement efficiency, gravity, reciprocity, weight, release, and the links between an engaged mind and a knowing body (Fortin 1993; Clarke, Cramer, Müller 2011; Bales, Nettl-Foil 2008; Brodie, Lobel 2012).

The idea of "releasing," or the term "release techniques," is an ambiguous one. Various interpretations include: releasing oneself *from* things such as old habits; codified forms of moving and tension; releasing *into* suspension or new relationships (Beavers 2008: 128); or, alternatively, a Zen-inspired method of release as "'letting go' in the sense of opening oneself to other possibilities—as well as being open about the ways to utilize these new possibilities" (Wittmann 2011: 274). All of these interpretations have somatic connotations. Philosopher Don Hanlon Johnson speaks of somatic movement as the process of letting forms of movement emerge from within rather than imposing them upon the body (1986).

During the past decades, many dance artists and educators have been experimenting with cross-fertilizing different somatic modes in their practices or creating their own fusions. Prime examples of this interface are American choreographer Trisha Brown's research with Alexander Technique, Canadian educator Sylvie Fortin's work with the Feldenkrais Method, and late British dance artist Gill Clarke's Minding Motion method. Somatic modes continue to evolve, and there are now over one hundred different somatic practices that have been identified (Eddy 2015).

Core terminology: concepts within the Feldenkrais Method

The concepts and methods of somatic movement practices are multifold; however, they all recognize the power of awareness and self-regulation as essential for understanding the interrelation of sensing, feeling, thinking, and action in the development of a more complete self-image and a richer sense of agency (Fortin 1993; Sieben 2011; Eddy 2009; Brodie, Lobel 2007; Cohen 1993).

Moshé Feldenkrais described the reciprocal experiences between the ways in which one thinks, moves, feels, and senses as the self-image, which "governs our every act—and is conditioned by varying degrees by three factors: heritage, education, and self-education" (1972: 3). The self-image is an explanatory principle with no measurable psychometric or objective reality. It exists as a phenomenon within the configuration of all human beings. The self-image is intrinsically integrative, dynamic, and changing; it underlies and affects everything we do, and is shaped by learning experiences throughout life.[6] As the self-image continually (re)forms, it therefore unconsciously narrows our perception of ourselves and who we are. Feldenkrais trainer Elizabeth Beringer speaks of the dynamism of this conception as an action of becoming, of *selfing* (2001).

The nomenclature of the two forms in which the Feldenkrais Method is practiced, "Awareness Through Movement" and "Functional Integration," describes two principal concerns of the method itself. On the one hand, it aims to develop awareness of the interrelation of sensing and moving in order to optimize functioning, so that intention and action can harmonize. On the other hand, it intends to develop fine-tuning powers in order to discriminate among one's own kinaesthetic feedback to choose one's own course of action through processes of self-regulation and agency.

Awareness is a skill that permits the regulation of behavior in response to the feedback produced by individual action. The term indicates here the capacity to sense, feel, and also to think, specifically in the context of, and with regard to, the action of the living and sensing body (Joly 2004: 6). It is the ability of the self, as a combination of objective and subjective physical processes of lived consciousness, to focus simultaneously and clearly on one's internal experiences as they interact with the environment. Awareness exists because it comes from a living organism, with a body and a brain capable of representing the body (Damasio 1994: 46). The possibility to pause between the thought patterns connected to a particular action and the execution of that action is the physical basis for awareness (Feldenkrais 1972: 46). Bringing the dimension of awareness to movement is a conscious act. Awareness is **consciousness** combined with the realization of what is happening within it or what is going on within ourselves while we are conscious (Feldenkrais 1972: 50). Awareness and consciousness allow the individual to "know" that one's movement in the world is not predetermined, but needs to be discovered, self-formed, and created through the potential of acting on one's intentions. Feldenkrais distinguished between awareness and consciousness as follows:

> *I use the word "awareness" as conscious knowledge. ... I am conscious of leaving and returning home all through the years, yet I am not aware of the number of steps on the stairs. If I pay attention once and count the number of acts, such as shifting the eyes and performing whatever movements may accompany them in my head, arms, and legs, then I become aware that before I was only consciously mounting the stairs. Once I am conscious of how I am shifting my attention from one step to another I am aware of them and I also know their number. "Awareness" is used by me to denote conscious-of plus knowledge. (1981: 94)*

Self-regulation recognizes the possibility of choice in one's own actions. This implies a recognition or construction of alternatives for action and decision-making in relation to the situational environment in such a way that the choices for action can be argumentatively justified. Through self-regulation, one can develop and implement, with sovereignty, unique patterns of action in accordance with self-determined goals. Here, the inner representation of the intended action, the process leading up to it, and the action patterns themselves are emphasized. The internal processes of self-regulation are vital for determining bodily structure, and include the following abilities:

- Posing questions
- Making informed decisions
- Expressing needs
- Handling oneself with critical reflection
- Accepting the consequences resulting from one's independent actions
- Following one's interests in accordance with the context and in reflective alignment with the interests of others (Stinston 2000; Green 2000; Brodie, Lobel 2007)

Processes of self-regulation lead the individual to more successfully access their potential for agency and self-reflection. **Agency** refers to the individual's ability to be the willful initiator of their own action or the ability to handle things with the consciousness of volition (Gallagher 2005: 57). Invested with agency, one acts through self-regulative processes as one's own expert. Agency is a body-based awareness that establishes one's inner authority to connect empathetically with one's world. **Self-reflection** plays a decisive role in the constructivist pedagogies of somatic movement education, artistic practice, and psychology, among other disciplines (Langer 1997: 17). Self-reflection is conducted through processes of homeostasis, one's biological ability to self-regulate and self-organize, and is understood as somatically informed and consciously directed action. The following statement by Feldenkrais is often quoted in relation to this concept: "When you know what you are doing, you can do what you want" (1984: 68). Here Feldenkrais speaks of the ability to endow consciousness with awareness, self-regulation, agency, and self-reflection.

Embodiment and **situated cognition** stress how one is physically integrated with the world. Understanding of this union dates back to the concept of autopoesis formulated by Umberto Maturana and Francisco Varela, from which enaction theory partly developed. Enaction theory, first articulated by Francisco Varela, Evan Thompson, and Eleanor Rosch (1991), views cognition as grounded in the sensorimotor dynamics of the interactions that occur between a living organism and its environment. It represents a new approach to embodied cognitive science in which knowledge is constructed by an agent through their sensorimotor interactions with the environment, which are both interactively and intersubjectively connected. Noë states that "we enact our perceptual experience; we act it out" (2004: 2). Both enaction and somatic theories concede a preeminent place to processes of socialization and the influence of the environment in the formation of the soma and the regulation of its interactions in the world. These theories assert that a person's particular body image, the shape(s) into which their body grows and changes, is created through social exchange (Noë 2004; Kampe 2015). Somatic education is about being present in oneself, while at the same time being present in and active and reactive to the environment in relation to which one is acting. Enaction theory, which evolved in part out of a constructivist model, stresses the growing consensus that the individual is not the representation of a preestablished world by a preestablished mind but is, rather, the enactment of a world and a mind resulting from the history of the variety of actions that a being in the world performs (Varela, Thompson, Rosch 1991: 9). Enaction aligns with a somatic appreciation of dance practice and performance, since both resonate with self-reflection, autonomy, and embodiment, as well as sense-making and intersubjective interaction (Warburton 2011: 67; Batson, Wilson 2014: 91).

Summary

This frame of thought positions focus on the self, specifically the idea of self-conception (typically understood as *Selbstverständnis* in German terminology). Self-conception relies on the components of awareness, consciousness, self-regulation, agency, and self-reflection. Similar to the concept of self-image described above, it is a dynamic understanding of the interrelation between how the individual perceives values and acts. Self-conception transcends mere self-understanding and denotes intrinsic interest in, as well as motivation and empathy for, ongoing learning and development.

Thomas Hanna locates the heart of the somatic process within the "interlocking reciprocity between sensing and moving—a process that constitutes its own unity and continuity by constant self-regulation" (1995: 345). This chapter has offered the reader a viewpoint on the subjective first-person perception through which a somatic approach to learning and living can emerge. It identified synergy between the complementary yet discrete fields of dance and somatics, and located the Feldenkrais Method within the broad spectrum of somatic movement education. The concepts and ideas discussed here provide a foundation on which the subsequent chapters build.

---

1 "Social somatic theory draws on the ideas of writers such as Don Johnson and Elizabeth Behnke who addressed issues of bodily authority and demonstrated how our bodies are shaped by the cultures in which we live. From this perspective, Western culture creates the myth of a body/mind split. However, this split does not simply separate our minds from our bodies and favour mind over body. There is rather an active obsession with the body as an objective, mechanical entity. There is a focus on the body, but as a mechanical instrument rather than as a soma. ... It should be said that this theory might be used in an affirmative way as people are afforded more agency as the body is used as resistance to cultural norms" (Green 2015: 13).

2 These institutions are the Palucca University of Dance Dresden, the School of the Hamburg Ballet led by John Neumeier, the Folkwang University of the Arts, the Center for Contemporary Dance at the University of Music and Dance in Cologne, the University for Music and Performing Arts in Frankfurt am Main, the University of Music and Performing Arts in Munich, the Inter-University Centre for Dance in Berlin, the John Cranko School—the Ballet School of the State Theater in Stuttgart, the Berlin State Ballet School, and the Academy of Dance at the Mannheim University of Music and Performing Arts.

3 The Bologna Process is a collective effort of public authorities, including the European Commission, universities, and representatives from industry. Since its inception in 1999, its primary objective is to ensure more comparability, compatibility, and coherence among the systems of higher education in Europe. The process introduced the three-cycle system (bachelor/master/doctorate), which seeks to strengthen quality assurance and simplify the recognition of qualifications among participating countries. To date there are fifty-one participating European countries.

4 Funding from the German Federal Cultural Foundation made the Tanzplan Deutschland initiative between 2005 and 2010 possible. Equipped with a budget of 12.5 million euros, this nonprofit organization supported the recognition of dance as an art form of equal value to music and the dramatic arts, brought about greater visibility for dance in the public sector, and encouraged networking and dialogue among institutions. It instigated the development and implementation of hybrid BA and MA programs, sponsored conferences, workshops, and training sessions, generated impetus for publications, and created a comprehensive online database. Other outcomes of this initiative include the founding in 2007 of the Ausbildungskonferenz Tanz, a national organization that represents publically funded tertiary dance programs in Germany to cultivate interinstitutional exchange and lobbying for dance education.

5 Somatic practices were at first acknowledged as adjuncts to, or particularly recuperative support for, dance techniques (Brodie, Lobel 2012). Through the past decades, somatic practices have now come to be seen as fundamental strategies for organizing technique (Fortin 1993) and for understanding the integration between action and perception.

6 The philosopher Shaun Gallagher's concept of body image aligns with Moshé Feldenkrais' view of self-image, as both regard the body image/self-image as a transformative process that occurs throughout life. Gallagher proposes that the body image "consists of a complex set of intentional states and dispositions—perceptions, beliefs, and attitudes—in which the intentional object is one's own body" (2005: 25). Body image is constituted through developing self-perception. The awareness of the parts of one's body is responsible for constructing one's mutable body image.

2. THE FELDENKRAIS METHOD

Jenny Coogan

The manner in which people learn and form habits is a central concern of the Feldenkrais Method. Practicing this form of somatic movement education brings conscious attention to one's customary patterns of action. The method employs functionally based processes of differentiation and integration, and uses permutations and variations in the sensorimotor system as a means to elicit novel behavior that may lead to new and unexpected modes of thinking, feeling, and action (Beringer 1997). Intentional action, kinaesthetic feedback, decision-making, choice, and (re)enacting with adaptations and variations constitute the method's forms of learning. Indirect approaches of seemingly aimless playfulness of movement and visualization, and the sensory experiences of self-observation, offer the necessary strategies for training somatic skills such as awareness, attention, and response. By deploying these strategies, the Feldenkrais Method can offer the practitioner a richer experience of dance.

The following chapter describes central concepts within this method and its modes of practice. It begins with a biographical account of the life of Moshé Feldenkrais, which is interwoven with the tenets of his system. These connections aim to demonstrate the inseparability of a life journey from the method that was created. In common with other visionaries from his generation, Feldenkrais shared an ethical perspective that looked beyond individual self-improvement toward a vision of society in which all individuals could flourish and humanity evolve (Reese 1985: xxxiv).

Biography

The method is named after its founder, Moshé Feldenkrais (1904-1984), an integrative thinker, scientist, and athlete. His life was shaped by astute self-observation, transdisciplinary scholarship, expert judo practice, and an insatiable drive for self-development.

Feldenkrais was born into a Jewish family in 1904 and lived for the first years of his life in Slawuta, Russia, now a part of the Ukraine. Fleeing unrest and upheaval in the aftermath of World War I and anti-Jewish persecution and pogroms, he traveled alone at the age of fifteen to Palestine, where he was finally able to complete secondary school. While in Palestine he worked as a surveyor, became involved in Jewish self-defense groups, and taught himself jujitsu, known as the "art of yielding." Teachings of moral nonviolence, resiliency, and adaptability, espoused in the martial art forms of both jujitsu and judo, guided Feldenkrais throughout his life (Reese 1985).

Feldenkrais displayed an early interest in autosuggestion and hypnosis. During convalescence after a soccer-related knee injury, he wrote a chapter about autosuggestion in a publication on this subject and subsequently translated the entire volume into Hebrew. Parallels exist between these two methods and his own, as autosuggestion, hypnosis, and the Feldenkrais Method all propose that the effort to succeed interferes with the fulfillment of one's intentions. They postulate that success is linked to reducing resistance and effort, and employ indirect approaches of guided exploration to tap into unconscious sensorimotor experience in order to reduce overly conscious direction. Through this process, undesirable behavioral patterns that impede success can be interrupted (Reese 1985; Zeig 1980).

Feldenkrais spent the 1930s in Paris, where he earned a PhD in mechanical engineering from the Sorbonne and worked in various laboratories, including the Pasteur Institute, collaborating with researchers in atomic fission, magnetics, and ultrasound. During this time, he began training in judo and became one of the first Europeans to earn a second-degree black belt. Feldenkrais was influential in introducing judo to the European community, and practiced, taught, and wrote books and articles about judo throughout his life. Escaping the Nazi invasion of Paris in 1940, he fled to Scotland, where he worked for the British Admiralty in anti-submarine research and trained paratroopers in a variety of self-defense techniques. While stationed on a submarine, his chronic knee injury resurfaced. To cope with this situation, Feldenkrais began a process of self-observation and experimentation that led to his discoveries in movement (re)education.

Upon his relocation to London after the war, Feldenkrais remained active in both scientific and somatic research. His many interactions with somatic movement pioneers, such as Gerda Alexander, F. M. Alexander, and Heinrich Jacoby, the neurophysiologist Charles Sherrington, and later with scientists and psychologists, including Milton Erickson, Gregory Bateson, Heinz von Foerster, and Karl Pribram, demonstrate the circuitous, transdisciplinary route that led to the crystallization of his method. The first publication that articulated his research, *Body and Mature Behavior: A Study of Anxiety, Sex, Gravitation, and Learning* (1949), grew out of lectures he gave to the Association of Scientific Workers. Feldenkrais later proposed that "when you have a theory, then your experience teaches and qualifies your understanding and your future experience. That's how science works" (2010: 204).

In 1951, Feldenkrais returned to the newly founded state of Israel (in 1948) and briefly directed the army's Department of Electronics before devoting himself fully to the practice and dissemination of his method. He taught extensively in Israel, Europe, and North America, and directed professional training programs in Tel Aviv (1969-71), San Francisco (1975-77), and Amherst (1980-83). Hundreds of hours of lessons in his method recorded in audio and video document his teaching legacy. Today professional teacher-training programs are offered around the globe.[1] Feldenkrais' publications are scientific, but also contain practical exercises. They abound with anecdotes and humor, which help to make them accessible to a broad audience. *The Potent Self,* his most comprehensive work, was published posthumously in 1985. He withdrew from public teaching in 1981, after suffering a stroke, and died in Tel Aviv on July 1, 1984.

Feldenkrais was both a refugee and a foreigner who dealt with the strains of adversity, historical change, upheaval, and physical injury throughout his life. Over the course of forty years, he created a method in response to, and in dialogue with, other twentieth-century non-dualistic systems of somatic movement education. His method is influenced by his own investigations into the Western sciences of physics, systems theory, postural biomechanics, evolutionary biology, neurophysiology, and developmental psychology using thought-altering practices, such as meditation and hypnosis, and the martial art of judo. He fused these disciplines and ideas in order to construct and operationalize a system that examines the harmonious connection between structure, function, and achievement. (Steinmüller, Schaefer, Fortwängler 2001: 160; Peters, Sieben 2009: 25).

Feldenkrais described his method as one of "learning how to learn," which is "a special kind of learning: that of knowing oneself, learning to know how one is acting, and thus being able to do what one wants—the intense living of avowed, and sometimes declared, dreams" (2010: 58). For Feldenkrais, the potential for self-realization that he referred to as "mature behavior" lies in one's ability to effectively decipher the nature of motivation and to modulate the dynamics of actions freed from the dependency of compulsive behavior. Based in neuromuscular organization, the method gives precedence to the inherent neurological competencies of every human being and is thus resource-oriented, emphasizing one's potential, not one's shortfalls (Feldenkrais 1972; 1981). Feldenkrais defined learning as the individual's biological capacity to self-regulate, as well as to generate, internalize, and act with intentionally focused movement patterns to achieve self-determined goals (1981). He believed that, throughout life, self-education is uniquely open to everyone, and appreciably subject to individual will (Feldenkrais 1972).

Feldenkrais challenged a prevalent hypothesis of his time, which speculated that the brain was hardwired, losing both neurons and the ability to learn new functions with each passing day. His paradigm, one that has since been validated by neuroscience, was that of brain plasticity, which posits that throughout an individual's life span, the brain has the ability to recover lost functions, modify existing organizations, and create new patterns (Doidge 2015). Learning is thus a consequence of how one uses one's biological potential. The neuroscientist Gerald Hüther reinforces this notion, stating that "the structure and thus also the functioning of our brain depends in a very critical way on how we use it and what we use it for" (2006: 8). Practicing the Feldenkrais Method exercises the brain's flexibility, and thus the individual's potential to uncover their innate potential for growth, (re)form, and change. An objective of this practice is to create conditions that make the "impossible possible, easy, pleasurable, and finally aesthetically pleasing" (Feldenkrais 1981: 92). Thus, that which was once elusive or out of one's reach can be brought into the realm of the apparent and serviceable.

Learning with Feldenkrais

The Feldenkrais Method utilizes movement as the individual's favored access point to the knowledge that movement, contact, and relationships with one's environment (re)form the self-image (see chapter 1). As a result, the biomechanical and energetic properties of movement are appreciated as embodied, intentional, and contextual. The method explores the self-organizing properties of the nervous system and the open-endedness of the contexts for action they generate.[2] Its methodology aligns with the epistemological underpinnings of radical constructivism. This perspective precludes the notion of an objective reality. Knowledge is thus an ongoing, self-organized creation based on the relation of an individual's past experiences to present ones (von Glasersfeld 1995). With Feldenkrais, one attends to intentions with an experimental attitude, rather than to the achievement of a goal, recognizing that learning takes place from the place where one is in the present, not from where one wishes to be (Sheets-Johnstone 1979). Feldenkrais wrote that learning is:

> *individual; and without a teacher who is striving for results within a certain time, it lasts as long as the learner keeps at it. This organic learning is slow, and unconcerned with any judgment as to the achievement of good or bad results. It has no obvious purpose or goal. It is guided only by the sensation of satisfaction when each attempt feels less awkward as the result of avoiding a former minor error which felt unpleasant or difficult. (1981: 30)*

The codependent interaction between student and teacher avoids judgment and interpretation. The environment encourages participants to move from one to the next present moment, freed from anxieties connected to the past or the anticipated future in a process of self-(re)discovery. Discernment in movement is predicated on the positive kinaesthetic feedback loop of ease, lightless, and pleasure. Therefore, the practitioner recognizes well-coordinated movement when its execution is easy (Feldenkrais 1980: 4). The purpose and function of lessons in the Feldenkrais Method arise organically and are revealed to the individual in the process of doing. Trainer Dennis Leri quoted Feldenkrais as saying that "when you learn how to learn, you will realize that there are no teachers, that there are only people learning and people learning how to facilitate learning" (1975: 50).

The practice

This method is practiced in two complementary forms: manually led lessons between a teacher and single client called Functional Integration (FI), and verbally directed lessons between a teacher and a group of students called Awareness Through Movement (ATM). FI and ATM are variants of the same process; they aim to refine kinaesthetic sensitivity, disrupt habitual modes of behavior, relate differentiated and undifferentiated movement patterns to one another, and create novel or unfamiliar learning situations. Both forms are similar to choreographic processes, infused with self-questioning and composed of permutations triggered by variations, repetitions, constraints, and alterations in orientation.

During lessons, students are guided through explorations of deceptively simple movement sequences structured around functional themes, such as breathing, rolling, crawling, and locomotion that reference both phylogenetic and ontogenetic patterns.[3] Small actions focusing on one or two joints, and their relationship to major body parts, grow into movements of greater complexity, range, and speed (Reese 1994). The client/student becomes aware of how the musculature, skeleton, and indeed their entire personality are involved in every movement. Lessons demonstrate the holographic nature of the nervous system, meaning that effecting a change in one part of a system creates a change in the whole (Sieben 2011; Pribram 1971).

FI and ATM draw the students into a state of relaxed concentration from which they can attend to the sensorimotor feedback loop that informs the self-regulating powers of one's nervous system. Developmental psychologist Jean Piaget has stated that "life is auto-regulated" (1971: 26). Similarly, Moshé Feldenkrais postulated that the more one accepts knowledge of the automatic regulating functions of the nervous system, the greater freedom, ease, control, or coordination one gains (Czetczok 1995). Factors pertaining to coordination, including timing, duration, extent, and range in terms of their relation to intention, are usually regulated automatically in the background of one's awareness in the place where self-balancing and self-regulating powers operate (Doidge 2015). Feldenkrais said the following: "Don't you decide how to do the movement; let your nervous system decide. It has had millions of years of experience and therefore it knows more than you do" (quoted in Reese 1994).

Powers of sensory and proprioceptive discrimination can be sharpened by, for example, focusing on isolated motions in order to detect the slightest signals of change in bodily feeling. In doing so, attention can be directed to what one is actually doing and not to what one thinks one is doing. By thus separating intention from action, one can access more deeply one's self-logic, thereby clarifying functional efficiency and the outward representation of intention (Feldenkrais 1972).

What passes between clients/students and the teacher during a lesson is informative and not prescriptive. Students do not receive instruction about how to reproduce a movement or "fix" a problem. The teacher offers tailored and contextual information and suggestions for movement with the intention of stimulating processual and embodied self-questioning. A series of simple and concrete instructions and suggestions, which are delivered either verbally or manually, "put into question" the how, why, and what of the action, thus reinforcing the individual's self-instructing capabilities.[4]

Functional Integration (FI)

Communication in Functional Integration (FI) is delivered through touch and tailored to the specific concerns of the client. Lessons, which last for approximately one hour, are given on a specially constructed table or some other firm base. In these one-to-one exchanges, the teacher's touch moves with the client in non-verbal dialogue through movement explorations that are initially experienced in a fragmented way before they are brought together and integrated into a whole. The teacher's listening hands hold presence; they wait for the proprioceptive signals of the client that signal permission to continue. Feldenkrais described the essence of FI in the following way:

> *These hands sense at the same time as they direct. Both the touched and the toucher feel what they sense through the connecting hands, even if they do not understand and do not know what is being done. The touched person becomes aware of what the touching person feels and ... alters his configuration to conform to what he senses is wanted from him. When touching I seek nothing from the person I touch; I only feel what the touched person needs. (1981: 4)*

The teacher kinaesthetically paces and leads the client's breathing and muscular tonus, remaining responsive to and in dialogue with when and how, and indeed whether, the client can accept and integrate the neuromuscular information offered. After a lesson in FI, one may experience an enhanced sense of ease and well-being, and a fuller and more integrated self-image.

Awareness Through Movement (ATM)

In Awareness Through Movement (ATM), students are verbally directed through meticulously structured compositions of movement sequences. The clarity of the language used is instrumental in guiding the exploratory process, as it is one that requires little, if any, representational modeling. The teacher's words alone provide the conditions necessary for students to follow the lesson. Therefore, the verbal instructions offered, using language that is directive, conditional, and suggestive, help the individual to separate intention from action, thus eliminating the necessity to achieve a goal (for example, "Allow the right knee and left elbow to move in the direction of one another," rather than "Join your right knee to your left elbow"). This manner of cuing has been described by phenomenologist and Feldenkrais teacher Sondra Fraleigh as a language of permission (2014: 252).

ATM often begins with body scanning in a supine posture, where one pays attention to sensations arising in the body, thus enabling one to experience the nervous system's ability to surrender unnecessary muscular resistance into the support of the gravitational field. Typically, lessons take place in different orientations on the floor, since the immediate and relatively non-variable feedback of this "partner" allows one to more effectively discriminate between felt differences. Throughout the practice, students revisit this supine posture to assess change.

Many lesson themes reference developmental movement patterns that have been self-taught in early childhood and which provide the innate functional efficiency that permits independent and bipedal movement through the environment. The contextual conditions of an individual's life can often alter neurological circuits that produce counterproductive movement or "bad habits." In returning to these primary processes of motion, inefficient links can be revealed, unraveled, and then reconnected in ways that aim to improve coordination. Much of the floorwork practiced in contemporary dance is built on these patterns; their (re)investigation paves the way for acquiring greater efficiency in executing the complex and virtuosic variations called for in dance practice and performance today.

Dance visionary Martha Myers has proposed that "language conditions our mental habits and thought processes, just as movement conditions our physical habits. The two interact on unconscious and conscious levels. Language is therefore integral to the sensations we experience" (1983: 21). Movement patterns give a diversity of simultaneous commands to one's entire motor system; the sensory-based language of ATM separates different aspects of these complex occurrences. At the kinesiological level, language is utilized to help the student gain information about the orientation of the skeleton, muscles, joints, and the forces of action as momentum. On the representational level, language serves to conjure up images in the students' minds that will lead them through structured movement sequences. The functional use of language reflects efficiency and the interdependence of function and structure; at the cybernetic level, language helps students to understand the interrelatedness of individual parts that combine to form the conceptual and complex whole.

The teacher also aims to vary the language used in order to deliver information that best supports students in the process of individualizing their embodiment of the spoken words' associated images. For example, starting from a position where students are sitting on chairs, a teacher may say: "Begin to elongate the right femur forward. What other parts of you can you invite to participate?"; "What is the trajectory of the right thigh when you rotate your pelvis to the left?"; or "Turn to look over your left shoulder—does your right leg move in response?" The juxtaposition of the integrative, nonlinear learning espoused in the Feldenkrais Method and the sequential, linear linguistic transmission employed in ATM might seem incongruous. However, the ambiguity of language gives rise to images that evoke multiple interpretations and may possibly provoke the kind of disruption that leads to self-questioning. Thus, both words and movement seek out meaning; introspection grasps toward the language of thought, as action and reflection unfold in the same temporal space.

A sense of community often arises during the course of a lesson. The shared atmosphere of questioning, and the teacher's leading and pacing, induce both a synchronization of action within the group and the cultivation of a condition wherein each student can transform the subjective impressions gained from internal sensory stimuli into objective representations in the external environment (Feldenkrais 2010). All participants are invited to "grasp that [one's] small world and the great world around are but one, and that in this unity [one] is no longer alone" (Feldenkrais 1972: 54). Moving forward in this state of awareness can help one to realign and reorient in new relationships and to reach a place where one can welcome serendipity.

Principles of the method

The instructive strategies of the Feldenkrais Method use movement as the source of information to enable the (re)organization of the sensorimotor loop (Steinmüller, Schaefer, Fortwängler 2001).[5] All learning processes are related to sensorimotor stimuli. Students working with Feldenkrais are guided in reducing muscular effort in order to more finely discriminate between subtle changes in sensorimotor stimuli, as well as to "attune" themselves to their movement in its relation to energy expenditure in the gravitational field. Lightness of effort stands in direct relation to the rate of learning and the level of finesse that can be attained in movement. Improvement ceases when one no longer senses difference in the relation between effort and movement (Feldenkrais 1981; Batson, Schwarz 2007).

Reducing effort

The Feldenkrais Method guides students toward lowering the threshold at which differences in body orientation, movement organization, and muscular effort can be perceived, all of which facilitate kinaesthetic sensitivity and, therefore, allow for improvement in physical prowess.

The physiological law of Weber and Fechner,[6] to which Feldenkrais specifically refers, states that discrimination is finest when the stimulus is smallest, and the muscular synergy between agonist and antagonist produces a proportional and comfortable distribution of energy throughout the entire body (Peters, Sieben 2009). The reduction of tension enables efficient movement; inefficiency is sensed as effort that prevents one from doing more and doing it better. Acting with the minimum of energy for maximum efficiency, one can recover to a more neutral state of increased structural sensitivity, leading to well-coordinated exertion that is healthy, powerful, easy, and pleasurable (Feldenkrais 1980). Homeostasis is thus achieved by yielding and softening, instead of applying strong pressure and force. Attention to effort is key in helping one find a balance between the yielding and the pushing necessary to find resilience and choice in one's actions.

Creative self-questioning

The manner of questioning generates sensations and images that arise through movement and the observation of self and other (Kampe 2015). Lessons are propelled by participants' self-generated questions that attend to the means of achieving a goal and not to the goal itself. One fills the time with a quality of "free time," patiently allowing oneself time to move forward and backward, posing and following one's own questions. Educationalist Alfred Petzelt eloquently illuminates this concept when he states that "questioning is innate to human beings; it belongs to them. It is not acquirable. In speaking of an individual human being, one speaks of the questioner in the same moment" (quoted in Steinmüller, Schaefer, Fortwängler 2001: 165; translation author's own). Through this method of questioning, time can be appreciated as both content and measurement. Feldenkrais commented that his method provides learners with "conditions where they can learn to think. They have to think without words, with images, patterns, and connections. That sort of thinking always leads to a new way of action" (2010: 88). Oscillating between the doing of and conscious reflection on action, one "learns to act while [one] thinks and to think while [one] acts" (Feldenkrais 1972: 60). Feldenkrais referred to this as "reflection in action" (1981). Both Feldenkrais' practice and contemporary dance engage with "reflection in action," in recognition that the cognitive and physical components of any action are two different perspectives on the same function.

Novelty in repetition, attention, and variation

Finding novelty in repetition is linked to embodied questioning and reflection in action (see chapter 7). Repetition is fundamental for learning any skill; movement patterns become inscribed in the nervous system through copious processes of repetition. Neurophysiologist Nicolai Bernstein described learning as "repetition without repeating" (1996). This definition implies that the practitioner's repetition of an action or actions, carried out with an attitude of curiosity and wonder, helps them discover the range of possible responses to similar stimuli. With this approach to iteration, dancers can better distinguish between mindful repetition (see chapter 4) and mechanical drill, which is important as the former can broaden their repertoire for dynamic, expressive, and autonomous action (see chapter 7).

Directing attention to specific kinaesthetic and proprioceptive signals attunes one's perception to neuromuscular changes (Ginsberg 1988). Therefore, shifting the focus of one's attention is an additional strategy for promoting fresh approaches when dealing with the "same" movement material. Once a change or difference is internally perceived, it can be appreciated in the movement's outward representation and expression (see chapter 9). Crafting subtle variations with the material, for example by changing the familiar spatial orientation of an action, disassociates it from its habitual context. A small variation of this kind affects muscular effort, creates new spatial relationships, triggers kinaesthetic discernment of change, and thereby changes the action itself. Variations can lead to instability, a necessary condition for learning (Rywerant 1983). Mindful repetition, shifts in attention, and subtle variations are processes that search for alternatives, rather than attempting to determine and repeat a single solution.

Imagining

As students become familiar with movement patterns that surface in a Feldenkrais lesson, they are encouraged to systematically reduce the energy they expend until the felt and differentiated movements occur with a minimum of mobilization. Visualizing images and imagining are tools that have long proven effective in facilitating neurological change and promoting performance enhancement (Batson, Wilson 2014; Sweigard 1974). Enactivist approaches to imagery, including sensory-, verbal-, and motor-based ones, and imagining without moving, or "not doing as doing," are practiced extensively in the Feldenkrais Method (Kampe 2015; Sieben 2011). Lessons often employ reciprocal one-sidedness, meaning that that a lesson is organized between the right and left side of the body. In one part of the lesson, when dealing with one side of the body, one physically executes the movements, while on the other side of the body, one kinaesthetically imagines the movement sequences without actually doing them.

Rest, pause, and reversibility

Lessons are examples of distributed activity (Batson, Schwarz 2007) and the pacing of a Feldenkrais lesson aims to strike a balance in the autonomic nervous system between activity and resting, and pausing in the recognition that learning happens both in conscious and unconscious states (Peters, Sieben 2009: 54). Rest is necessary as full attention can only be given in short intervals. When attention diminishes, automatic movement sets in; therefore, moments of rest are essential for integrating the newly learned into one's system and refreshing the brain (Steinmüller, Schaefer, Fortwängler 2001). During lessons, students are given sufficient time to become aware of paying attention, as well as to incorporate moments of rest needed to maintain attention.

By slowing down, giving time to assimilate the idea of the movement, and leisurely finding novelty in the situation, one gains feedback on which the nervous system can build enhanced awareness and improve functioning (Feldenkrais 1980). Time is filled with the freedom to move, pause, pose, and follow one's own questions. Time can be appreciated as both content and measurement. Feldenkrais wrote that

> *to enable everybody "without exception" to learn, there should be plenty of time for everybody to assimilate the idea of the movement as well as the leisure to get used to the novelty of the situation. There should be sufficient time to perceive, and organize oneself. ... No one can learn when hurried and hustled. Fast action at the beginning of learning is synonymous with strain and confusion which, together, make learning an unpleasant exertion. ... When one becomes familiar with an act, speed increases spontaneously, and so does power. (1980: 3)*

The handling of rest and time aligns with the method's principle of reversibility. Feldenkrais has said that reversibility is demonstrated by the ability to pause, continue, or reverse action at any moment without any preliminary change of attitude or effort (1985: 113). He postulated that slowing down, delaying action, and prolonging the period between the movement's intention and its execution enables self-knowledge (Feldenkrais 1972: 46). Reversibility effects a kind of quintessential poise, which enables the individual to exercise choice at any moment during an action (Reese, quoted in Feldenkrais 1985: xvi).

Constraints

Bringing constraints into the practice narrows the multifarious possibilities for making sense of and organizing incoming information. Constraints set parameters, provide sets of scaffolding, and within this framework "scores" can be created that challenge and tease students to discover physically unfamiliar solutions to any given situation. In the Feldenkrais Method, self-imposed limitations fashioned by immobilizing parts of the body can form unusual relationships that inhibit movement along habitually organized routes. Maneuvering around these constraints enables the student to deconstruct and differentiate between known patterns, and to then reconstruct and reintegrate components into new permutations (see chapter 9). They create the conditions to generate new and unexpected movement, and the opportunity to move outside one's comfort zone.

Summary

In the Feldenkrais Method, one is asked to depart from certainty and recalibrate assumptions about where knowledge lies. The method draws on the individual's innate competencies for self-learning through processes of awareness, and engages both teacher and student in a mutual search for potential options for action. One can learn to "know" more clearly the function and felt organization of movement patterns, gain a more variegated sense of movement, and develop skills in order to improve one's ability to adapt with greater freedom of choice to the fluctuating circumstances of life. Experiencing the Feldenkrais Method can often result in enhanced artistic expression and a richer sense of personal agency and self-authority (Peters, Sieben 2009; Kampe 2015).

Of course there are myriad ways in which students respond to the information and suggestions offered during lessons. They may react with acceptance, indifference, or rejection. Signals of acceptance made apparent to the teacher can include independent exploration of the movement themes and their possible variations, a fuller breath, release of muscular tension, or adaptation to some encountered difficulty. Rejection may be evidenced through an increase of muscular tension, which can be taken as a sign of resistance.

For young dancers, an environment that challenges a goal-oriented approach to learning can be uncomfortable and unfamiliar, as familiar modes of practice may be disrupted. Often in dance, one resolves and strives to achieve one's goal as quickly and directly as possible. Factors that accompany a performance career in dance, including competition and compromised longevity, can cause stress. Reconciling the division between training modes that require pushing, working hard, and working fast, and those that attend to yielding, reducing effort, and slowing down often prove to be very challenging for young dancers (Brodie, Lobel 2012; Fortin, Vieira, Tremblay 2009).

It is not suggested here to replace one mode of practice with another, but rather to negotiate a balance between necessary levels of yielding and pushing in order to develop resilience and widen choice when dealing with the unpredictability of the profession. The research conducted with a first-year group of Bachelor of Arts students in the Dance program at the Palucca University of Dance Dresden juxtaposed the questioning, indirect, and explorative strategies of the Feldenkrais Method with more conventional and direct modes of training. Chapter 3 recounts and reflects upon the case study conducted with this group and examines the integration of somatically oriented pedagogical approaches into these students' contemporary dance practice.

---

1 Curricula and accreditation procedures are governed by national and international associations. The International Feldenkrais Federation (IFF) is the coordinating organization for these associations. It provides a forum for the international community, makes the original teachings available for teachers and students, and offers research and scholarship.

2 The Feldenkrais Method and theory of autopoiesis have similarities. Both reinforce the autonomy of the individual. Autopoiesis characterizes living systems as autonomous, closed organizational structures that generate their components by themselves (circularity). A set of particular organizational structures—relations between the distinct components of one system—define the system's identity (self-referentiality). The external world can only trigger the release of internally determined activity, which may possibly lead to structural reorganization without changing the system's identity (structural coupling) (Maturana, Varela 1985).

3 As is the case in the somatic movement systems of Bartenieff Fundamentals and Body-Mind Centering®, ATM lessons prioritize the following movement patterns: breath, core-distal, head-tail spinal, homologous, homolateral, and contralateral, referred to as developmental or early-childhood patterns.

4 An example of these instructions, while lying on the floor, could be: "Bring the right foot up again to stand as before, and review in your mind how you brought it up. Was the foot passing from one place to another in the air or was it dragged along the floor? Was there a moment when the foot left the floor? Notice if you felt any intention to stop breathing."

5 The sensorimotor loop can be understood as a recurrent feedback system between sensor readings and motor reactions. Feldenkrais bases his work on this intimate relation between the sensory and movement systems. The former plays a key role in orienting, guiding, helping to control, coordinating, and assessing the success of a movement. Executing finely tuned movements of body parts with an increased awareness, in turn, creates a subjectively lighter and more relaxed experience of these body parts due to a more differentiated representation in the brain's map. Finely tuned movement can thus help to reorganize the motor cortex and the nervous system (Doidge 2015).

6 The Weber-Fechner law states that subjective sensation is proportional to the logarithm of the stimulus intensity; the just perceptible difference between two stimuli is proportional to the magnitude of the stimuli and the subject's sensitivity (Feldenkrais 1949).

EXPERIENCE IN DANCE ART: REFLECTIONS IN THE PALUCCA COMMUNITY

IN CONVERSATION WITH MATTHIAS MARKSTEIN

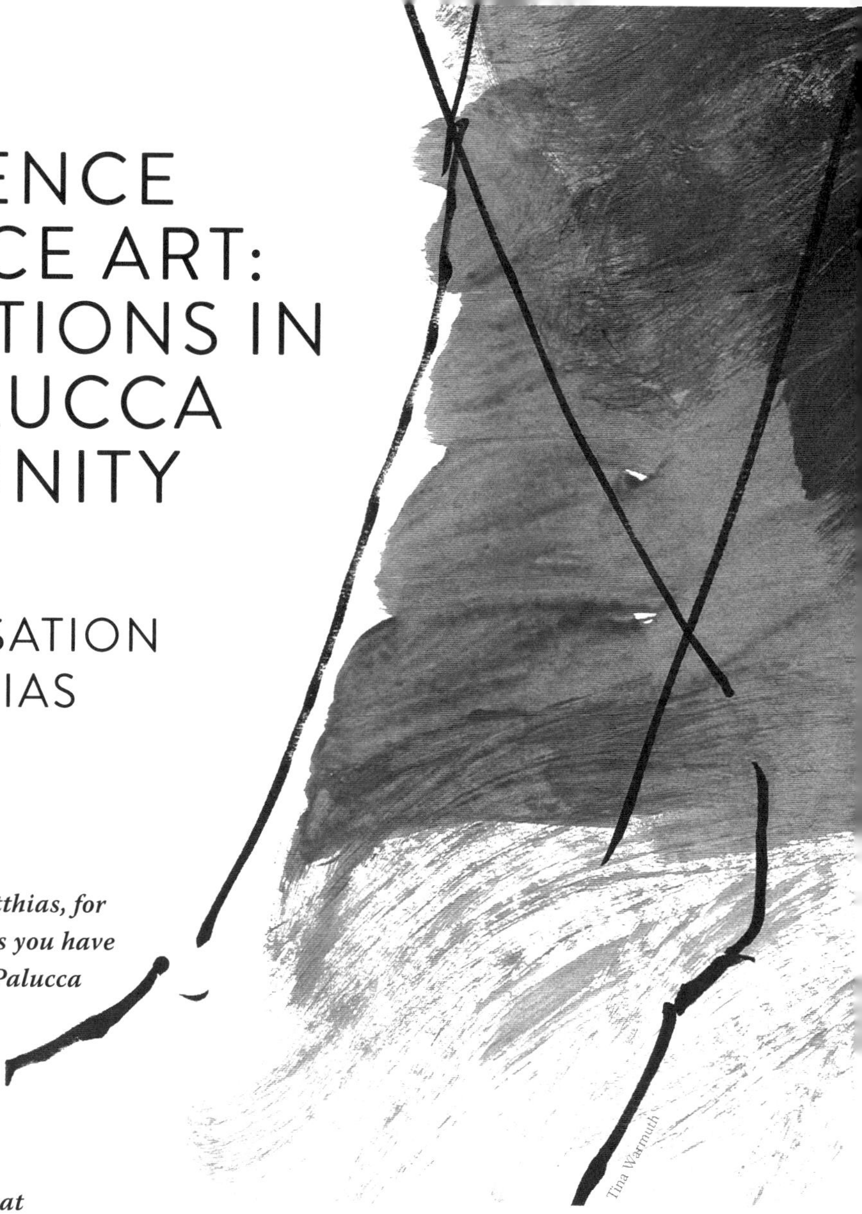

Jenny Coogan: Matthias, for nearly twenty years you have been a part of the Palucca community, as a student and for the past six years as a teacher and choreographer. What changes have you noticed to the professional demands that confront dancers today, as well as to the curricular structures within which they train at this institution?

Matthias Markstein: When I first joined the Palucca University of Dance, I felt very much at home in the subject of improvisation, since that was where my role as an artist was most evident. Emotion, and intention resulting from emotion, still play a major role for me today. For Professor Hanne Wandke (Gret Palucca's successor), emotion could be a source of inspiration for generating improvised movement, particularly in the interplay with live music. The diversity of musical styles and genres played an important part in the process.

All in all, the university's profile has not really changed much over the past years. It is still based on the three pillars of practice: ballet, contemporary dance, and improvisation. But when I was a student at the Palucca University, there was a stronger emphasis on the performance of improvisation rather than on improvisation as research-oriented exploration. Today the tendency is to expand one's self-concept by accessing one's own internal landscapes. Greater value is placed on somatically oriented learning and on the center of our own bodies. Of course both aspects can never be separated fully, but there is currently more differentiation in the concept of improvisation. I think this tendency is noticeable throughout the contemporary dance scene.

J: You have begun a program in Laban/Bartenieff Movement Studies. Is this, in part, because you feel that a somatic approach is likely to enhance the competencies now required from prospective dance artists?

M.: The integration of a broad spectrum of somatic approaches is definitely becoming more common in the world of dance. In particular, elements from the Feldenkrais Method are much more common today. You, Jenny, integrate them differently in your lessons today than you did in the past. Laban/Bartenieff Movement Studies are becoming much more differentiated with regard to the art of dance and are closely linked to body work. They automatically have a high priority in dance classes. Forsythe Improvisation Technologies are firmly embedded in the curriculum of this university. Likewise, workshops in GAGA movement language are offered to the graduating class. Forsythe Improvisation Technologies and Laban Movement Studies tend to focus more on the cognitive component of somatic work whereas, in my view, Gaga and Bartenieff Fundamentals address a stronger physical and emotional component.

In general, I've also noticed that a lot more somatic approaches have been integrated into contemporary technique classes today. After all, somatic work and the transmission of imitative movement vocabulary do not exclude one another. The pedagogical challenge here is to support the teaching of prescribed movement vocabulary through somatic approaches. For this purpose, the vocabulary should first of all be disassembled, so that the underlying movement principles become apparent. This, in my view, is what contemporary dance is all about.

In addition, I would love to have more time in class for communication, interaction, and encouraging each student to develop autonomy within the group. This is happening on a small scale already. For example, when I look at our current second-year class in the Bachelor's Dance program—i.e. the student group for your case study, Jenny—I can see their exceptional openness when it comes to feedback and interaction. These young men and women can express their opinions freely; I notice how they do not restrict their answers to what they think I might want to hear from them. And this is what I find particularly inspiring and challenging as a teacher, and also as a choreographer, or indeed for any community that meets to perform art together. I think that our university structures could put even more emphasis on interaction and autonomy.

J.: I have observed that many students in the Bachelor of Arts program in Dance feel pressed for time. What is your view on this?

M.: I agree. I really think that, at the beginning of the program, students should be given more time to arrive, and to experience what their present state is and how they can build from it. To discover answers to the questions "Who am I?" and "How did I get here?" The site-specific weeks of dance and music improvisation in the summer on the islands of Hiddensee and Sylt were one of the events I experienced as a student myself.

I consider this project to be a great source of inspiration for any performing artist. The setting allows one to come fully into contact with oneself and then to slowly drift into an explorative state from which creativity can emerge. For this reason, these project weeks are one of the most significant annual events at our institution.

Fundamentally, our curriculum aims to train dancers to develop diverse physical competencies. When I observe the dancers of our graduating class, I see some highly trained and physically "perfect" dancers, who really enjoy explorative and interactive processes.

J.: How do you integrate somatic approaches in your work with secondary school pupils?

M.: I have observed that our youngest students, who join us in the fifth grade, are still very autonomous. They don't have preconceptions and are adventurous. Exploration is the determining factor during this phase of their training. This means that class plans can usually be implemented in a very playful way. By grades nine or ten, during adolescence, I have found interactive processes harder to establish. The students do communicate with each other, but self-exploration in artistic processes poses a real problem. In addition, they can often find communication with me as their teacher rather tedious.

The challenge for my work with students at this age is to evoke emotions by offering them tasks in which they can find themselves. I don't ask the students to talk about their emotions, but I expect them to reflect on who they are and on their inner driving force from which they make artistic decisions.

At the moment, I am teaching a ninth-grade class, a group with whom I worked last year. I have constructed a system for these younger students, in which specific themes are initially explored somatically through movement with improvisation. Out of this exploration, movement phrases are developed either collectively or, if necessary, by me alone. We then work with them, paying attention to the themes that were initially identified.

J.: You aim to encourage a reflective and autonomous practice for all the students with whom you engage.

M.: Yes, I do not doubt that all students are capable of this. However, as I have mentioned, adolescent students often have difficulties with interaction and do not always succeed in implementing the learned movement material in artistic practice. The challenge for our students is to follow through with the interactive processes they experienced in the early, explorative years of their training and not to shy away from making their artistic decisions transparent. I think that dancers are so preoccupied with their own identity in adolescence that they just don't want to interact with their environment as much as in earlier years. Nevertheless, the biggest pedagogical challenge I face at the Palucca University today is to draw out a certain amount of openness from adolescent groups of students, so that they can develop further and get to know themselves more deeply.

J.: I thank you Matthias for this informative interview.

Maria Katherina Franz

3. SOMATIC APPROACHES IN CONTEMPORARY DANCE CLASS: A CASE STUDY

Jenny Coogan

Introduction

The following question steered this case study: How can a somatically oriented pedagogical approach informed by the Feldenkrais Method contribute to both empowering young dancers with personal agency and supporting their self-reflection within a German conservatory environment? The pedagogical methods of this project aimed to offer young dancers strategies for attending to their physical, affective, social, and cognitive domains. In addition, it intended to help them navigate their studies with enhanced awareness and self-regulation, and to potentially carry these methods of knowledge into other areas of their lives.

One of the primary motivations for conducting this study grew out of my own observations and reflections gleaned from years of teaching at the Palucca University of Dance Dresden. As part of my responsibilities at this institution, I have worked daily with first-year groups of Bachelor of Arts (BA) students as their primary teacher in contemporary/modern dance and as class advisor. Supporting freshmen to manage issues related to self-responsibility, authority, independence and interdependence, socialization, and interculturalism, as well to negotiate a variety of styles and concepts within dance and dancing—all challenges that await them in the professional field!—has strengthened my conviction that somatically informed pedagogy should be integrated into the curriculum from the beginning of conservatory education. Somatic methods can support autonomous learning and the development of ethically conscious, self-determined, and self-caring human beings. These are essential skills for enabling dancers to become more fully equipped to navigate their way through their studies and the professional landscape.

This case study was implemented in the contemporary/modern dance class for first-year students of the BA program in Dance. The research team included experts in the fields of dance, sociology, pedagogical psychology, and business education. Research associate Nina Patricia Hänel shared teaching responsibilities with me and—together with the research assistants Anja Balzer, Fanny Barz, and Karin Matko—contributed to data capture and analysis. Professors Jürgen van Buer and Susanne Narciss offered invaluable support as expert academic advisors. All of the above participated as unobtrusive observers and critical friends throughout the research period.

The following chapter identifies the study's theoretical, methodological, and pedagogical underpinnings. It outlines the research setting, participant group, and the planning and operationalization of the study. A description of the processes of data capture, its results, and a critical reflection close this section of the volume.

Theoretical background

As a researcher and teacher, I work within somatic, socio-constructivist, and post-positivist paradigms. The manifestations of these models view the world as being made up of social constructions that can be changed (Schwandt 1994), posit the existence of multiple realities in personal meaning-making (Robson 2011), and consider the *Leib* to be a non-permanent body-self, which is formed and transformed through the context of an individual life (Shusterman 2008). Knowledge and the knower are not static but rather are emerging and transforming, experienced individually or in relation to others. Socio-constructivism emphasizes the collective generation and transmission of meanings between people, as they form their relationship with the world (Long 2002: 14). Philosopher Don Ihde proposes that:

> *We all are situated beings with a history of our own. In the postmodern perspective, knowledge is related to the local and particularized experiences through which we construct our practices, understandings, and conceptions. (2002: 67-68)*

Post-positivist paradigms understand situations as socially constructed realities that are in part determined by the researcher's position in the world. They aim to introduce a critical perspective to the investigation and to work toward change in the teaching, learning, and research processes. Therefore, as in the case study described in this text, teaching and research often overlap (Green, Stinson 1999).

Therefore, epistemologically and ontologically speaking, this case study aligns with the experiential elements of being, and acknowledges both the plurality of truths and the sociocultural aspects of subjective experience that construct identities. It harvests from interdisciplinary thought, including enaction, and somatic and educational theories.[1] These have evolved in part out of constructivist models, which stress that the individual is the enactment of a world and a mind resulting from the history of the variety of actions that a being in the world performs (Varela, Thompson, Rosch 1991: 9). Presence is sought in oneself, while at the same time one is present, active, and reactive, in one's world (Eddy, Williamson, Weber 2014: 174).

Early twentieth-century educationalist John Dewey's humanistic and experiential philosophy of learning reflects these propositions. Its profound simplicity has retained contemporary relevance. Dewey identifies reality with experience, not with external phenomena. He speaks of learning as a natural phenomenon that proceeds from the individual's engagement with the world; such learning can be understood as a spiral-like form of readaptation to one's environment (1997). This cyclical process illustrates that the observation of one's present actions, infused with knowledge of those that are past, endows learning with meaningful purpose. As is the case in the Feldenkrais Method of somatic movement education, themes are revisited in order to discover them anew, to view them from different perspectives, and to engage with them using enhanced discrimination and refined skill.

Furthermore, Dewey highlights the individual's fundamental dependence on larger environmental factors, as he defines the self in terms of habit, and insists that habits must engage with and assimilate into the environments in which they function (quoted in Shusterman 2008: 214). Dance is inherently a socially organized process of shared and experiential learning. Meaning is created individually in ongoing negotiation with and accommodation of the social environment. Therefore, what is learned cannot be separated from how it is learned and how it is utilized (Luhmann 1995). Dance scholar Laurence Louppe writes of "the essential idea of a body not given but discovered, even invented" (1997: 40), and her contemporary Susan Leigh Foster has argued that "the repertoire of metaphors learned in class functions not only to define the dancer's body but also to establish the epistemological foundation for performing dance" (1997: 241). Stimulated by this social, cultural, and artistic thinking, the research team strove to recognize, accept, and value the aesthetic and socially constructed systems of beliefs and attitudes the dancers hold, in addition to the individual bodily inscribed histories of the participants, as the known was incorporated with the yet undiscovered in our dance practice together.

Methodology

Action-research methodology provided the operational scheme for this study, and grounded theory gave us the procedural frame for data capture and interpretation. Phenomenological in nature, action-research seeks to understand and interpret the meanings of individual human experiences as they are situated in culture and society (Robson 2011; Giguere 2015). Questions arise through rigorous processes of observation, participation, reflection, data gathering, analysis, and action planning that, in turn, lead to new cycles of thought informed by the learning that has taken place (Giguere 2015; Creswell 1998). Among the defining factors of this methodology are: ongoing self-monitoring and self-reflection; privileging the voice of the participants; active participation; and the desire to create change (Wilson 2009; Wisker 2001). The inductive processes of grounded theory align with the iterative processes of action-research; as a result, they are often employed in tandem. Both methods of qualitative social research look to create procedures rather than to produce results. In grounded theory, an analytic appraisal of each piece of newly captured data is used to shape the development of subsequent data-gathering processes. Throughout the study, there was a constant interplay between the gathering of data, its analysis, and the generation of new data. This process led to revision and (re)evaluation both in regard to the study's conceptual planning and the sequencing of the teaching modes.

Pedagogical approach

Somatically informed pedagogy

Somatically informed pedagogy examines the structure and function of the body in terms of the processes of lived experience, perception, and consciousness (Joly 2004). By consciously expanding awareness, improvement in the function, efficiency, and qualities of movement can be supported without the levels of tension or effort normally associated with attempts toward advancement (Holdaway, Kovich, Simmonds 2002). As Sara Reed, quoting Rosemary Butcher, states in her essay in this publication, "[t]he body comes to be understood with a sense of democracy and ownership" (see chapter 10).

Somatic approaches in dance training reflect a paradigm shift in education that increasingly recognizes the teacher's role as primarily one of steward and facilitator, rather than master. Teachers/facilitators set parameters in which students are encouraged to be decision-making agents, and are motivated to assume ownership of their own processes and questions. Thus students are encouraged to loosen themselves from dependence on their teachers. As a result, power relations that have traditionally existed within conservatory environments can be disrupted (Shapiro 1998; Green 2002a; Burnidge 2012). As somatic principles underpin all efficient movement, and are inclusive enough to accommodate a variety of teaching styles found in conservatory education, a comprehensive grounding in these principles can provide students with a sound base to explore a variety of dance styles and genres (Holdaway, Kovich, Simmonds 2002; Fortin 2003). The eclecticism of today's dance world requires teachers/facilitators and students alike to be willing to practice a variety of methods and formats, to engage with their work from multiple perspectives, and to be open to meanings other than their own in an acknowledgment of one's own prejudices (Reed 2015; Ginot 2011). Cultural theorist Gesa Ziemer proposes that "strength lies in the in-between, in the gap which develops out of different perspectives" (2011: 243).

A tradition of disruption

Dancers may have explicit expectations and assumptions about dance training and technique, often summed up by learning fast, pushing hard, sweating, and being corrected. Usually their goals are identified at an early age and dancers strive to achieve them in the most direct way possible (Buckroyd 2000). Somatically informed pedagogy, one that emerged out of a tradition of disruption, takes the dancer off a linear path of learning and goal achievement (see chapter 1). Working somatically, dancers may encounter destabilization or disruption to their familiar ways of training, and experience ambiguous sensations, thoughts, or feelings that may be associated with new ways of moving and thinking about movement (Rouhiainen 2008). They may become disconcerted or frustrated, or experience a sense of loss when known measures for weighing and balancing the physical sensations of effort and movement are recalibrated (Holdaway, Kovich, Simmonds 2002: 36). However, destabilization offers potential for learning as it can reveal alternatives to one's habitual actions. In liminal moments of uncertainty, learners are invited to adjust their ingrained systems of knowledge, expectation, and value (Whatley 2015). The somatic emphasis on individual decision-making and experimentation may foster a richer sense of personal agency. A consequence of this, however, may be the disruption of one's customary manners of accommodating external authority and hierarchical structures (Green 2001; Burndige 2012). The result may be to challenge social conventions in one's environment or the ability to interpret these conventions while paying greater attention to one's self-regulatory needs (Shapiro 1998).

Methods

The pedagogical methods and strategies of this study provoked change by introducing unfamiliar ways of working to the contemporary dance class. Students experienced and processed this change in very different ways; for some, it produced motivational and/or cognitive dissonances (see chapters 4 and 6). Dancers were asked to relax their expectations that training should necessarily prioritize external modeling and fast-paced assimiliation of prescribed material. They were also asked to slow down in order to pay attention to the sensations and experiences that create space for body awareness and proprioceptive sensitivity. In an atmosphere of shared responsibility for learning, questions were developed to which students were encouraged to discover their own answers. This situation challenged all participants to recognize multiple perspectives, to learn self-governance, and to become conscious of the consequences of choice.

Research setting[2]

Embedded in the conservatory model of education, the BA program in Dance at the Palucca University is comprised of three equally weighted pillars of practice: classical dance, contemporary/modern dance, and dance improvisation. The admission process is highly selective, requiring proficiency in classical dance and a curiosity for improvisation. As familiarity with contemporary/modern dance is not one of the criteria that is prioritized for acceptance, students begin the program with varying degrees of experience in these styles. Classical dance provides the frame of reference for incoming students. The curriculum is predominantly comprised of required courses; there are few elective offerings. The aspirations of most graduates are to work under contract in dance companies; some choose to pursue freelance careers.

As a member of the same community, I am invested in daily happenings both as observer and participant. Students, faculty, and staff spend their days together in close physical proximity, as most of the institution's infrastructure—including dance studios, dormitory, cafeteria, classrooms, and administrative offices—is housed in a single building. "The Palucca family" is a phrase that is often heard at the school, and expresses the sense of shared identity. Students exude pride and feel privileged to have been accepted into this community; they adapt to its social norms and regulations, and hold similar aesthetic dispositions. Ultimately, practice is the shared histories of learning (Wenger 1998: 95). Phenomenologist Maxine Sheets-Johnstone proposes that:

> *Moving harmoniously with others is pervasive in everyday life, in our lives in play, and in aesthetic creativity and appreciation. Whether we are moving individually with another or moving as part of a group, our harmonious moving together is the result of real-life, real-time experiences of the qualitative dynamics of movement. (2016: 61)*

Belonging provides anchoring. Indeed, one can feel an unmistakable sense of belonging in this environment.

Participant group

The case study took place in the contemporary/modern dance practice of the first-year BA students and in supplementary workshop sessions scheduled intermittently throughout the year. It spanned a period of thirty-four weeks. This dance class is a required course for the students; however, participation in the processes of data capture was based on consent. The regulatory ethical procedures for ensuring informed consent were fulfilled. All students agreed to participate in the study and contributed data in varying degrees throughout the research period.

The study began in September 2014 with a group of twenty-one students, fourteen female and seven male, ranging from fifteen to nineteen years of age. Seven of these students had either graduated from the institution's secondary school or had been enrolled as guests during the previous year. Fourteen joined the program from other German or world locations. Midway through the study, two students exmatriculated as their career objectives changed. Nineteen students completed the academic year.

Ten nationalities and seven languages were represented in the participant group: Austrian, Australian, British, Belgian, French, Italian, German, Serbian, Spanish, and Russian. The impact of language in teaching and learning in this program can be compromised due to its international profile and the fact that many of the foreign students matriculate with only rudimentary skills in the primary languages (German and English) used for instruction at the institution. As language is physical, the precision and imagination with which it is used, which is both visual and kinaesthetic in explorative teaching and learning in contemporary dance and somatic practices, is essential for students to truly profit from the material that is offered. Throughout the course of their studies, students accrue language skills in both the German and English languages and thereby gain confidence.

Contact hours with the participant group varied for each semester. For the eighteen weeks of the winter semester (September 2014 to February 2015), I taught the majority of the daily contemporary/modern dance classes and worked with the students in supplementary afternoon sessions. During the sixteen weeks of the summer semester (March 2015 to June 2015), we met for studio practice twice weekly and continued to meet in afternoon workshops. The extended research period (thirty-four weeks) and the density of contact hours afforded the research team the opportunity to observe development and change in the working environment, and to gather, review, and interpret a diverse pool of data.

Research design and research questions

Frame

The principles and strategies of the Feldenkrais Method were woven into the contemporary dance practice in ways that engaged the students in sustained discourse structured around the higher-order processes of problem-solving, critical thinking, and decision-making. Emphasis was placed on the direction and focus of attention, self- and peer observation, finding the novelty in repetition, and forming one's own questions. The sequencing and variegation of the material took into account the different learning styles and personalities of the group, and aimed to balance somatic approaches with teaching strategies found within a more traditional dance class. Dance artist Kirsty Alexander shows how the cross-fertilization of dance and somatic practices can be achieved by working with existing vocabulary through which students can use kinaesthetic experiences to discover their own language (2003: 20). The class structure alternated between exploratory tasks, improvisation, and the transmission of prescriptive movement material that had a shared focus on sensory awareness and kinaesthetic feedback. Its pacing allowed space for self-directed movement research, discussion, dialogue, and critical-analytical reflection and writing.

The practice was grounded in functionalism and coordination. The interrelation of the following aspects was stressed: attention and intention; gradations in effort and muscle tone; the interplay of weight and gravity; congruence between breath and movement; the availability of the pelvis as a center of motor function; and the fluid quality of spinal movement. Students were asked to observe themselves in quotidian movements and fundamental movement patterns in order to identify their personal movement preferences and habits, and reflect on how these might affect their alignment and coordination. Attention was directed toward "tuning in" to movement initiations and the manifold ways in which they spread through the body and are expressed outward into space. Working within these parameters, a repertoire of floor, standing, and locomotive material was generated and developed in length and complexity over periods of two to three weeks. The environment prioritized action-oriented learning and the explicit rendering of the interrelatedness of sensing, feeling, acting, and thinking.

THE QUESTION STEERING THIS RESEARCH WAS:

- How does a somatically informed pedagogical practice develop dance students' self-reflection and personal agency?

THE FOLLOWING RESEARCH QUESTIONS WERE DERIVED FROM THIS PRIMARY ONE:

- Wherein lies the potential for the coexistence of a somatically oriented pedagogical practice alongside the diversity of skill-based training practices and choreographic styles in a conservatory environment?
- In contemporary studio practice, what strategies and methods might support young dancers in learning to locate themselves with self-efficacy in the inherently collectively organized structure of dance education?
- Within a German conservatory environment, what conditions are necessary for dancers to find value in a somatically informed pedagogical practice, with particular emphasis on the Feldenkrais Method, as an integral component of their contemporary/modern dance practice?

Research design

The study was carried out in five phases. Term breaks and periods of examination dictated the apportioning of time for each phase. The table overleaf provides a structural overview of the complete case study and is followed by a more detailed description of each individual phase.

PHASE	DURATION	THEME	FOCUS
1	6 weeks	Orientation and contextualization	To provide contexts for contemporary and modern dance; to introduce somatics as part of the class fabric and a support for forming the social group; to bring knowledge from a greater range of sources into class
2	7 weeks	Indirect leadership though the practice of team teaching	To create a lively climate and culture of interaction encouraging the development of symmetrical exchange among all participants in the learning situation
3	5 weeks	Explicit integration of the Feldenkrais Method	To focus on self-perception as a way to experience and contend with the complexity of contemporary dance; to use movement sensation to track one's own progress
4	4 weeks	Peer-assisted learning	To support autonomy and self-reflection thorough a laboratory-like environment of peer-centered learning; to enhance performance skills
5	12 weeks	Integration and evaluation in processes of shared decision-making	To work with an individual combination of the tools, methods, and strategies investigated during the course of the study; to support self-directed and self-generated learning processes

Students are quoted throughout the following section of this chapter (all quotes are presented in italics). The unconventional inclusion of student voices in this part of the report is intended to highlight their individual responsiveness to the processes that took place in the learning environment. The initial evaluation outlined below provides a base for the summative evaluation that follows.

Biographical interviews

The first step in this research process was to identify what systems of reference and value were embedded within the dancers' previous experiences, and how these systems might affect their engagement with the present. Thus structured individual interviews, with an ethnographic and phenomenological focus, were conducted with each of the research participants during the first week of the study. Information gleaned from these interviews helped the research team to clarify the context at the beginning of the study.

A collection of typical student responses to three central questions are included below:

Can you say in three words what dance means to you?
Responses expressed with the most amount of regularity were: *"feeling; expression; emotion; pleasure; passion; joy in performance; giving to and receiving from the audience; a way of life; discipline; hard work; concentration"* (recorded interview, 09.09.14).

What does contemporary and modern dance mean to you?
Responses included: *"freedom put into movement; individual and experimental; whatever you want it to be; Contemporary dance is not written like ballet. Every teacher has their own technique; Contemporary and modern dance provoke emotions and a reality that can be diverse and confronting. It has no boundaries, and it's an integral part of development as an artist"* (recorded interview, 09.09.14).

What does/do somatics or somatic practices mean to you?
Few responses were forthcoming. Many students were familiar with Pilates, and one person contributed the following: *"I had some classes in somatics, but I can't really say what it is."*

The responses revealed the students' strong emotional connection to dance, demonstrated great variance in their conceptual understanding and experience in contemporary and modern dance, and showed that they had little or no exposure to a somatic way of working. Therefore, through the systematic integration of somatic methods in the teaching and learning environment, a disruption in students' familiar training practices was anticipated. This—coupled with the fact that many of the students were still fully immersed in the dynamic processes of the development of their personalities (puberty)—led us to expect that strong emotional and cognitive reactions to the teaching materials, their modes of transmission, and the reciprocal pathways of communication might emerge.

PHASE 1	ORIENTATION AND CONTEXT SUPPORT
Duration	Six weeks, five ninety-minute classes per week, six workshops
Teacher/facilitators	Jenny Coogan, Nina Patricia Hänel
Data capture	Individual biographical interviews; focus-group interviews; online mixed-modal questionnaire; quantitative survey identifying students' aims and objectives for the study year; video recordings

Focus:
To establish common ground with a heterogeneous group of students with diverse backgrounds in contemporary and modern dance (ZT/MT); to provide a conceptual frame for understanding these dance styles through physical explorations, text and film analysis, movement explorations in workshop formats, and the attendance of performance events; to introduce the field of somatics through physical practice in class and workshop formats.

Feldenkrais:
To attend to sensory information and kinaesthetic feedback; to notice how such attention might affect movement in both its expression and form; to establish somatic referencing strategies through body scanning and breath awareness; to practice self- and peer observation in classes and workshops; to encourage self-reflection through class discussion.

Teaching modes:
Class themes that combined individual movement research, improvisational tasks, and the appropriation of teacher-led movement material were explored. Particular attention was devoted to the experience of one's breath, movement initiations and their pathways through the body, weight release and recovery, and the regulation of muscle tonus. Floorwork sequences were referenced from the developmental movement patterns and prescriptive material was sourced primarily from the Humphrey/Limón lineage. The repetition and variation of sequences were prioritized in order for students to become more attentive to small approximations of movement and to discriminate between subtle differences. Attention was paid to generating somatic conditions in which students could experience moving and dancing that felt significantly different to their usual coordination. Some realized that in strong dance training they sometimes lost their awareness of inner sensations while moving. Their experience with Feldenkrais changed that awareness:

> *I felt like I was stepping on place in a way, but through these weeks and through the work and through the theory and through the understanding of what we're doing, yeah, through the whole process in the end, I found that this is still very important work I need to do, and which is maybe—*ja ein bisschen letztendlich vernachlässigt *(yes, ultimately a little bit neglected).*

In workshop situations, students became more familiar with the directions and stylistics of ZT/MT through engaging in small groups with text, film material, and physical explorations with or without guidance from a teacher. One workshop led the students through a physical and conceptual introduction to somatic movement education.

Foto: Karin Matko

Summary:
This phase combined the familiar mode of imitative practice with the unfamiliar somatic approach of slowing down in order to attune to sensory information and pay attention to subtle differences in movement. In addition, the careful construction and deconstruction of movement material was intended to encourage awareness of how each individual part contributes to the effective functioning of the whole. Students reported that this phase challenged them to focus on the subtlety of movement and

> *to really focus on the details and not to focus on "OK, I want to do all that stuff," but to take one thing and then try to work on that, and take the other thing and try to work on that. ... Then I actually feel improvement and feel that I can work more precisely with things.*

The fact that this phase concluded with a public presentation of the material during the annual open-house event encouraged students to endow their class work with similar attitudes and qualities that they bring to performance. In this way, "performing" the class material supported students in linking internal and environmental attention. Audience responses, as well as the students' own comments when viewing the video recording of the event, indicate that this connection was apparent both to the viewers and themselves. Most of the international students encountered difficulty in the reading and comprehension of texts, *"especially for those of us who don't speak good English or even German, it's difficult to read and try to understand these things."* At this stage of the study, contextualization acquired through physical practice and group discussion proved more beneficial than that acquired through text analysis.

PHASE 2	INDIRECT LEADERSHIP STYLES THOUGH THE PRACTICE OF TEAM TEACHING
Duration	Seven weeks, five classes per week, guest residency, three workshops
Teachers/facilitators	Jenny Coogan, Nina Patricia Hänel, Jason Jacobs, Monica Buckland
Data capture	Entire group: weekly text responses to the "theme of the week"; video recordings Focus group: for the remainder of the study an ethnographically diverse group of nine students participated in regular focus-group interviews and kept journals of their experiences in the study

Focus:
To create classroom situations that reveal how different perspectives in learning/teaching can occur simultaneously; to offer anatomically based movement explorations; to present a variety of learning strategies, including sensory and proprioceptive discrimination, analytical properties of observing and reflecting, and movement composition.

Feldenkrais:
During the two weeks of team teaching (Coogan and Hänel), attention was directed to the process of differentiation and integration, and the functional organization of the shoulder girdle. Classes explored the depatterning and repatterning of habitual ways of using the shoulder girdle. Self-reflection was exercised through the introduction of writing practice. As in all phases, repetition, variation, and perturbation of movement were emphasized, as well as self- and peer observation, and sensory discrimination.

Teaching modes:
As in phase one, there was a constant interplay between exploratory and imitative teaching both during the guest residency and in team-teaching classes and workshops. During the two weeks of daily team teaching and the two afternoon meetings with Coogan and Hänel, the students were confronted with a small amount of movement material that was investigated using constraints, variations in sequence, spatial orientation, and sensorimotor differentiation. The purpose was to understand the complex functional organization of the shoulder girdle, particularly in regard to weight support and locomotion in floorwork. The team teaching was carried out either through reciprocal leading and

following or the division of roles in which one person attended to the group in general, while the other offered individual feedback. Jason Jacobs introduced students to writing as a strategy for creating individual movement material. In workshops that fused music and dance, students created movement compositions with sections of the scores of minimalist composers. The themes of each of the final three weeks for this phase focused on different aspects of learning: sensory and proprioceptive discrimination, the analytical properties of observing and reflecting, and movement composition.

Summary:

Team teaching led us to identify shared objectives, provided an atmosphere of respect and trust, and enabled us to be willing to change course. Student comments suggest that team teaching made the continual process of negotiation, immediacy, and spontaneity that took place in the environment explicit:

> *For me it was sometimes just helpful to hear ideas and images with different and new words. Every teacher teaches at least a little bit differently. Small differences can have a big effect on my understanding of an exercise or principle. In addition, I had the feeling that the teachers felt comfortable in their cooperation with us. This made the atmosphere, for me as a relatively sensitive person easily influenced by mood, very pleasant.*

Students experienced the most diverse range of teaching and learning methods during this phase and their responses were varied. Classes with Jason Jacobs offered students a daily change of both focus and mode of transmission: working in pairs, with text, and with improvisation and composition. Team teaching in dance class explored one complex function from multiple perspectives; team teaching in music and dance workshop situations afforded students composition and performance opportunities. Students appreciated the variety and one identified that *"what we are aiming for in the class is to touch and try everything without any prejudices."*

PHASE 3	EXPLICIT INTEGRATION OF THE FELDENKRAIS METHOD
Duration	Five weeks, five classes per week, two workshops
Teacher/facilitator	Jenny Coogan
Data capture	Entire group: biweekly questionnaire; one workshop Focus group: interviews; video recordings; journal writing

Focus:
"To make sense out of sensation" (Scott Clarke, quoted in Reed 2015: 212).

To improve self-organization and coordination; to use visualization to enrich understanding of anatomical principles; to find the endurance and concentration to persevere with the "same" material in order to make more informed choices about one's dancing; to understand that a change in movement function can change one's awareness.

Feldenkrais:
To work with the following: differentiation and integration; self- and peer observation; novelty in repetition; reduction in effort to feel the forces that pass through the skeletal structure.

Teaching modes:
During this phase, emphasis was placed on the direct integration of mini-Awareness Through Movement lessons into the beginning of the practice. The pacing of the classes was slow, which allowed for the potential to sense and perceive one's movement, reflect on individual perception, and engage with kinaesthetic feedback. This phase invited the students to resist the tendency to focus on the movement's outward representa-

Foto: Karin Matko

tion, and to draw their attention to the subtle dynamic variations of its execution: *"I've done the movement so often, but now I have the feeling that I can feel every detail."* By working with partners in refining skills of self- and peer observation, students engaged with the idea that coordination can be understood as the proportionally efficient relationship between gravity and energy expenditure.

Summary:

By working in pairs with only small amounts of teacher demonstration, students were encouraged to move away from dependence on the teacher and toward positioning themselves in the material. A student statement illustrates this: *"I really appreciate the possibility to try things out in my own time and in my own authentic way. This is a creative right."*

However, as there was subtler dynamic variation during this phase, students found it more difficult to concentrate and struggled with the small amount of athletic movement: *"I don't feel like I'm moving enough, that it's getting me to the place that I want, that I see myself in."*

Some were able to make the connection between inner perception and its outward representation: *"It feels different, but I don't know if one can see the difference from the outside."*

Increasingly, students were asked to make, reflect upon, and accept the consequences of their own decisions. In class questionnaires, students were repeatedly asked to reflect on their somatic condition at a given moment in relation to their ability to fully engage in class (see appendix).

PHASE 4	PEER-CENTRED LEARNING, PERFORMANCE SKILLS
The fourth phase marked the beginning of the summer semester. During this semester, contact time in the studio occurred twice weekly. No workshops were scheduled during this phase.	
Duration	Four weeks, two classes per week
Teachers/facilitators	Jenny Coogan, Nina Patricia Hänel
Data capture	Entire group: video recording; mixed-methods questionnaire Focus group: focus-group interviews; journal writing

Focus:
To work on the interpretation of choreographic material in small groups; to take responsibility for individual composition and performance choices negotiated within the group; to collectively document the creative processes in written and digital form; to improve performance quality and social skills.

Feldenkrais:
To make refined proprioceptive distinctions, particularly in muscle tonus, in order to improve performance and physical skills; to carry out self- and peer observation; to discover novelty in repetition.

Teaching modes:
The class structure created conditions that facilitated students' self-generated learning. The role of the teacher was that of mentor. After a brief group warm-up, students worked in small groups with choreographic material in a laboratory-like environment. Each class offered tasks in relation to the movement material offered. These addressed movement qualities, phrasing, spatial orientation, and musicality. The musician ac-

companying the class worked with each group in creating a score for their composition. Each session concluded with the showing of each group's material and discussion. The showings were captured digitally and mailed through an internal Facebook account to all dancers. This offered the students the opportunity for feedback, self-evaluation, and discussion with other class members between sessions.

Summary:

Students appreciated the artistic freedom offered to them during this phase, and by the end had acquired the necessary skills to feel confident in this situation of self-directed learning. They could experience the fullness of the dance, explore their own creative processes, and bring a sense of artistry into their daily training that was both personally and socially satisfying, as one student elaborates: *"This was really great because we had the chance to learn from each other. The fact that we were in smaller groups, and that we had to show what we did with the others, gave me more confidence and really helped me to take more risks and to show what I have deep down in me."*

PHASE 5	INTEGRATION, SELF-DIRECTED LEARNING, AND SELF-EVALUATION
Duration	Twelve weeks, two classes per week, four workshops
Teacher/facilitator	Jenny Coogan
Data capture	Entire group: mixed-methods questionnaires; digital recording; final evaluation Focus group: journal writing

Focus:

To embody dance and dance training from a somatic perspective; to transfer learning from one situation to others that are independent of contemporary/modern dance practice; to encourage self-directed and self-reflective practice.

Feldenkrais:

To work with variation and permutations, differentiation, and integration, and the use of "constraints" (see chapter 9) as a somatic tool for (re)inventing the material offered.

Teaching modes:

The teaching strategies combined imitative, exploratory, and compositional processes. The themes and ideas experienced during earlier phases were revisited so that students could more clearly recognize changes in their levels of movement approximation and integration, particularly in regard to quality, muscular efficiency, and safety. After a group warm-up, students worked in pairs to create their own compositions derived from small modular units of material given to them by the teacher. This material was underscored with rhythmical ostinato and a polyphonic use of body parts. Variations, permutations, and changes in body and spatial organization were prioritized as compositional tools. Students applied their skills of somatic awareness to refine their performance. Each pair worked with the accompanist on the musical landscape.

Summary:
This phase was the most inconsistent in terms of regular class meeting times. Scheduling changes were implemented to accommodate for examination weeks and performance events. As a result, lesson themes during this phase did not evolve organically over longer periods of time, but rather changed with greater frequency. Thus students composed multiple duets in dialogue with the variety of thematic material. The flexible atmosphere and in-class sharing of the compositions helped students to work with the material following their own creative interests and trusting in their own artistic identity. A student reflected that: *"As soon as we put ourselves into a piece of work, it made a big difference to me because it kind of triggered my creativity or made me think: How can we make that work? We have this and we have that: How can we put it together? What possibilities do we have? "*

Students came to value reflective practice as a means to share experiences, renew learning, and to question and recognize the multiplicity of perspectives and responses that they gained through showing and discussing their working processes together.

Summary of the study's five phases

The design of the case study offered students a series of methods that interlaced Feldenkraisian strategies of learning with teacher-generated instructional material. Students were encouraged to develop both their physical skills and their comprehension of underlying anatomical and conceptual principles of movement. In other words, they were asked to reflect while in action (see chapter 2). As somatic practice is not an antidote to dominant dance practice (Ginot 2011: 12), the study did not strive to substitute one practice for another but rather to combine a variety of pedagogical approaches and methods to accommodate individual learning strategies and personal preferences. It strove to incite students' curiosity about how somatics can become an integral part of their dance practice. Throughout the course of the study, students employed higher-order thinking strategies, inherent to the Feldenkrais Method, such as problem-solving and critical thinking. John Dewey reminds us that "thinking is evoked by problems and questions—by perplexity, confusion, and doubt" (2008: 15).

Students were allowed the freedom to discover their own creative solutions for the tasks at hand, to explore movement from multiple non-habitual viewpoints, and to act using a refined sense of choice within a given framework. In a dialogic atmosphere, they shared verbal analogies for their physical experiences and reflected on the learning process through self-questioning, self-monitoring, and self- and peer observation. As students cultivated personal agency and self-reflection, they became better equipped at handling reciprocal learning methods (see chapter 6) and, in turn, became increasingly confident in making and taking decisions necessary for the task-oriented, self-directed learning that dominated the final phases of the study.

Foto: Karin Matko

Data interpretation and overview of the results

The case study looked to understand and interpret a specific situation, to pursue a critical investigation, and to work toward change in a specific teaching and learning environment (Green, Stinson 1999; Robson 2011). Its methodology was modeled on constructivist action research. The procedures for data capture followed a grounded theory approach. Exchanges with "critical friends" brought greater authority to the research process as they challenged an individual researcher's subjectivity, methods, prejudices, and interpretation of situations (Denzin, Lincoln 2013). The following subchapter provides a descriptive analysis of the study.

During each of its five phases, data was gathered through mixed-method questionnaires, individual and focus-group interviews, video documentation, and researchers' field notes. All nineteen students in the participant group contributed data in varying degrees throughout the entire research period. (An appendix at the end of this chapter offers several examples of the processes of data capture that were used in the study.) Interviews with the students were recorded and transcribed, while text responses to questionnaires and interview transcriptions were examined using the software program MAXQDA. Quantitative data was assessed statistically with the program SPSS Statistics. An analysis of the quantitative evidence is presented in chapter 4, "Students' Perceptions and Acceptance of Somatic Instructional Opportunities: An Analysis from a Psychological Perspective." This report describes and interprets the study's central outcomes exclusively through qualitative methods of data capture.

Students' participation in the study was independent from the ZT/MT courses' examination procedures. The final exam took place in the class of my colleague Christian Canciani, with whom semester teaching responsibilities for this course during the summer semester were shared. Therefore, any issues regarding grade coercion were irrelevant. However, the research team conducted a final evaluation with participants at the end of the research period. This included students' presentation of duets choreographed in class and written responses to scripted questions in review of all five phases of the study. A semi-structured group interview, reflecting on the individual parts of the study and the way it came together as a whole, brought this final evaluation to a close.

In considering the research questions and reviewing the data, four categories have emerged at the center of this analysis. These categories bring different and interrelated perspectives to the complex processes of situational learning. They are: atmosphere and social environment; self-reflection; personal agency; and sustainable learning.

Atmosphere and social environment

Students identified the class atmosphere as a primary factor in their ability to concentrate and learn. This is certainly connected to the fact that dance is a social activity and a collective generation and transmission of meanings between people. Their responses repeatedly demonstrated that atmosphere and the ability to "tune in" are intrinsically intertwined. One student said, *"There needs to be a certain atmosphere in class that allows for concentration without disturbance."* A somatic approach to teaching and learning heightens one's sensitivity, thus making the quality of the class climate a factor for successful learning that cannot be ignored: *"I feel the flow of concentration, energy, whatever—it's definitely a thing."*

Classes proceeded with an attitude of shared responsibility among all participants. Horizontal pathways of communication were prioritized. The class climate was one that was open for dialogue, discussion, and exchange; consequently, student voices were privileged. This condition heightened the need for the whole group's positive motivation in class, which many students acknowledged, including the statement that: *"It helps me so much if I have the feeling of 'we're all going there together.'"* Students articulated their opinions and desires and positioned themselves in relation to the materials and structures of the class. During the course of the study, students gained awareness of their responsibility as co-creators of the class climate, and began to consider the consequences of their actions with greater sensitivity. A sense of awareness encapsulated their movement, their interaction with others, and the way in which they worked in the environment (Holdaway, Kovich, Simmonds 2002). One student perceptively expressed this in the following way: *"I feel like appreciating everybody else and being aware of the group helps the awareness of each individual to grow."*

Reciprocal methods of student-centered learning and peer tutoring were emphasized throughout the study (see chapter 6: 2.0, 2.4), and these created direct and intimate exchanges that necessitated an environment of mutual trust and respect. Not all students were able to work within this learning paradigm. Some recognized divergent attitudes in this environment and offered comments such as the following: *"I did notice some discrepancies among my fellow students. I felt that some in particular were rude and judgmental when it came to the new approach to teaching."* In the middle of the study, some students were still unable to identify with this unfamiliar dance practice and began to participate with less frequency. As a result, the class climate transformed into one in which students could finally more effectively profit from its pedagogical opportunities. Below is one account of this change:

> *For me it was really prominent to actually see ... how certain concepts will click because a negative energy is brought out—it's just gone. Even within myself,*

letting go allows me to accept things more easily and faster, so for me atmosphere and energy in the group is pretty much everything.

However, the disruption of the cohesiveness of the class was met with disappointment from some in the group, one of whom described it as *"a shame, because I would have loved to finish this with everybody."*

The majority of students' statements pointed to both their strong emotional desire to proceed as a class unit, and their need for a positive and encouraging atmosphere for effective learning. In this instance, these two conditions could not continue in tandem. It was clear that with time students became increasingly willing to accept the change to the learning paradigm, identifying that the generative power of somatically oriented pedagogy needs time to unfold.

Self-reflection

In focus-group interviews, group discussions, and questionnaires, students were asked about their ability to navigate the changing contexts employed in the study. At the onset of the study, one student expressed that *"for me, engaging in my contemporary class means trying everything, and even more so things that I am not used to, so that I can evolve more."* Others aspired to have *"a curious state of mind."* These initial responses, which related to students' self-reflective abilities, were compared with ones made at later points during the study, such as the statement below: *"For me, to stay fully engaged and tuned into myself within this contemporary dance class, I need to understand. I need to be able to give context to what I am doing to facilitate the full potential of the exercise or concept."*

Another student described a growing willingness *"to learn something new, to totally give in to"* what happens in class. Yet the critical self-reflection also led to some uncomfortable realizations, such as recognition of the high expectations one places on oneself: *"I expect to do as much as I can in classes. It's just—I always kind of pressure myself to come back, and I expect to see improvement."* This issue of self-expectation appeared to be a difficult one to tackle, especially in an environment that aimed to reserve judgement and foster individual learning strategies. A student identified that *"It is important for me not to judge myself, but just to observe, experiment, and try as much as possible, thereby tackling problems in a constructive way."* Others began to allow themselves more time and patience, realizing that learning somatically cannot be forced: *"I need to gain further practice, to really feel, and just repeat, repeat, repeat."* Students also became more critically self-reflective:

I personally feel that I am engaged in contemporary class, and for me that means listening to the teacher, their opinions, corrections, and teaching experiments—with movement, various ideas and explorations for tuning into my body, what it's feeling and why. I'm also asked to question—question why some things work and others don't, how and why this will benefit me, and how I can improve, reflecting after class so the next day I can make progress and gain a stronger grasp on specific ideas or tasks taught in the previous class.

Another reported that what had become important were issues such as *"taking things and processing them. Not only taking them in, but maybe questioning them, answering them again."* It became clear that personal agency is not a one-way street, but a long and winding road.

In general, responses demonstrated that the open and student-centered learning atmosphere was an important condition for gaining self-reflection, and was essential for directing and evaluating one's own learning processes. Throughout the case study, pedagogical methods encouraged students to find verbal analogies for their experiences and to engage in learning with an attitude of self-questioning. Aspects of both self-directed learning and self-reflection are found in the student responses. These meta-cognitive facilities are discussed in depth in chapters 4 and 6. Responses offered early on in the study illustrate that these strategies were channelled exclusively toward improvement in dance skills. With time, students reported a growing recognition of the independent value of self-reflection as an ability that can lead to enhanced curiosity and openness to less familiar forms of dance and dancing.

Personal agency

The growth of personal agency throughout the project was apparent and evidenced by various indicators. One of them was reduced dependence on the teacher. A student phrased this in the following way: *"I'm actually doing something. I'm improving. And that's it. And even if people don't see that I have improved, I don't care, because I did. That's it. And that's when you start to be more settled and to enjoy everything even more."*

By being confronted with disruption to familiar ways of negotiating dance training situations, the group was brought into dialogue and discussion about both class content and the teaching methods. Students formed and articulated diverse opinions and positioned themselves with personal agency in this new context. One student commented: *"I have discussed this class a lot with my colleagues, as this is a new situation for all of us, and everyone has a different opinion about it."* Another student contributed that:

There was a more cooperative vibe between the students, which to be honest was much more enjoyable! Also, there has been an increase in communication between my colleagues and me about the new concepts that we have learned in and out of the studio, which I personally find incredibly interesting.

Personal agency is in part defined as being present in the moment. What effects does self-actualization have on stage performance? Do dancers become more "present" for the spectator? Does this relate to the ability to effect choices? The research team noticed a direct correlation between personal agency and convincing performance. Below is a student articulation of this thought:

To know this is the present right now, this is happening right now, I'm standing here right know. So that I can't get distracted by, I don't know, things that happen in the room, or things that happen outside of it, or things that might happen tomorrow morning, or things that happened yesterday evening.

In the end, personal agency is crucial for artistic work, which dancers reported in the following way:

Within that directness (in phase 4), there was quite a lot of freedom, which was really good. Because I feel that gave you so much choice and opened up so many options, and it's interesting to see how different groups interpreted different things. It really shows what an artist is.

Students' experiences in the phases that emphasized interpretative and performance skills were overwhelmingly positive both in their impact on the class climate and the development of self-actualization. This was noted in the following statement: *"It was a really open environment, and I really enjoyed that because it enabled us to find different ideas."* A student also commented that:

The different focuses in each lesson were great because they showed that we could go even further—we have the skills to do it. It's just that we normally don't think of using them. And the teachers were really supportive during these classes, which were great. This made me feel more secure.

The link between self-realization and self-reflection became more pronounced throughout the year. Students acknowledged the cumulative nature of the learning process: *"It was the continuity of our process of learning, and without what we did to begin with in the classes, it would have been hard to find."* When challenged with complex choreographic material, students reflected upon the processes that brought them to the moment of performance. Elaborating on this thought, one student felt that:

> *The movement themes of previous phases led up to the big movement pattern we dealt with over the last few weeks. That's why, even if the material might have been a little difficult to handle in the first place, it didn't totally overwhelm me. Principles like the starfish, ideas about how to work and roll on the floor, or even whole steps were familiar to me, and therefore made it easier for me to deal with the complexity of the phrase.*

Not only were students accessing personal agency, they began to self-evaluate. Higher-order thinking—prerequisites for sustainable learning according to the literature—had thus become rooted in students' practice. The group of nine students who engaged in journal writing reported that they developed an array of strategies for finding reciprocity in their dance and writing practice, which is a further means for enriching self-efficacy (Gläser-Zikuda, Hascher 2007).

Sustainable learning

The idea of "giving in to" the methods and materials of the class accompanied the students throughout the entire case study. Increasingly the students, who participated with a willingness to learn something new and a curious state of mind, accepted that learning does not always follow a linear path. It takes time. Toward the end of the research period, a student ruminated that *"I give myself the time I need. I not only use my body but also my imagination to learn."* Students who persevered with the process (fourteen out of nineteen students) commented on situations that had been uncomfortable, tedious, or dissatisfactory during the study. In hindsight, the value of the process was acknowledged in the following way:

> *It felt like especially for me when we were doing a lot of Feldenkrais at that period of time that I didn't find it very beneficial at all. But now coming back and distancing myself from it, now I can actually see how it helps me and why certain things are easier now. But unfortunately in that period of time I was just not so into it, but now I appreciate it a lot more. So I think that it is a good experimental phase, and I think that other people might feel the same.*

Reflecting on their own somatic work during the year, students commented that *"when you learn things, you either choose to take it on or you don't take it on, and sometimes things take longer."* Another student observed the need to evaluate the material with which one is confronted, rather than accepting it blindly: *"Sometimes it's good if you don't really take everything on from the beginning, because then you think more about it, and it stays with you more because you processed it."* Only at the end of the study did students begin to notice a transfer or influence of the somatic work on other parts of their lives. These different experiences were described in the following way:

> *If I think about applying somatics, it's just moving. If I want to do an exercise, I really think about myself and how my body moves through space and how I do something. I just feel like all the bumps in my phrase have smoothed out. That's a really cool feeling. Like when we do floor phrases. I mean one of the first ones we did lasted two weeks. It was long, but I feel like when you're applying somatics, then things come fluidly, and you don't necessarily understand why it's fluid, but it just happens.*

> *I had some really strong sensations about it. It feels normal and integrated as well, so I am happy that I can feel it in my body. I can feel it even more actually when I do really physical things, for example in different classes. And then I try to find a different way to do it, and then I think "How would I do it if I were in Jenny's class or in Nina's class?" And then I kind of find a different impulse or different way, and then it sometimes actually works faster as well, as I try to think how I would approach it in a somatic kind of way.*

The sequencing of the five phases of the case study included various somatically oriented methods of teaching and learning: instructional, exploratory, cumulative, cyclical, and associative that all link to memory, images, and emotions. (Deese 1966). The ways in which dancers navigated this field sprung from their individually organized, nonlinear, and associative processes of learning (see chapters 4 and 6). Striking a balance between different teaching modes afforded students the opportunity to engage in somatic processes in a variety of contexts in their contemporary and modern dance classes, and to carry these experiences into other parts of their lives.

During the year, students became less dependent on personal feedback or "corrections," and more eager to exchange and share experiences with one another. The hesitation at the beginning of the year to work in pairs or small groups was replaced with an eagerness to engage in cooperative learning and peer-tutoring frameworks, as they could work from a place of personal agency, knowledge transfer, self-reflection, and self-confidence. This all required time.

Critical reflection and summary

In this case study, students were invited to do the following: to attune themselves to their own movement, whether improvised or prescriptive; to learn how to listen to their own sensorimotor information; to move with intention; to reduce tempo and force in order to develop discrimination and differentiation in regard to the fine nuances of movement; to shift from goals to experimentation; to find novelty in repetition; and to trust their own thoughts and be open to uncertainty. Students handled situations in accordance with their own interests in an atmosphere of shared responsibility between student and teacher.

The pedagogical approach created disruption as many students were brought out of their modi operandi to repeat past experiences that felt good to them. The methods of the case study required stamina on the part of the students to work through discomfort. Persistence, self-monitoring, and open-minded, flexible attitudes were required to deal with uncertainties and new questions.

The repetition of learned patterns of movement was a thread throughout the study. By finding novelty in repetition—directing, shifting, and playing with attention—one can move onto higher levels of approximation, organization, and expression. Although one learns through repetition, and particularly in dance training repetition is an ever-present theme, many students found repetition in the somatic dance class tedious. The ability to discern and notice change is predicated on recognizing the positive feedback of ease, lightness, and pleasure. This is a different register of energy expenditure than that which is commonly identified in the dance class. At times, students expressed a desire to "dance more" and to learn a greater range of movement material. This desire was met during the first phase of the study in preparation for the open-house showing, the second phase through interactions with guest teachers, and the fourth and fifth phase through work with choreographic material.

The study challenged participants to deal with novel situations in terms of class structure, personal relationships, expectations for studio practice, the nature of the movement material, and individual decision-making processes. In addition, the simultaneity of teaching and research was a first-time experience for all students, and therefore it was essential for the team, and particularly for me as primary researcher, to import to the students my continuing role as teacher/facilitator/mentor, and not solely researcher.

As language influences how one perceives one's body (Myers 1983; Ruge, 2002), I attempted to use language in class that conveyed authority without being authoritarian. Often the teaching language I employed was conditional—it posed questions, suggesting rather than stating. This was challenging for young dancers as they were not told exactly what to do, but allowed to make their own decisions within given parameters.

At times students responded to my questioning with phrases such as *"Tell me what you want"* or *"Don't ask what I want or how I think I should do it."* For these students, the invitation to make choices was perceived as cognitively tiresome and time consuming. Other students became aware that by embodying intentional thinking, they could change the way their bodies are aligned and how they move. This indicated that some students had allowed themselves to become more independent from the teacher.

One of the outcomes of this study clearly showed that variety in the teaching and learning environment, as well as a variety of teaching staff for a particular course, is helpful as a means to address different people's learning strategies, desires, and values (see chapter 6). The reduced amount of contact time with the participant group during the second semester of the study proved conciliatory, as the unfamiliar ways of practicing dance were more equally balanced with habitual approaches. Throughout the study, many students began to recognize and find value in the quality of the investigation that allowed them to engage with dance from multiple perspectives and to make their own informed choices: *"I feel like somatics is kind of a thing ... you have to understand. It can't be 'OK, I get an explanation, and now I understand it.' ... You have to go through it—you have to do it and experience it."*

The final evaluation demonstrated that the fourteen students who actively participated throughout the course of the study profited from learning through embodied self-awareness, self-observation, and self-reflection. Somatic processes had been understood conceptually, and applied in dance and life experience.

However, a somatically oriented pedagogy can only gain in effectiveness when it is integrated fully in the curricular and regulatory structures of the given institution. It asks one to reconsider individual biases and presuppositions, and to encounter a juxtaposition of viewpoints and epistemologies in working processes with acceptance and empathy. In working somatically, one values difference, accepts perspectives other than one's own, and invites a space for everyone in the community to discover and pursue their own truth.

Appendix: Examples of instruments used for data collection during the case study

PHASE 3: FELDENKRAIS IN DANCE CLASS

The following questionnaire was distributed to students on a biweekly basis during phase 3 of the case study. It was filled in at both the beginning and end of their contemporary dance class.

Dear students,

On the accompanying disk-shaped diagram, please identify four points of interest or goals that are important for you in today's class. Write these in the four corners of the disk. Use the symbol "I" in the four fields to correspond to the importance of these goals for you today, and use the symbol "C" to correspond to how confident you feel of your ability to achieve these goals. The closer you set your "I" and "C" to the center of the disk, the more relevant these goals are for you.

Next, using the symbols "M," "A," "T," "MA," "MT," and "TA," please mark in the appropriate fields how you feel the criteria below will help you to achieve your goals. The closer you set your below symbol to the center of the disk, the more helpful you feel the criterion is for you.

Please mark with:

My own facility will help me to attain these goals.	M
Only the atmosphere of the class will help me to attain these goals.	A
Only the teacher's input in the class will help me to attain these goals.	T
The combination of my own facility and the atmosphere of the class will help me to attain these goals.	MA
The combination of my own facility and the teacher's input will help me to attain these goals.	MT
The combination of the teacher's input and the atmosphere of the class will help me to attain these goals.	TA

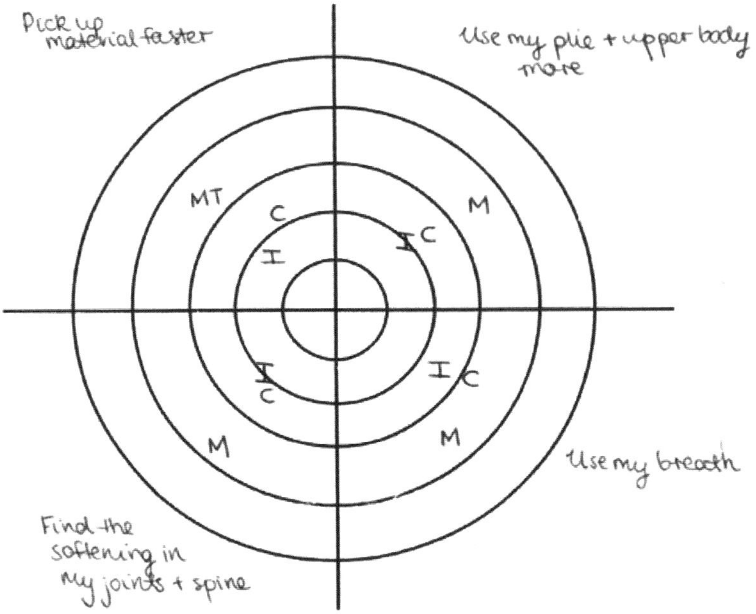
Pick up material faster
Use my plie + upper body more
MT
M
C
I
M
Use my breath
Find the softening in my joints + spine

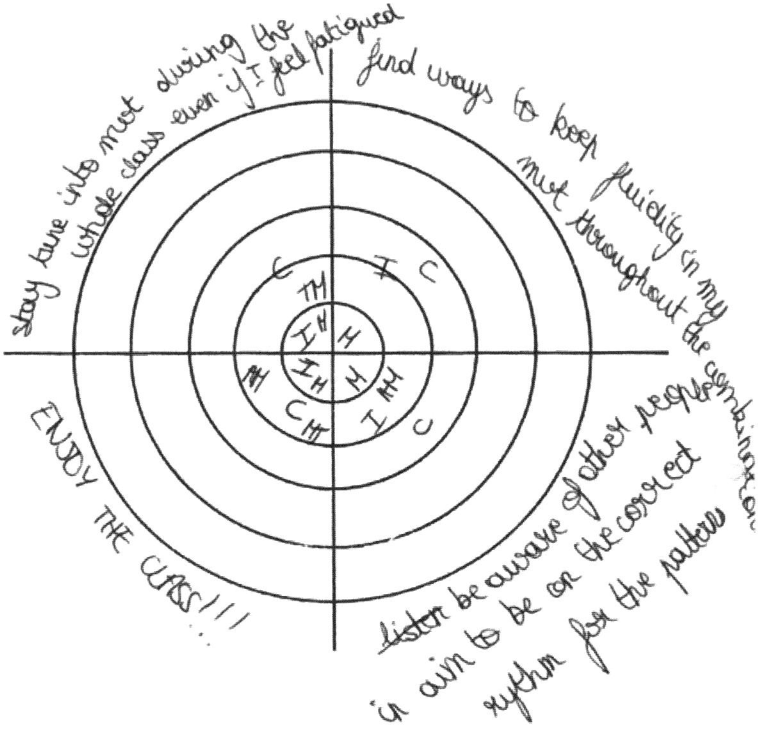
stay tune into mvt during the whole class even if I feel fatigued
find ways to keep fluidity in my mvt throughout the combination
ENJOY THE CLASS!!!
listen be aware of other people in aim to be on the correct rhythm for the pattern

PHASE 4: PEER-ASSISTED LEARNING

Students received the following questionnaire at the conclusion of phase 4. The initial section of this questionnaire is shown in its original format. The subsequent pages list only the items of the survey.

Dear students,

Please complete the following questionnaire by marking the appropriate SMILEY and by adding, if you wish, your own COMMENTARY in the boxes below.

1. SMALL-GROUP WORK

Overall, working together in my small group with the material...				
- helped me to work with the material more fully				
- offered me the opportunity to express my own ideas				
- provided enriching exchanges with others				
- inspired me to try out other people's ideas				
- created a productive atmosphere				
- created an atmosphere of trust and acceptance				
The small group work supported my understanding of:				
- Fluid coordination				
- Phrasing				
The small-group work supported my ability to apply the following qualities in practice:				
- Fluid coordination				
- Phrasing				
The small group work helped me improve my performance skills				
Comments relating to the statements above:				

2. DIGITAL FEEDBACK

I used the video material as a tool to give myself feedback.

Using the video supported my self-reflective and physical processes.

Sharing the video with others invited discussion.

Comments relating to the statements above:

3. TEACHING FORMAT

The non-changing warm-up gave me the space to tune in to myself.

The teachers' mentoring during the phase was helpful for me.

The sharing, dancing, and observing with the whole group at the end of the class was:
- Satisfying
- Irritating
- Important
- Helpful
- Scary
- Enjoyable

The format of these sessions encouraged me to explore different approaches in:
- Learning given material
- Interpreting and performing given material

Comments relating to the statements above:

4. SPACE AND TIME FACTORS

The division of time between warm-up, learning and reviewing the material, working in small groups, and sharing with others was appropriate.

I would have preferred to have more time for:
- Warming-up
- Working on the phrase material with the whole group
- Working on the phrase material in my small group
- Sharing the dance with everyone

The amount of space in the studio for working in my small group was sufficient.

Comments relating to the statements above:

5. LAST BUT NOT LEAST

Could you make connections between the movement themes in this phase with the movement themes introduced to you during other phases of the case study?

Do you have any issues that you think should have been addressed more closely during this phase?

Can you describe which format(s) for the final phase of this study you think would best further your artistic development? Consider the teaching/learning formats you have experienced thus far in this academic year.

We thank you for your participation!

---

1 German educationalist, Andreas Helmke incorporates these ideas into his theoretical model: process-mediation-product framework of instructional effectiveness (2009). This theoretical frame delineates conditions that contribute to the processes of teaching and learning. It offers a structure for evaluating the learning environment in relation to the learning objective; it identifies learning needs, and the propositional, procedural, and conditional approaches to knowledge acquisition; and it proposes the possible effects that these considerations might have on learning appropriation. The model distinguishes between individual and institutional contextual factors, pedagogical materials and approaches, as well as the characteristics, systems of value, and life worlds that the teachers and students bring with them into the learning situation. This model served to support the construction and implementation of the case study. It is often cited as a best-practice model for learning and teaching, and is used as a theoretical model in chapter 4.

2 The Palucca University integrates a secondary school (grades five to ten) with BA and MA programs in Dance and Dance Pedagogy, an MA in Choreography, and a portfolio-organized *Meisterklasse* (masterclass). Approximately 200 students are currently enrolled in its various programs. The BA program in Dance transmits established canons and the aesthetics of Western theatre dance, as well as hybrid mixes of contemporary practice. Seminars in dance history and analysis, music theory, Laban movement analysis, and anatomy augment the studio practice. All studio practice is accompanied with live music.

4. STUDENTS' PERCEPTIONS AND ACCEPTANCE OF SOMATIC INSTRUCTIONAL OPPORTUNITIES:

AN ANALYSIS FROM A PSYCHOLOGICAL PERSPECTIVE *Susanne Narciss and Karin Matko*

Jürgen van Buer

Students participating in the Palucca University case study delineated in chapter 3 were provided with instructional opportunities aimed at enhancing self-reflective and self-regulatory skills. Students experienced a shift from teacher-centered to peer-oriented and self-regulated learning. Moreover, they were asked to engage in decision-making and decision-taking as a way to develop greater awareness of their minds and bodies.

This chapter will describe and analyze insights from educational psychology concerning how students with diverse individual needs perceive and make use of instructional opportunities. The starting point for the description and analysis is the Process–Mediation–Product (PMP) model of instructional effectiveness (Praetorius, Lenske, Helmke 2012). According to the PMP model, the extent to which students take advantage of instructional opportunities provided within an educational scenario is a central mediating factor influencing if and how much students perceive such opportunities as valuable, and this factor can improve learning within this scenario. This chapter focuses on student motivation, attitudes, and mindfulness with regard to their use of, and reactions to, various instructional opportunities.

Throughout the study, students' attitudes and reactions were collected and assessed by the research team through questionnaires, focus-group and individual interviews, feedback sessions, and in-class video recordings. During the final phase of the study, three questionnaires were administered that addressed: (a) students' general use of learning strategies (adapted from Berger, Karabenick 2011); (b) their mindfulness, according to the Freiburg Mindfulness Inventory (Walach et al. 2006); and (c) students' perceived levels of satisfaction concerning their innate psychological needs for competence, social relatedness, and autonomy (adapted from Vlachopoulos, Michailidou 2006). In analyzing and interpreting the data, the phenomenon of U-shaped developmental trajectories—well known in the field of interventions, training, and instruction (Pauls, Macha, Petermann 2013; Stavy 2012)—was taken into account.

U-shaped curve of changes in instruction and training

Learning and training processes are complex and dynamic, and the changes observed throughout these processes are often not only linear (i.e., monotonic, cumulative increases in the abilities being trained), but also follow nonlinear trajectories (i.e., variability in the growth of competencies). This means that growth in learning and instruction occurs sometimes quickly, sometimes slowly, may sometimes be interrupted by periods where little or nothing appears to change, or may be affected by periods of time when performance temporarily deteriorates. One nonlinear trajectory, which can be observed in a variety of contexts regarding changes in behavior, learning, performance, and development, is the so-called U-shaped change curve (Pauls, Macha, Petermann 2013; Stavy 2012; see figure 2). U-shaped patterns of change are considered to be a hallmark of developmental processes (Marcovitch, Lewkowicz 2004; Gerschkoff-Stowe, Thelen 2004).

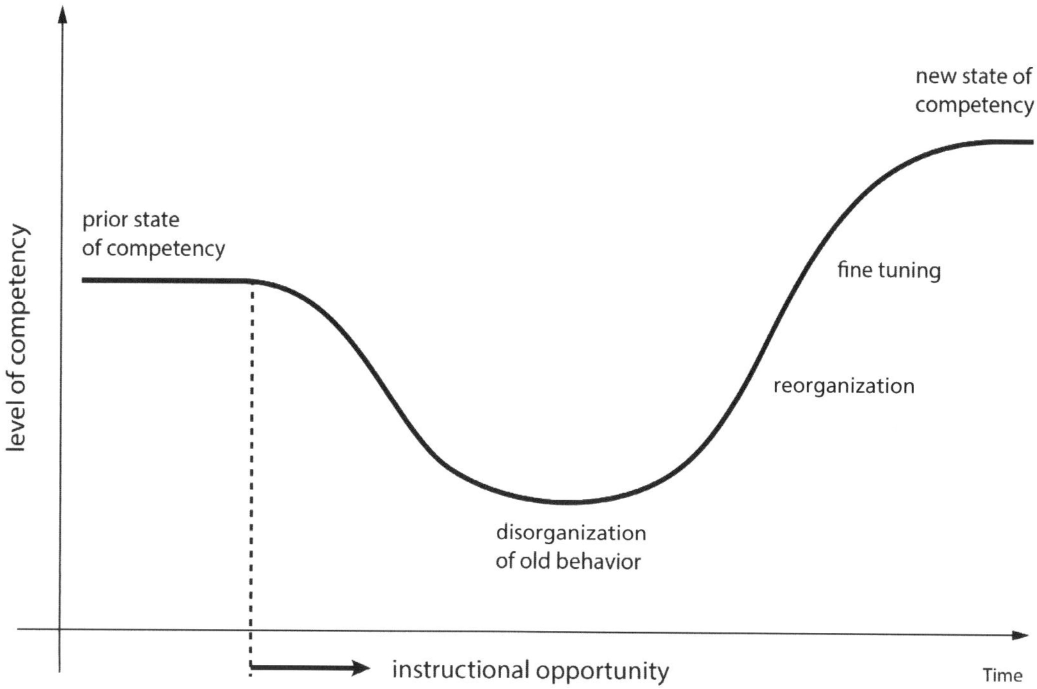

Figure 1: U-shaped curve of changes in competency within training and instruction

U-shaped trajectories of change occur because learning and development require students to not only acquire new strategies or competencies but also because they need to reorganize knowledge and skills in order to achieve new levels of competency. By doing so, students often have to experience states of disorganization in which learned strategies and sometimes automatized patterns of behavior come to be considered inadequate, but new competencies cannot yet be applied successfully. At this point, students experience a decline in performance ability that can be frustrating and result in a loss of motivation. A successful application of new competencies requires students to invest time and effort in training and fine-tuning new knowledge and skills. Thus, in many instructional contexts, a learner's experience with new instructional opportunities can be more positive at the beginning rather than later on, at which point they experience disorganization and have to fine-tune new strategies or competencies. Learners who do not invest enough time, effort, and persistence in reorganizing and fine-tuning their competencies will not achieve a new level of competency, and will remain at their previous level of competency. Learners who persist, however, will achieve a new level of competency and experience the benefits of the instructional opportunities.

Interview data from the case study provides evidence that students' reactions and experiences follow the phases of U-shaped changes. At the end of the first phase, students reported having their first "aha!" experiences regarding the benefits of somatic approaches in contemporary dance class.

A sample of student statements, October 2014

At the end of phase 1, after six weeks of dance education in a new school with new teachers and the introduction of new learning methods, students reported the following regarding their motivation in dance class:

> *You always have to push yourself and there is a certain level of discomfort, of course, but after working like this, to a certain extent, you feel happy, like, I conquered a lazy part of myself ... and then you are proud of yourself afterwards and say, I managed to achieve something today.*
>
> *I can also feel a change in my body, like you said before. I realize that I'm still on the way—sometimes I feel it and sometimes I can't. ... I realize that I need to work even more on that, and I need more time—I have to give myself more time.*
>
> *By working on this particular exercise so very slowly and really taking every section at a time—I remember sometimes we spent an hour and a half on one exercise—at the end I really felt that I'm able to do this and I'm able to do that in a good and healthy and smooth way for my body. That was pretty impressive to me.*

But when students reached the phase that required most effort, restructuring existing competencies and fine-tuning new competencies, they reported difficulties.

A sample of student statements, January 2015

At the end of phase 3, which coincided with the end of the first semester, students from the smaller focus group were asked about their experiences with this new learning approach and how they view their own future.

> *I feel that when we take a movement and we break it down and find what's initiating the movement, which is similar to a Feldenkrais sort of thing, I find that my movement pattern is more clear. And I can really concen-*

trate on the line through my body. But I can't say that I can transfer it into other classes necessarily.

My body felt different. I can't even explain exactly what it was, but I was pretty much aware of what I did and was internally focused. It's kind of hard to do it once and then maintain it for the rest of your studies. ... I kind of lost that feeling because I was thinking of other things, and I'm not in that state of mind anymore.

As a result, during the middle phase of the case study, some students' levels of engagement and motivation for mindfully applying instructional opportunities dropped to an extent that hindered them from achieving a new level of competency. Those who persisted and maintained their engagement with the material until the end of the case study, however, successfully achieved a new level of competency and were able to perceive the beneficial effects of learning with a somatic approach.

A sample of student statements, July 2015

In the final feedback session at the end of the year, students were asked to recapitulate and reflect on their experiences in the different phases of the case study. Students reported having experienced delayed "aha!" experiences.

I'm actually doing something. I'm improving and that's it, you know. And even if people don't see that I've improved, I don't care, because I did. That's it. And then you start to be more settled and to enjoy everything even more because you have changed, and you go back to your thing changed, like the way you look at the world.

It felt for me, especially when we were doing a lot of Feldenkrais at that period of time, that I wasn't finding it very beneficial at all. But now coming back and distancing myself from it, I can actually see how it helps me and why certain things are easier now. Unfortunately, in that period of time I was just not so into it, but now I appreciate it a lot more. So I think that it was a good experimental phase, and I think that other people might feel the same.

I feel like you have to go through it [somatics], and you have to do it and experience it.

Students who acknowledged the usefulness of somatic awareness in dance class also reported experiencing a higher level of mindfulness.

In the following sections, the U-shaped curve of change will serve as a framework for describing, and analyzing in more detail, if and how the following factors related to changes were experienced during the case study: self-reported learning strategies and motivation; perceived satisfaction of the psychological needs for competence, social relatedness, and autonomy; and self-reported mindfulness.

Self-regulated learning

One of the main aims of the study was to offer students opportunities for self-regulated learning. Researchers in educational psychology view learners as active participants in the learning process and thus emphasize that self-regulated learning (SRL) in particular is as an active, constructive learning process that involves setting goals as well as monitoring, regulating, and controlling learning activities and motivation (Boekarts, Pintrich, Zeidner 2005; Pintrich 2004). This process requires students to master a number of demands, including: (a) constructing their own meanings from the instructional opportunities provided, as well as incorporating information from prior experiences; (b) setting learning goals and monitoring the progress made toward these goals; (c) selecting and applying appropriate learning strategies; and (d) regulating their motivation and volition efficiently. SRL research reveals that mastering these demands is a challenging task for many students, and certain contextual and/or individual factors may constrain such mastery (Pintrich 2004).

Students' self-reported learning strategies

Research on self-regulated learning reveals that students require knowledge about different types of learning strategies, as well as knowledge about when and how to apply these strategies (Bjork, Dunlosky, Kornell 2013; Dunlosky et al. 2013). Learning strategies can support the learning process either on a cognitive level (i.e., organizing or elaborating information to be learned), a metacognitive level (i.e., monitoring learning progress and selecting adequate control activities), or through the management of resources (i.e., seeking help; Berger, Karabenick 2011). Effective self-regulated learning requires learners to engage in higher-order or deep-processing learning strategies, since it has been determined that superficial processing of information (i.e., memorizing by repetition and without reflection) is inefficient for learning (Bjork, Dunlosky, Kornell 2013; Dunlosky et al. 2013).

In order to investigate if and how the students used various learning strategies differently, they were asked to respond to a learning strategies questionnaire adapted from Jean-Louis Berger and Stuart A. Karabenick (2011). This questionnaire comprised three scales addressing cognitive, metacognitive, as well as resource-management strategies. Eleven students from the group of nineteen responded to the questionnaire. Statistical analysis revealed that, on average, all learning strategies were used similarly by these students, indicating there was no clear preference for any particular learning strategy. We find it noteworthy that students' self-reported use of superficial learning strategy and deeper learning strategies was comparable. The use of superficial learning strategy did not correlate with the use of deeper-level learning strategies. Yet, we found significant positive correlations for the deep learning strategies, indicating that the more students reported using one kind of deep learning strategy, the more they also agreed to use other deep learning strategies.

Students' motivation

Student motivation is a key factor for effectively using instructional opportunities in contexts that require self-regulation (Berger, Karabenick 2011; Pintrich 2004). Motivation research in educational psychology is concerned with the energization and direction of learning behavior. Specifically, it examines the role of motivation in learning processes and learning outcomes by investigating individual and situational factors that influence a student's choice of tasks and activities (directions of behavior), as well as examining the effort and persistence invested in the chosen activities and tasks (energization of behavior) (Schunk, Meece, Pintrich 2012). Theoretical frameworks such as expectancy-value models of motivation (Wigfield, Eccles 2000) and humanistic approaches concerned with the satisfaction of basic psychological needs (Deci, Ryan 2000) may serve to determine the factors for and consequences of motivation in learning and teaching.

Expectancy-value models of motivation suggest that student motivation is the result of a complex interaction of expectancies and values within a specific instructional context. Core expectancies in instructional contexts refer to students' belief in their capabilities to successfully accomplish required learning tasks and activities, or self-efficacy, and their belief that successful accomplishment of learning activities will lead to desired outcomes or an expected outcome (Bandura 1977). According to Wigfield and Eccles' model of motivation (2000), the following value components can be distinguished in instructional contexts:

(a) Intrinsic value (e.g., the enjoyment gained from doing the task)
(b) Attainment value (e.g., the importance of doing well in the task, experiencing success through mastery)
(c) Utility value (e.g., the usefulness of the task in pursuing future goals or attaining tangible rewards for engaging in the task)

(d) Cost (e.g., all negative aspects of engaging in the task, such as anticipated effort or lost opportunities for more attractive activities)

Based upon the expectancy-value view of motivation, the following conditions are necessary for students to mindfully use instructional opportunities: First, they should consider themselves capable of accomplishing the learning tasks and expect positive outcomes at the completion of the task. Second, they should consider the benefits of the learning tasks to be more valuable than the costs of accomplishing them.

The statements in the three sections of student statements in this chapter reveal changes in student motivation. When students experienced gains from learning, they perceived the utility of engaging in classes that demand intense cognitive processing along with physical practice. Yet, in the phase of reorganizing learning strategies, the gains from learning were not immediately apparent. Those students who persisted with learning throughout this period reported benefiting from the somatic approaches in contemporary dance classes.

Deci and Ryan's theory of self-determination states that the satisfaction of basic psychological needs, namely the need for autonomy, competence, and social relatedness, plays a key role in student motivation (2000). The need for autonomy refers to the individual's desire to be the origin of their own behavior and to experience a certain degree of freedom with regard to their behavior. The need for competence refers to one's aspiration to have an effect on one's environment and to experience opportunities that exercise and express one's capacities. The need for social relatedness reflects the desire to feel connected to others, to give and receive both appreciation and care. The satisfaction of these nonhierarchical, innate, and universal needs facilitates natural growth processes, such as intrinsically motivated behavior, and leads to higher overall motivation, performance, and well-being.

To explore if and to what extent basic psychological needs were met when taking advantage of the instructional opportunities and contexts offered, students responded to an adapted version of the Basic Psychological Needs in Exercise Scale (BPNES; Vlachopoulos, Michailidou 2006). Analysis of the BPNES data shows that students perceived higher levels of satisfaction in relation to the need for competency and social relatedness than to the need for autonomy. This finding is in line with previous findings in the field of exercise science (Vlachopoulos, Michailidou 2006). This makes evident that, despite intermediate phases of disorganization students may have experienced during the case study, those who remained engaged recognized the value of a somatic approach in supporting their development. These students particularly appraised their new level of competence.

Interview data showed how students valued the phases of collaborative and peer-oriented learning, thereby reflecting a high level of satisfaction in meeting the need for social relatedness.

Satisfaction of basic psychological needs

In phases 4 and 5, the instructional opportunities centered on exploratory, peer-centered learning in pairs or small groups. Student statements at the end of this phase included the following:

> *This last part was definitely my favorite. The fact that I was with people that I am used to working with was really great because we had the chance to learn from each other. The fact that we were in smaller groups and that we had to show what we did to the others gave me more confidence and really helped me to take more risks and to show what I have deep down within me. ... The different focuses in each lesson were great because they showed that we could go even further, and that we have the skills to do it. It's just that we normally don't think of using them.*

> *We had opportunities to do what we wanted to do. ... I enjoyed that, and I really enjoyed watching the other groups as well. I felt that it was interesting to always have some task or idea to go into and really work on for almost an hour, and then step out and take a look at other people and go, "Oh wow, they did it totally differently!"*

In summary, the findings emphasize the importance of providing students with opportunities to find their own ways of applying and expressing their skills and to present the results of group work to peers.

Somatic instructional opportunities and mindfulness

Somatic approaches in dance education aim to increase students' awareness of internal and external processes during learning (Enghauser 2003). To achieve this, a certain level of "mindfulness" is necessary. Mindfulness is "a process of regulating attention in order to bring a quality of non-elaborative awareness to current experience and a quality of relating to one's experience within an orientation of curiosity, experiential openness, and acceptance" (Bishop et al. 2004: 234). Mindfulness is currently receiving increased attention in research as its cultivation has positive effects on well-being and health (Eberth, Sedlmeier 2012). Based on the current state of research, one may assume that there is a close relationship between students' use of instructional opportunities rooted in somatic approaches and mindfulness (Caldwell et al. 2013).

In order to investigate to what extent mindfulness relates to self-reported learning strategies and the perceived satisfaction of basic psychological needs, students were asked to respond to the Freiburg Mindfulness Inventory questionnaire (Walach et al. 2006). Descriptive data analysis revealed that those students who persisted in mindfully using the instructional opportunities reported, on average, the same level of mindfulness as people without any meditation experience have been found to report (Walach et al. 2006). The correlation analyses yielded moderate to high positive correlations between mindfulness and self-reported use of higher-order learning strategies (correlation coefficients range between .41 and .78), as well as between mindfulness and satisfaction of the three basic psychological needs (correlation coefficients range between .42 and .65). These findings indicate that the higher the students' mindfulness, the more they reported using higher-order learning strategies and the more they perceived their basic psychological needs as being satisfied. This finding is in line with prior research on the role of mindfulness (Brown, Ryan 2003; Vago, Silbersweig 2012), and is also reflected in the interview data.

A sample of student statements, July 2015

In a feedback session at the conclusion of the study, students were asked to reflect upon their experiences with somatic approaches during the year. They reported the following:

> *I can feel it, and it feels normal and integrated as well, so I'm happy. ... And then I find a different impulse or different way, and it sometimes actually works faster as well—trying to think more about how you would approach it in a somatic kind of way. And I felt it in different classes too.*

> *If I want to do an exercise, I really think about myself, how my body moves through space, and how I do something. I just feel like all the bumps in my phrase have been smoothed out. That's a really cool feeling. You know you're applying somatics when things become fluid, and you don't necessarily understand why it's fluid, but it just happens.*

Conclusions

This chapter adopted a perspective based on theoretical and empirical insights from educational psychology, namely insights gained from research on instructional effectiveness (Praetorius, Lenske, Helmke 2012), self-regulated learning (Pintrich 2004), and the U-shaped trajectories of change observed in many fields of human development, learning, and instruction (Stavy 2012).

Data collected on the basis of these psychological insights illustrates and confirms several key findings from prior research. First, the benefits of providing students with instructional opportunities (derived here from somatic approaches in dance education) may not be visible immediately but only after a certain delay, since learning and development require students to reorganize their competencies in order to achieve a higher level of competency. Second, the core conditions for experiencing the benefits of instructional opportunities include the mindful use of these opportunities, as well as student willingness, motivation, and persistence in passing through states of disorganization or reorganization in order to achieve a new level of competence. Third, if these conditions are fulfilled, students experience increasing empowerment as self-regulated learners and dancers.

On the basis of present and prior findings regarding the impact of somatic approaches in dance education, a significant implication is worth noting. Teachers, teaching institutions, and their students should be cognizant of the findings regarding U-shaped trajectories of change in order to encourage patience and persistence when coping with the difficult phases of reorganization, during which students might experience stagnation and frustration (Krasnow, Wilmerding 2015). If they do not have this knowledge, there is a risk that student engagement with new instructional opportunities might be reduced or even halted before they have the chance to experience the benefits.

Photo: Jürgen van Buer

5. KITCHEN-TABLE TALK:

A DISCUSSION AMONG STUDENTS AND GRADUATES

A conversation with Alexei Bernard, Valeria Danhauser, Nadja Güsewell, Luke Hayward, Swane Küpper, and Lars Reinschmidt
Moderated by Jenny Coogan and research associate, Fanny Barz

Jenny: This "kitchen-table talk" offers an opportunity to share experiences you have had with somatics and dance during the course of the InnoLernenTanz (ILT) project. You have all participated in various phases of this research: some of you were involved in the initial exploratory phases; others engaged with interdisciplinary projects in cooperation with the Motion Bank Group; others were part of a somatic and dance pilot study; and several of you participated in an extensive case study that investigated somatically oriented methods in teaching and learning processes in contemporary dance practice at the Palucca University of Dance.

Fanny: To begin, we would like to hear what "somatics" means to you.

Lars: I think somatics means "the body perceived from within." Especially for me, dance-wise, it's about feeling the body from inside, analyzing your own movements, and being able to teach yourself.

Swane: I think somatics is about awareness, even in daily life. It's about watching myself in my surroundings, spreading attention toward myself and the surroundings with which I engage.

Valeria: For me, it's a quality of visualizing and imagining what I feel. It's something for the brain as well. I don't only feel—I *think* about what I feel so I can visualize it in my body.

Alexei: It's like seeing what's happening in my body from above. Like an ability to be inside and outside of my body at once.

Nadja: For me, somatics means being really honest with myself and with my surroundings. And especially dance-wise, in the first weeks of working together, I realized when we were with you, Jenny, how honest I could be with myself and how far that brings me and my attention into the space and to new experiences of my body and the people around me.

Swane: We as dancers can be very judgmental about what we do. I mean, we are always trying to go somewhere; we are always trying to achieve something or to do something better. For me, with somatics you go into a state of just taking things in, just seeing things and dealing with them, rather than actually judging on the spot and saying "This is better or worse" or "I have to change this in a certain direction."

Nadja: It's about acceptance of what you do and making decisions—to respect what happens and what is going on. And I think that's very important for dancers.

Luke: It's about how you are using your energy, and noticing if you're using it in a necessary or unnecessary way. In a somatic mindset, you actually figure out how far your pelvis might move or how much range or rotation a movement has, and then you are able to apply that understanding in a dance class.

Nadja: I think about habits. If you want to figure out how to change them, you also have to listen to what you're doing, and I think that's where somatics is really helpful. It is a great support for ridding yourself of bad habits and learning where these habits are coming from.

Swane: Yeah, because you have to be able to take things apart to find the detail. For me, it's like a big machine or a big puzzle that has lots of little *Zahnräder* (cogs) and little things where maybe one thing is going slightly wrong or doing a loop that it shouldn't do. You can't really see that if you take a look at the whole picture—you just see it bleeping and blinking—but if you take the little things apart and look at them individually, take them out and maybe change something, then when you put them back together, you can see what it has done.

Valeria: Somatics is seeing within yourself.

> ***Fanny: Can anyone offer an example of where you have used what you have learned from somatics in your life?***

Alexei: In our first year, you were getting us to really consider what we were doing and how we were doing it so we could make decisions about what we were doing, because you can do the same thing for years and not actually evolve. And somatics means learning methods to change an approach to movement, because you have a perspective, so you can look and see what is happening and what could be different. It's a crazy thing, but you can get better at *grand allegro* when you work on awareness.

Lars: Especially in repeating movements over and over again, I felt completely different. I didn't learn the movements and memorize how to do them. I learned about my body and that, no matter what the movement was, I knew how my body would take it, and that my body knew how to arrange itself. I learned to analyze my own body and listen to my body, because every body is so different.

Swane: It is more in retrospect. Sometimes in class we worked in ways that actually might have helped me with my *grand jeté*, but at that moment I was not aware of the fact that the somatic method could have benefited me. Now, even after we have changed contemporary teachers and are doing different stuff, it is still so incredibly related to all the things we were doing last year with Jenny.

Nadja: I've learned a lot about how to look at dance as well. When I see the teacher showing a combination, then I'm already in this kind of absorbing and observing mode. I try to see the starting point of the movement. I didn't do that before. Before I tried to pick up the movement as fast as possible, and this didn't always work well for me, and it made me feel completely overwhelmed.

Swane: You were just like looking at the movement rather than looking *into* the movement. Maybe one example would be from contemporary class—rolling on the floor, like we did with Jenny so many times, finding the connection between head and tail, and how to curl and open up again, and cross-lateral and homo-lateral—learning how to do all of these things. Then we took it to the next level, from up to down on the floor and then standing. We did that basically for the entire year and now that we have a new contemporary teacher who does a lot of floorwork, and you find yourself in a situation where it could be overwhelming, you still find your body doing the movement properly because you understand the principle. Then you kind of just look back and realize, "Well, now it just works."

Valeria: We did a really nice experiment that was part of a multidisciplinary research project—in cooperation with Motion Bank, tamed, and Bielefeld University—about learning processes in dance. We traveled to Bielefeld, and the experiment took place in the motion-capture lab there. We were asked to learn two phrases of movement in two different ways, one phrase just from a video and the other from verbal instruction. We watched the video without words, so we just saw the movement and tried to put it on the body or copy it. It's different to verbal instructions because there you had more pictures and images to use to find intentions in the movement, like imagining the wind blowing behind your back. So it had a totally different feeling.

Alexei: That experiment was incredible. When you saw the video without the verbal description or the details behind it, you did this sort of copying; you put the movement on yourself like a suit, but it isn't in you.

Valeria: Yeah. And for me, the movement phrase I learned through verbal instruction felt more like it could be my own, more for me. And the other one, from the video, was like, "Am I doing this right?" or "Does it look right?"

Jenny: This is very much about taking ownership of what you are doing.

Alexei: That's when somatics gets really interesting—when you start actually making decisions.

Swane: And that's basically somatics for me—being conscious of what you are doing.

Fanny: Could you give further examples, both within and outside your daily dance practice?

Nadja: Riding my bike, for example. When I ride home there is one part of the path where it gets a bit harder, a bit steeper. Before I was putting as much force as possible into my legs to try to get up the hill. And after your classes, Jenny, I actually was trying to release more and use less energy and that helped.

Luke: An example for me would be my shoulders. I used a lot of muscle tension and energy in my shoulders. It took a while for me to understand how to lift my shoulders without always using the chest muscles, without going back into this tense "hulk" posture to find the neutral position. I had never heard of Feldenkrais or somatics, so I had to discover what they were. It takes a while to realize how to use your energy to find out how far you can go or what is meant by "trying." Once I was able to better understand the reasoning, the thinking, and analyzing behind it, I understood how to respond to Jenny's directions.

And it took a while into my second year, when I was taking the Feldenkrais lessons separately from the technique class, to actually feel the sensations of how, and to what degree, I can move my arms with ease in a position that's comfortable for me and that looks good too. Obviously I cannot look in the mirror to see if it feels comfortable for me. What I experienced in Feldenkrais was to focus totally for the whole hour and a half, not just for, like, the first fifteen or thirty minutes, on understanding what we were doing. And I would feel this sensation in Feldenkrais, especially the ease, and try to keep this feeling. But that was hard and the feeling would disappear, so it took a while to apply this in my dancing. As the sensations became clearer and I noticed when the sensations changed and what is good for me, I could start to apply this approach in my ballet and contemporary classes.

Now I identify when I am using a lot of muscles, when I am pulling back, and why something is not working. Maybe this is why I think you have to really get back to closing your eyes and sensing yourself. That's my example of really discovering how I can use somatic work in my dancing, how it's been effective.

Valeria: I realized it the most during a summer school in Brussels. I took a floorwork workshop that was really tough. And the first two days I was just pushing and going through the motions. Everyone was sweating like crazy. And then I thought, "Okay, let me try to work efficiently." I thought I could maybe organize my body in a different way, where I didn't have to use all my muscles to be efficient. That is how it got easier. And it also felt even more settled and calm.

Swane: Related to what Luke was saying, in Feldenkrais we do a lot of things on the floor, and you do a lot of things with alignment. You use lying down on the floor, and a different sort of support from the floor, to teach your body how it is correctly aligned and in balance. By training the sensation for correct alignment and balance lying down, it is now a lot easier for my body to find and reconstruct this feeling while standing upright. The body now automatically moves into a more balanced, aligned position while standing.

Nadja: I have the feeling that I am more attuned to my body in general, to the way it's moving, and that I take more care with my body and really try to listen to it the whole time. I feel this a lot in contemporary class, not that much in ballet yet as I don't give myself the chance to really feel what I'm doing there sometimes. But I want to get there one day too. Maybe that's also about habit, like you're so used to doing something in a certain way, as I'm now used to taking contemporary class from a different approach. Also in daily life when I'm injured, for example, I really try to help my body by using my body without medicine. You know, like through normal movements.

> ***Fanny: The last question you were asked to consider was about positive and negative memories you have in relation to your experiences with somatics. Is there something you would like to add?***

Nadja: Well, the beginning of the year was difficult. I had never done something like this before, and you really have to be open, ready, and willing—otherwise it is not a good experience. It changed into a good experience for me. And I noticed that even at the end of the year some people in our class were still not open to accepting what was offered. You have to be open in order to accept it.

Alexei: I find it interesting that there is always a kind of rebellion against the introduction to somatics during the first year of the Bachelor's program each year. I remember hearing students pass on advice to the younger ones, telling them "Don't give up!", "It will be worth it," "Make it happen!" And I think that's kind of inherent in somatic practices, that there is a moment where you can decide to be open, which is not always so easy to take because you don't get immediate rewards. The somatic way takes you out of normalcy, and you have to wait to get results. But it can be really worth it. And people always look for immediate rewards, some you get from "Get the legs higher, point your feet more!" But how am I getting better, and in what way?

Lars: At the beginning of my first year, I just didn't understand it. Halfway through the year something clicked, and I noticed rapid improvement. From then on I really enjoyed every single moment of working this way. And it really gave me the ability to teach myself; it really let me learn to teach myself.

Alexei: I think it brings self-dependence to life in general.

Swane: The most difficult or strenuous thing for me was finding the ability and the strength to *be* that much with myself—to *stay* that much with myself. I didn't know that little things needed so much concentration, so much focus ... actually intellectually. That was sometimes that was really hard for me.

Luke: I kind of knew in the first year how it was going to help me. I didn't know exactly how to apply lots of it, and I'd get frustrated at myself for not being able to figure it out. I know I was very eager to learn. The only "bad" thing would be that it took me a while to know how to warm up my body and to figure out how my body works. I now know what I need to do in order to prepare myself for contemporary, ballet, or Feldenkrais class. Before Feldenkrais, I really get my body ready. In that mind-set I can focus on myself and be more aware of details in the body. After Feldenkrais class, I actually feel good; I'm much more awake, can feel my body, and go to the next class prepared. It helps you to discover what you need in order to dance or perform.

Lars: It was in my last year that I had a really completely new mind-set, that I had fully adapted my mentality and approach to dance. A big help with that development was the GAGA classes. However, what I found incredibly difficult and rough was to become so fully aware of my body in these classes, exploring and experiencing my body, and then going directly afterwards to a ballet class where I was forced to look at movements purely from an aesthetic viewpoint and to use more power than necessary simply "because then it's right."

Valeria: For me it was a different experience. The first time that I had fun in ballet was after the GAGA class—because I felt myself.

Lars: I realized that I really want to be my own person, I don't want people to be constantly telling me what to do. I think somatic teachings have completely let me find myself, not only in my body but as a person.

Lars: I think to work professionally you need to be open to somatics.

Alexei: It makes sense to have somatic practice at the beginning of a Bachelor's program because we all got to the point of actually thinking about what we were doing and how we were doing it—rather than just doing it.

> ***Jenny: You have to ask yourself to notice your progress using measures that may not be so familiar to you. It does take some time to find out how to maintain attention when working very slowly and gently on the floor. And this kind of work is not something you can** make **happen; you have to** let **it happen and be patient.***

Swane: It does create friction, and it's also necessary to go through that process.

Luke: I didn't really do contemporary until I came here. I did jazz, tap, ballet, and gymnastics in my hometown so I had to really educate myself, to actually realize why I am doing this. What's the reason behind it? And what actually is "seeing"? Especially now that I'm in the third year, I can see more clearly that it is you who needs to figure it out, otherwise it is not going to be of any help.

Nadja: What I really enjoyed about somatics was that it didn't matter where you came from or how much you already knew, there was still the possibility for everybody who was open to it to accomplish the same amount. The possibility was always there.

Swane: You need to be able to take whatever people chuck at you and deal with it in a certain way and be open enough to be like, "Okay, what am I going to do with this? What is the most I can get out of it?" And if you can't do that with somatics, you probably can't do it with the choreography somebody chucks at you or with a company situation or with a contract. For me, it's mind-set and how you deal with situations that are maybe not the most comfortable or whatever you've always imagined. It's a lot of responsibility, and that's not always comfortable. But to do something with somatics, you have to have that quality—self-responsibility.

Alexei: Jenny, how would you define somatics?

> ***Jenny: Well, I think you've all hit on it. I would say that it is paying attention to one's self as a subject. To notice sensations and subtle differences in order to make the connection between sensing, feeling, moving, and thinking. To attend to your inner world and know that how you sense yourself inside informs how you appear in the outside world. And it's not about indulging yourself, closing your eyes, and retreating from the outside world but being aware of yourself in your relation to your environment. Everybody is different, everybody comes from a different place—and part of a somatic way of being is the ability to recognize and appreciate how someone else's differences affect and inform your "being." And you all identified the relationship between attention and effort, which is very important.***

Lars: I think it's like a circle because it doesn't matter where you start. There is no single right or wrong place to start and finish. If you start with small exercises, you will learn to become more aware of small details happening inside your body, and you will be able to find similar intricacies in the larger actions. Similarly, the larger movements and impulses will make connections between individual sections of the body, and you can then use your experiences to find better connections on a much smaller scale. No matter where you start, you will also learn to listen better to the other side of things. And when you have spent quite a bit of time with one aspect, and move on to the other only to feel your limits with that one too, then you can go back to where you were originally and go even deeper, because it is a never-ending cycle.

> ***Jenny: The cycle never ends but this conversation has to find a conclusion! We thank you for joining us at the table today in such an active exchange about your experiences with somatics and dance.***

INTERMEZZO: REFLECTIONS OF DANCE EDUCATORS

TO BE CONNECTED TO STAY CONNECTED

Karin Munters Jameson

"You are a good and skillful dancer, but to date you are only a product of your education and the choreographers with whom you have worked. In order for you to become interesting for me, you have to find your own manner of expression. You have to become your own." These words were uttered by the choreographer Per Jonsson when I was a young dancer who finally found the courage to ask him if he wanted to work with me. Through my education, I was trained in imitating, remembering, and doing the "right" thing—filled with a desire to shape and discipline the body into the form of what I understood to be a "dancer's body." I had learned to take control over my body, but was not really in contact with it. There was no space for notions such as identity or personal expression. Through the conversation with Per, it became clear that I had no clue what "personal expression" or being "one's own" actually meant and that I knew even less about how to search for knowledge about this idea.

During a summer course in 1992, I first encountered Klein Technique™. I was immediately affected on a deep physical level that I could not express

Tina Warmuth

in words. Although it was only a short experience with a few exercises from it incorporated into a dance technique class, I realized that this might be a way of getting closer to an understanding of what Per was referring to years earlier. This meeting became my starting point for several years of intense study in the Klein Technique™.

At that point in time, my identity was primarily that of a pedagogue. This first encounter with the technique encouraged me to reevaluate both my movement material and myself as a pedagogue. With Klein Technique™ as a base, I have continuously developed both my artistic and pedagogical practice.

The greatest challenge for me as a pedagogue is to create a space for the desire and curiosity of the students to unfold so they might explore extended possibilities for movement and bodily expression. I strive not to emphasize their limitations but, instead, to strengthen the students' ability to throw themselves into the unknown so they might reach a place of—selfdirected, critical reflection in relation to their personal development.

I meet young dance artists on a daily basis and, although it has been about thirty years since my own time as a young student, I see students still have the same desire to control, command, and shape the body. There is often a conflict between striving to do "right" and to throw oneself out there, into the unknown—a conflict that often makes it difficult for the student to stay with the actual exploration and to continue to work through the insecurities of not knowing where the work will lead. Perhaps this is a result of how the Swedish educational system is structured—with limited time, competitive grading, and the idea of being "ready" when the education is completed. I wish we could, instead, encourage students to dare to trust their inner strength, to understand the potential of not knowing, and the importance of allowing a process to take time—along with the insight that a dancer will most probably never be "ready."

The field of dance today is one with a much greater perspective on both what dance is and has the potential to be than was the case when I was young. It demands of us (as pedagogues and members of institutions) that we prepare students for a reality different to the one for which I was shaped. Also, the role of the dancer looks different now. In the past, a dancer was more or less a tool for interpreting someone else's vision. The dancer of today is more likely to be a co-creator of movement material and a contributor to the conceptual scope of work. Such tasks demand a strong artistic identity, as well as personal integrity, and they make it imperative that young students encounter practices and techniques to challenge and encourage the exploration of material as well as identity. In this way, we can educate students to take responsibility for generating new knowledge. Such a process takes time and does not ever come to an end, but through learning to continuously reevaluate one's knowledge, new doors will be opened toward new insights. This can in itself be seen as a process of producing both material and identity.

The fundamental structure for my work in contemporary dance is based on the Klein Technique™ and its movement analysis. This technique offers both theoretical and practical knowledge. It is a central part of my teaching in that it provides students with knowledge about the body and its ability to develop and articulate movement. In order to reach a deeper understanding of the body and its function in movement, physical and anatomical structures such as the form, function, and mechanics of the skeleton are, in dance, connected to weight, spatiality, and gravity. Movement creates space and space creates body, just as the movement of the body in space creates time. Understanding these connections brings forth tools for understanding one's own body and its expression, both as a concrete tool and as an opening toward reaching the ungraspable.

> *One could say that Klein Technique™ is the hypothesis and that the questions, and the formulation is my body. A great reason for my interest in the technique is that it includes both a philosophical and a bodily aspect. Not only does it allow my body to have the structure that it has, but it also brings out my potential to affect its capacity. It proposes both an analysis of how things are and how change can happen. Since the training form insists on everything being inconstant, there is no "final station" for the practice. (Student comment, Dans och Cirkushögskolan/School of Dance and Circus (DOCH) 2010)*

> *In your classes, there is a precision in the movement that is about the body always being directed in space. It is a certain type of movement that happens in a certain part of the body that is directed in a certain direction in space. In the same way that I experience how the mechanics of the skeleton constitute the source of inspiration for the movement material we do in your classes, I also perceive that the directions are a part of that. If one wishes to be a bit phenomenologically philosophical, one can perhaps say that we, through the insight of the directedness of the body, not only work with the consciousness of how we direct ourselves in body and space, but also that this in itself is the actual aim of the movement. (Student comment, DOCH 2011)*

The world we live in today is fast, in constant flux, and demands that we stay updated, connected, reachable, and flexible. For a student to stick with such a seemingly slow process as Klein Technique™ can consequently be very challenging. However, that said, I believe it is absolutely essential. I want to challenge the students to take the time to find the inner peace needed to search through specific elements that, in turn, can open up something much larger, and even much deeper.

What the Klein training has added to my other experiences is a sense of being through stillness with a greater empathy for myself, what I know, and who I am. And also in relation to others and everything else. (Student comment, DOCH 2012)

I want to communicate a strong and nonhierarchical relationship, as well as connection between body, space, and time, by starting with the physical craft of the Klein Technique™. Because it is there, in the concrete body work, that the possibilities for development start—both the development of one's own identity and one's own artistic expression.

THE BODY: A WORK IN PROGRESS

Jan Burkhardt

Our body is a vital, constantly constructing and deconstructing organism. It is *in process.* Consequently, I like to treat a class or rehearsal like a living organism, as opposed to a predesigned set of exercises.

What is a process? It is a vital, multi-relational course of change. What we perceive as "us" is contributing to, and affected by, this ongoing transformation—similar to how a synapse functions as part of a network of neurons interacting in their larger context.

My personal somatic background is mainly informed by Laban/Bartenieff Movement Studies, Body-Mind Centering™ (BMC), and my training as a physical therapist. These are all characterized by scientific, physiological knowledge that is brought to life by subjective experience. The core value in somatic-based practice, for me, is that I become more conscious of somatic information and its contextual value. The application of a partly analytical system like Laban/Bartenieff Movement Studies, in combination with a more subjective (sometimes suggestive) exploratory system like BMC, provides an ideal setup because the work can reveal the importance of form in relation to sensation. Both systems are based on early childhood sensorimotor development, which sets up this very relationship in the first place.

Working with set movement patterns and subjective sensations provides both the facilitator and student with the possibility to navigate practice according to collective or individual needs; in short, to provide options for the practice and potential contextualization of what is happening. This, in turn, can help to build trust in the process and in each other.

I like to treat a dance studio as a laboratory for life rather than a separate study room. Somatic exploration can prepare a person to become a physically virtuosic dancer, as well as widening one's philosophical horizon or empathetic capacity; it all depends upon what the person allows themselves to "open up" to or be emphasized. When facilitating, I frequently begin by proposing a specific physiological focus. For example, I might ask students to find a partner and explore each other's bones (or skin, organs, etc.) through movement and touch, and then suggest tracking specific physiological information. This manner of practice sets up both an objective frame, through the scientific base of physiology, and a collective focus. Both then function as an anchor to which one can return later in the process. In addition, this framework leaves space for individuals to follow up on their own impulses, needs, and desires.

I then often let the focus zoom into experiencing relationships based on the given somatic frame. This is a crucial part of my practice as, in my view, the question of how specific physiological experiences feed into what we do, and from which context we move, is often left too undefined. I might ask the following questions: "How do you relate to each other when sensation is emphasized, for example, in the bones?", "How do you relate to space, and how does space relate to you?", "What is the relationship between your sensations and your feelings?", "Which associations (images, memories, etc.) emerge?" As wide as this field can be, I ask for the experience to remain as specific as possible, since this allows for a common focus in the group and prevents randomness in both experience and expression. In addition, it enables us, in retrospect, to more easily and precisely track what happened. This is especially important, for instance, in a choreographic process, when building movement material, or when one is simply trying to be precise about the specifics of a particular form of artistic research.

In my experience, physiological research can efficiently function as a foundation for reference, mutual agreement, or for sharing with one another. In comparison, emotions tend to be more subjective and concepts can often be too abstract to relate to. Moreover, physiological exploration does not polarize emotions and concepts but, rather, helps to frame and define them.

Monitoring myself is another crucial layer in my practice. I always aim to be in the practice and reflect on it at the same time. This not only opens up a tremendous field of options for me on which to act, but also creates a communicative base from which to work in the first place (i.e., my own body). For this inside and outside relationship, the system of proprioception functions as both an amazing example and metaphor. The proprioceptive sensors provide feedback on how the body is positioned by measuring the length and tension of the tendons. The nervous system simultaneously translates this sensation into a projection onto the vision fields of the brain, making me see the position of my body. Thus I am able to virtually look at myself. I can also visualize my body from any perspective within the space while simultaneously looking into the space from within my body using my eyes. For me, the complexity of this feedback is crucial for training myself physiologically, emotionally, and intelligently. This interplay mirrors the core of theater and performance—the physical within the virtual, a distance, shape, or tension that triggers projection for performer and audience member alike.

Allowing depth in the process also invites the resolution of the duality that often arises in dance practice between "technique" and "experience." For someone who is used to practicing pirouettes many hours a day, the experience of rolling on the floor and sounding into the liver for several hours might be completely inaccessible, at least in the beginning. By building a bridge between form and exploration, we can expand

and specify our practice. For example, a student might encounter difficulties with her pirouettes and cannot see how she would benefit from spending time sensing the weight of her organs while rolling on the floor. After having done so for some time, however, and having become conscious of the fact that what prevented her from turning efficiently on a high level was a lack of core support and connection to the floor, she is very likely to find her pirouettes improving more than had she simply continued to practice turning.

One of the biggest challenges for us as facilitators is helping students trust that time and space are necessary for this process, since somatic-based work often doesn't reveal results right away or at least not the expected results—especially when one is new to working within such an approach. Also, somatic work often seems unconventional for young students who frequently come from a result-oriented education and need to allow a change to their paradigm of learning. For this, the only way again—paradoxically—is "results." One frequent inroad to somatics opens up when healing an injury through a repatterning of the body's habits or when experiencing a consequent release of a strained body part or body system.

Once students grasp the complexity and multitude of possible outcomes of somatic practice, they might find agency for such an approach in the evolving complexity of the field of contemporary dance, where the requirements for training are constantly developing. Building a dance practice from a somatic approach can generate more vitality and expressive range in the students. It can also create a multitude of choices about how to direct one's practice, as well as how to become part of a larger whole by being connected to a deeper, cellular level within the body.

In this sense, contemporary dance is an exemplary mirror for the often overwhelming complexity of contemporary life itself, with which it is becoming more and more challenging to deal. A certain way to position oneself within this challenge, being with oneself while being connected to one's environment, is a somatic-based practice that fosters the development of personal ownership, emancipation, and empathy. This, in turn, supports the ability to be at the source of creation, at the birth of each moment—which is to live fully.

Jürgen van Buer

6. ATTRIBUTES OF SUCCESSFUL TEACHING:

NEW FINDINGS FROM RESEARCH ON TEACHING AND LEARNING *Jürgen van Buer*

Section 1: Reliable knowledge about successful teaching?

School and teaching are phenomena whose external appearance, contours, interior structures, and processes vary—sometimes radically—according to the observer's viewpoint and perspective. This is true not only of everyday knowledge, but also of research into education systems, school, and teaching. By the time the discussion turns to the meaning of "successful teaching," the varying viewpoints begin to clash unmistakably. For this reason, it is important to outline briefly the context in which the findings presented in sections 2 and 3 emerged. Pursuing the question at hand—"For what aspects of school and teaching do reliable findings exist?"—exposes the fact that those findings' richness and perspectives rest on both their underlying research traditions and on investments into specific research fields governed by education and research policy.

(1) Placing the empirical findings about school and teaching into political context: In the early 1970s (see Ingenkamp 1971, as an example of an initial study), the "empirical turn" gained ground in German education studies. Owing in major part to systematic research support from the German Research Foundation (DFG) and the research programs of the German Federal Ministry of Education and Research (BMBF), the past three decades or so have seen the establishment of a highly dynamic research process. This process aims to investigate: (a) the (success) factors for teaching processes; and (b) for their systemic and institutional contexts; (c) those processes themselves; and (d) their outputs among students (for an overview, see Achtenhagen 2006).

(1a) National and international performance studies as drivers of development: This development was supported by performance studies, both national and international, such as the Program for International Student Assessment (PISA). These made it possible to compare students' learning outcomes across countries. Likewise, in Germany, they permitted the systematic comparison of "success" across federal states. (For examples of national performance studies, see Brandenburg's QuaSUM study by Lehmann et al. 2000.) At least in Germany, this process of empirically "screening" school and teaching has been perceptibly influenced by research questions aligned with the concerns of educational policy and the interests of state and federal governments. (For examples, see the studies on discrimination against children and teenagers from underprivileged and immigrant backgrounds, such as the essays in Allemann-Ghionda, Stanat 2010.)

(1b) Evidence-based educational policy as a control framework: Hence, the control process employed for the educational system has increasingly relied on implementing "evidence-based" educational policy (Bromme, Prenzel, Jäger 2014). The educational reports published by the German federal government (e.g., Autorengruppe Bildungsberichterstattung 2014) and individual states play a major role in this regard. These reports attempt to draw broad-based, but sometimes also thematic, conclusions about the current state of the education system, educational institutions, and teaching and its learning outputs. In reports on the learning output, in turn, the students' skills acquisition play a central role.

(2) (German) educational research's focus on cognitive aspects of teaching and skills acquisition: After an initial preference for assessments of institutionalized educational processes in the school subject of mathematics (see the Trends in International Mathematics and Science Study (TIMSS); Baumert, Bos, Lehmann 2000), the focus of empirical investigations expanded from the late 1990s to other fields, such as science lessons (see the essays in Petersen, Cotter 2015), lessons in students' native languages, and students' acquisition of their first foreign language. The emphasis of these and comparable studies is placed on the cognitive aspects of individual learning and development, and thus also teaching processes. Research questions about motivational processes (see Möller, Schiefele 2004) have likewise been founded on notions of motivation that stress its cognitive underpinnings. Emotional aspects have been slow to gain focus in empirical educational research (see Ledergerber 2015). Investigations into motor learning are merely marginal in the overall trends described above, almost entirely restricted to sports studies and physical education studies. Assessments of somatic learning, the focus of this handbook, are essentially absent from the literature about empirical research into teaching and learning outlined here. Even perspectives that so much as reference the significance of such viewpoints are lacking from the conclusions and "prospects for future research" sections of the studies named.

(3) The role of meta-studies in the framework of evidence-based education policy: One of the outcomes of the practically explosive diversity of empirical studies about school and teaching is the critical view on whether their results "fit each other." For it has to be mentioned that the studies are designed from different perspectives, which alone leads to varying findings. Consequently, this calls into question the reliability of the knowledge arising from such studies—a concern especially pertinent for education policy. Indeed, this is one of the central questions of both empirical educational research and evidence-based policy strategies: How can chains of causation be identified that are stable across the various studies? The basic premise is that these chains' effect sizes can serve as a springboard for planning and implementing systematic changes to school and teaching. "Meta-studies" offer indispensable aids toward identifying this desirable "solid" knowledge. These grand studies use statistical methods to compare the effects demonstrated by individual studies, such as the impact of teaching methods on students' learning success, across a large number of investigations and then summarize them comprehensively. The meta-study that has drawn the most worldwide attention over the past few years is that of the New Zealand-born education researcher John A. C. Hattie, who teaches in Australia (2009; for more, see section 2).

In summarizing the main trends in empirical educational research, the same central focus on questions about the cognitive aspects of teaching and learning, discussed above, coalesces around meta-studies. In addition, the scope of most of these studies is indisputably restricted to schools for general education. Therefore, in the context of this handbook, the following critical question presents itself: How can empirical education research contribute solid knowledge about teaching in order to promote and support individual learning and development processes in dance lessons?

Section 2: Learning factors for successful teaching—results of the Hattie study (2009)

(1) The Hattie study's context, structure, and reception: The Hattie study had a largely positive reception in the associated fields of education studies. Nonetheless, in Germany as elsewhere, the study's weaknesses and limitations were also debated, at times fiercely. The German press acclaimed the investigation by Hattie as an "epochal work" (*Der Spiegel*, April 15, 2013). Accordingly, the study was received with great acceptance from the German states' educational administrations (Terhart 2014: 8). According to Hilbert Meyer (2014: 120f.), a "battle of interpretations" has long been waged, at least in Germany, over the central takeaways of the Hattie study and how to implement them in concepts for educational policy. This "battle" will continue for a while to come.

In his meta-meta-analysis *Visible Learning*, Hattie (2009) draws on around 800 meta-studies of previous investigations and distills them once again (for his methodological approach, see 2009: 8ff.). Ultimately, his study is based on more than 50,000 smaller original studies covering more than 80 million students. This approach is certainly vulnerable to criticism. It remains unclear whether the categories used in the statistical analyses, the institutional contexts, the schooling and teaching processes, and their outputs are in fact comparable across individual studies (see Pant 2014: 137f.). Hattie is quite aware of this line of criticism (2009: 10ff.). As a result, he does not consider the findings of his meta-meta-study to be a solid, unshakable list of factors that are proven to be relevant to learning at school. Rather, he sees these factors as a starting point toward narrowing down the questions about the effects of school and teaching, and critically reassessing the findings' unquestioned structures and interpretations. Thus the author speaks of an "explanatory story, not a 'what works' recipe" (Hattie 2009: 3).

Altogether, Hattie identifies more than 130 school and teaching variables that affect learning (listed in appendix B of his 2009 book). He classifies variables as clearly relevant to learning if they have an effect size (d) of at least 0.40 (Hattie 2009: 17f.; the indicator d is a unit for measuring deviations from the mean value).

(2) Findings from the Hattie study about teaching effectiveness: According to the Hattie study, variables connected to the education system, the type of school, and individual schools' institutional variables, such as leadership behavior and school administration, are relevant, but have a much weaker impact than teaching variables on students' learning directly (2009: 72ff.). Hans-Günter Rolff (2014) relativizes these findings, at least for the German education system, pointing to the highly robust results of the PISA studies that indicate medium- or higher-effect sizes for different school types on students' cognitive outputs (for the PISA studies, see OECD 2016: 137–170). The Hattie study demonstrates particularly clear effects on students' learning and development for variables related to (2.1) the curricula in place, (2.2) the learners themselves, (2.3) the teacher and, especially, the teaching approaches (2.4).

(2.1) The effect of curricula on students' individual development (Hattie 2009: 129ff.): The Hattie study has virtually nothing to say about the curricula discussed in this handbook. However, the following effects related to language skills can be seen as relevant to dance education as well. First, the study discusses the significance of programs that systematically promote students' reading competencies and vocabulary (Hattie 2009: 129ff., 131ff.). Indeed, across curricula, these areas generally pose one of the most critical foundations for successful learning, above all for students whose native language is not the language of instruction. Second, Hattie highlights the major significance of creativity programs and tactile stimulation programs (2009: 155f., 153f.). Hattie (2015: 186) derives this insight from the findings of Steve Higgins, Elaine Hall, Viv Baumfield, and David Moseley (2005: 31ff.), who highly stress the interactive relationship among developing comprehension abilities, such as between the self-sufficient formation of concepts/ideas and strategic, deliberated thinking. The latter primarily relates to individuals' process of contending with their own metacognitive strategies, such as how they manage their own learning or their own value judgments. One approach that seems to have an exceptionally positive effect on learning is systematically incorporating different communication strategies in teaching, shifting between a focus on visual representation and nuanced verbalization. As a pleasant by-product, this also has significant effects on students' individual argumentation skills.

(2.2) Contributions from the student to successful learning (Hattie 2009: 39ff.): An almost mind-boggling number of empirical studies have demonstrated that in addition to socio-biographical background (family home, living environment, etc.), the students' previous domain-specific knowledge, their underlying cognitive resources, their motivation, and their self-efficacy expectancies are particularly impactful variables. The Hattie study fundamentally confirms these variables' significant effect on development, learning processes, and learning outcomes. However, because the Hattie study places the aspect of motivation within an extended overall spectrum of personality variables (2009: 47ff.), its significance is narrowed here. Instead, self-reported grades and the Piagetian stage of cognitive development come in first and second place in the full rankings of the Hattie study. In his comments (2009: 44), Hattie points out that self-reported grades are a fairly accurate substitute for students' actual quantified achievements. However, this is less true for students from minority groups and also varies by gender.

(2.3) The teacher's effect on students' learning and development (Hattie 2009: 108ff.): In the German discourse, the findings of the Hattie study are frequently listed as evidence of teachers' exceptional impact on learning, especially in regard to their subject-matter knowledge and their didactic competencies. While the teacher's personality has visible, but rather moderate, effects according to Hattie (2009: 129ff.), the effects of competencies in methodological teaching processes, such as microteaching, especially microcommunication during lessons, are demonstrably large.

> *Hattie (2009: 112f.) describes "microteaching" as a didactic concept that emphasizes the following aspects of teaching: a coherent vision of good teaching shared by the teacher and students; the use of "well-defined standards of practice and performance" (113) that serve as benchmarks for coursework; and taking into account the social contexts of learning.*

In addition, the variables of communication and interaction during lessons, as guided by the teacher, are highly meaningful for students' successful learning (see section 3). The teacher-student relationship plays a central role in this area, demonstrated in daily interactions through elements such as respect of self and others, individualized feedback, and individualized support strategies (on the teacher's part, see Hattie 2009: 118f.). The same applies to articulating high teacher expectations. This should not be paired with labeling students (Hattie 2009: 124ff.), a process that quickly proves harmful to development. Teacher clarity (Hattie 2009: 125f.) acts as a kind of "common anchor" for the markers listed above. Clarity enables teachers to communicate their expectations, their ideas about teaching, and the didactic concept underlying each stage of teaching so that the stakeholders develop a shared understanding of the teaching approach. The clarity of the teacher's language plays a prominent role toward this end.

(2.4) Contributions from teaching approaches for successful learning (Hattie 2009: 108ff.): Hattie devotes chapters 9 and 10 of his meta-meta-study to this aspect. In the fields of planning, implementing, and evaluating or assessing teaching, both models of general didactics and special didactics use a remarkable variety of categories and constructs to describe teaching approaches and outputs. When discussing these factors across countries, as the Hattie study innately does, these categories and constructs are strongly based on specific national traditions and therefore often exhibit visible cultural specificity. It is thus unsurprising that the study's critical reception in German education studies, general didactics, and special didactics has particularly come from this area (see Brügelmann 2014: 42ff.).

The Hattie study shows the special relevance of didactic concepts founded on individualized support and individual instruction (such as mastery learning concepts; 2009: 170f., 198f.) and those that use "advanced organizers" to pace the learning process (2009: 167f.). Adapting the time allotted to each task to the needs of individual learners is shown to be valuable. The value of feedback (Hattie 2009: 173ff.) and frequency of testing (Hattie 2009: 178ff.) points in the same direction. Successful learning processes are further supported by spaced practice (Hattie 2009: 185f.) that integrates massed practice as well as support measures such as peer tutoring (Hattie 2009: 186f.) and mentoring (Hattie 2009: 182f.). Since the 1960s, time-on-task models (for another recent contribution for German-speaking Europe, see Helmke 2003: 10ff.) have indicated the particular value of the active use of learning time (or engaged learning time) by learners, as cumulative effects are especially apparent in cases of underutilization and among lower-achieving students. The Hattie study corroborates this (2009: 184ff.). Meta-cognitive strategies have a central significance for successful learning.

> *This is especially true of learning techniques (Hattie 2009: 189ff.), such as self-evaluation, positive self-consequences, and self-control, but also time management, visualizing the learning objects/imagery, and the design of a suitable learning environment. The techniques of self-verbalization and self-questioning (Hattie 2009: 192f.), by which learners articulate learning processes concurrently and in retrospect, can also be classified within this spectrum.*

Overall, it becomes clear that these repertoires of meta-cognitive strategies and techniques especially encourage learning when the learning techniques and the student's learning style are well matched (Hattie 2009: 195ff.). The effectiveness of the variables listed is supported by a formative evaluation of the teaching approach, in other words one that is close to the "action" of teaching (Hattie 2009: 181). Ideally, this should return directly into the feedback for the learner. It can also help the teacher to adjust and improve lesson plans and teaching activities. In terms of the implementation of teaching methods (chapter 10), the factors of reciprocal teaching, problem-solving teaching, and cooperative learning have outlier effect sizes (regarding gains and losses in cooperative learning, see Dubs 2007: 149ff.).

> *Reciprocal teaching (Hattie 2009: 210ff.) emphasizes a focus on dialogue during lessons in which students often take on the role of teacher. The practice of*

"scaffolding" plays an important part in this. After observational learning through expert examples, scaffolding enables students to transform into stakeholders who actively guide their own learning processes (Fernandez et al. 2001). Problem-solving teaching (Hattie 2009: 210ff.) emphasizes the holism of the full procedure—all the way from defining the question to identifying problems and potential solutions to reaching and evaluating a solution. This goes along with visibly student-centered teaching strategies and small-group learning, which in turn encourages cooperative learning.

Section 1, paragraph 3 above alludes to the following point—for a long time now, a "battle of interpretations" has been waged over the Hattie study, in Meyer's words (2014: 120). This battle has taken place in various media and across groups of affected stakeholders, from educational researchers to school administrators to parents' associations to practitioners, and the debate has been both fierce and quite controversial. In his review of the Hattie study, the educator and didactics expert Meyer (2014) stresses that the communicative "surface structures of teaching" and the "deep structures" dictating learning are often not matched to one another during lessons (124ff.). Consequently, the variables that the Hattie study identifies as significant to learning cannot be used as a list of successful attributes that could be deployed independently in any configuration and temporal sequence within the teaching process as a whole. Instead, Meyer contends, it comes down to implementing the deep structures of teaching that have conclusive effects on learning. The central aspects of such deep structures of teaching might be these:

Establishing a mutual understanding of the learning in question—by the students and teacher in equal measure; approaching teaching as a field that the stakeholders should continually investigate anew for themselves; independently defining and assigning development tasks; respecting one's self and others during lessons—again, applied to students and teachers in equal measure (Meyer 2014: 19ff.); and, finally, designated structures of self-directed learning (Wirth, Leutner 2008).

Section 3: Interactive communicative structures of teaching processes

(1) Communication and interaction—conceptual clarifications: The structuring of communication and interaction in teaching is manifested in part by the verbal, language-related, and nonverbal repertoires at the disposal of the lesson's stakeholders (Retter 2002: 10ff.). This structure is also revealed in the preferences according to which the stakeholders use their repertoires during lessons.

(1.1) Communication: According to the Austrian-American communication theorist and therapist Paul Watzlawick, "it is obvious that [human] communication is a *conditio sine qua non* of human life and social order" (Watzlawick, Beavin, Jackson 2007: 13). It can consist of one or more messages. These are primarily conveyed via verbal codes comprising national languages and dialects as well as different registers within a given national language (Biber 2006). The latter can vary depending on markers of social background (Bernstein 1971; Labov 1971; for examples of variation in German, see Marossek 2016) or age (for teenage slang, see Pauli 2011; Müller 2013). When these clash during lessons, it can lead to comprehension problems but also—often hidden—emotional problems and stigmatizing labeling (see section 2, item 2.3).

(1.2) Interaction: While the concept of communication is limited to one or two messages, interaction is commonly understood as the mutual exchange of statements between two or more people (Watzlawick, Beavin, Jackson 2007: 22). Thus the concept of interaction applies to longer sequences or cycles of social activity, as is also typical of teaching approaches. For the psychologist Friedemann Schulz von Thun (1981), the interplay that the sender and recipient jointly enact is manifested in communication, but even more so in interaction. To a large extent this occurs consciously—in other words, it is intentionally designed—yet it is also partially unconscious. With his four-ear model, von Thun calls attention to the following: in addition to the subject reference and the relationship reference (see communication axiom 2 in Watzlawick, Beavin, Jackson 2007: 56), this interplay of communication/interaction makes—largely conscious—self-representations manifest. However, self-representation is inextricably linked to unintentional self-exposure to one's counterpart.

(1.3) Language-related and nonverbal elements of communication and interaction: The language-related and nonverbal aspects of communicative/interactive behavior play an especially critical role in this unintentional self-exposure (van Buer, Niederhaus 2010). At least in the European cultural sphere, most stakeholders are unconscious or only partially conscious of using these repertoires (Oomen-Welke 2004). It is therefore unsurprising that the impact of language-related and nonverbal signals on human communication is often underestimated, not least when it comes to teaching (Rosenbusch, Schober 2004: 1). Thus Charles Galloway (1976), in the very title of his book, calls nonverbal behavior "silent language," and not without reason. According to Heinz Rosenbusch (2004: 141), successful teaching and learning processes require all stakeholders to safeguard "communicative hygiene as a prerequisite of teaching."

(2) Teaching as an interplay of communication and interaction: Through its "surface structure" first and foremost (see the concluding remarks of section 2), teaching can be seen as significantly dictated by verbal communication and interaction. At this juncture, it is not possible to further investigate the extent to which this also applies to dance lessons in which nonverbal behavior—"body language"—plays a prominent role. Nevertheless, in regard to these settings of teaching and learning, it is worth noting that the stakeholders' statements in these lessons are primarily manifested in verbal behavior. As the most essential objective of the "deep structures" of teaching, learning largely occurs by way of language—be it the establishment of knowledge or the acquisition of meta-cognitive strategies for the reflexive management of learning (see section 2, item 2.4). Hence, it is only logical that Bernd Switalla called attention to the following as early as the 1980s (in 1982): the stakeholders' verbal repertoires are rarely congruent, especially not when the stakeholders come from different social milieus, verbal traditions, family skill sets, and so on (see item 1.1.). Accordingly, communication difficulties, which for many students lead directly to learning problems, would at least accompany day-to-day lessons, or even dictate them in some cases. In regard to the Hattie study (see section 2, item 2.1), this highlights the following: measures to promote language skills and the learners' verbal repertoires prove to be highly relevant to successful learning. As Eveline Wuttke (2005) shows, microcommunication during teaching—and the language used—play a particularly decisive role in the process of knowledge acquisition. For students whose native language is not the language of instruction, measures to promote language skills not only have direct effects on language acquisition but also lead to a general emphasis on the verbal basis of communication during lessons. These measures prove to be especially effective when they focus on the repertoires of relevant jargon at hand. Finally, one could conclude that the didactic concepts only achieve their impact by way of the participating stakeholders' communication skills and the day-to-day microstructures of communication during lessons. In particular due to the ritualization of communication and interaction during lessons via the institution of school and its teaching traditions (Bellack et al. 1966), these microstructures can also be described in terms of the precarious balance in the interplay between mutual understanding and misunderstanding (Dobrick 1985), which in some cases the participants deliberately exploit. As Wuttke (2005: 87ff.) has determined in her compilation of empirical results from the relevant studies, mastery of the communication rules by every stakeholder is an indispensable prerequisite for both the "traditional" and "innovative" conceptualizations of teaching. To this end, the language-related and nonverbal repertoires of the lessons' participants play a much larger part than commonly assumed.

Section 4: Successful communication in teaching as a prerequisite for successful teaching

(1) The critical-communicative model of didactics as a point of departure: "Conventional" models of general didactics (as summarized in Porsch 2016, for example) tend to aim at analyzing, planning, and evaluating the broad conceptual management of teaching and its reflexive legitimation (in regard to the relative effectiveness of such concepts and teaching strategies, see also section 2, item 2.4). In contrast, the critical-communicative model of didactics is highly focused on the dialectical structure of schooling and education on the spectrum between freedom/autonomy and commitment (Schaller 1971), and between authority and emancipation (Schäfer 1971a). As both authors indicate, these two dichotomies are always in fragile balance and sometimes in an oppositional relationship in state-run educational institutions. In this respect, according to Alfred Schäfer (1971b: 144ff.), the microstructuring of the communicative field of action is particularly important. The reflected execution of symmetrical and asymmetrical education, punctuation, and of meta-communication plays a prominent role here (see also the axioms of communication by Watzlawick, Beavin, Jackson 2007: 53ff.). Fundamentally, the processes of communication and interaction during lessons should not be seen as linear paths of development, but as generally open-ended systems involving diverse feedback among the participating stakeholders. This applies both to mass communication in society and to communication in one of its prominent institutions: school and the teaching that takes place there.

(2) Successful communication, a normative construct: From the perspective of critical didactic theory, the Göttingen-based pedagogical theorist Klaus Mollenhauer outlines seven desirable attributes for a pedagogically designed situation:

> *Involving each partner in defining the situation; enabling flexibly defined relationships; maintaining role distance; maintaining tolerance for ambiguity; achieving empathy; negotiating the identities of the stakeholders participating in the situation for each new situation or partner; and enabling meta-communication. (1972: 107)*

The implementation of these attributes in day-to-day teaching poses a major challenge. Even if the primary goal of teaching methods is the acquisition of subject-matter knowledge, the call to acquire a differentiated understanding of verbal, language-related, and nonverbal communication and their interactions, as well as day-to-day "communicative hygiene" (Rosenbusch 2004: 141ff.), plays an indisputable role. Only by regularly renewing the naturalness of such communicative hygiene and by ensuring the equal participation of all stakeholders can the didactic and specialized "deep structures" of teaching make a suitable impact. This is distinctly true for a conceptualization of teaching that employs fairly open-ended, student-centered design, systematically promotes students' self-organized learning, and includes elements of cooperative and reciprocal learning (for the latter two, see Hattie 2014: 240ff., 250ff.; chapter 2, item b4).

That leaves the question from the end of section 1: To what extent can the considerations and findings of empirical educational research provide solid evidence of attributes of successful dance teaching? As laid out in section 1, educational research emphasizes the cognitive aspects of teaching and skills acquisition, while most studies are restricted to the "traditional" subjects at a school for general education. For that reason, it is virtually impossible to guarantee beyond doubt that any of the findings reported here apply to dance lessons. Nonetheless, Hattie's meta-study (2009), and the exploration of the communicative and interactive structures of teaching, offer clear indications of which configurations of attributes offer higher prospects for success. However, to narrow that statement—and this must be emphasized—these prospects are only qualified.

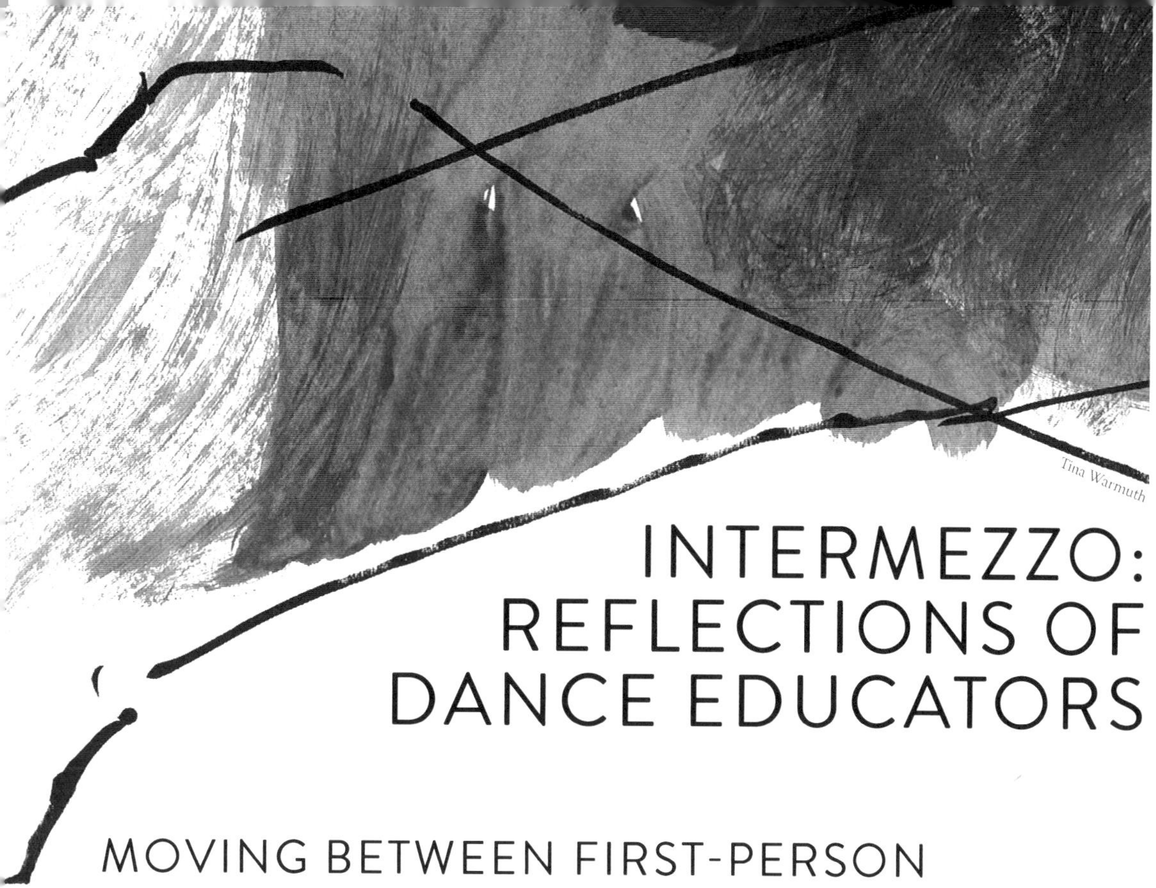

INTERMEZZO: REFLECTIONS OF DANCE EDUCATORS

MOVING BETWEEN FIRST-PERSON AND THIRD-PERSON BODIES IN DANCE TEACHING

Jennifer Roche

I am currently a lecturer in dance at Queensland University of Technology (QUT), Brisbane, on a dance performance course for pre-professional dance training, which integrates many elements of a conservatory model within a university program. The Bachelor of Fine Arts degree program in Dance Performance delivers intensive daily training in ballet and contemporary dance alongside other practical subjects such as choreography, partnering, body conditioning, and the creation of new works with guest choreographers. This is supported by theory-based subjects, such as dance analysis and contextual studies.

Somatic approaches have informed my dance teaching for many years. More formally, I recently engaged in a short study with Avril Huddy, a colleague at QUT, on the integration of somatic approaches for first-year dance students who are making the transition as learners from private dance studios into pre-professional training.

This involved a four-week program at the beginning of the semester in which students were introduced to somatics and subsequently supported in making links between this approach and learning in dance technique classes. The outcomes of this study were reported in a journal article, titled "Creative Adaptations: Integrating Feldenkrais Principles in Contemporary Dance Technique to Facilitate the Transition into Tertiary Dance Education" (Roche, Huddy 2015). From this study and my knowledge of similar research undertaken in the field (Fortin, Vieira, Tremblay 2009; Kampe 2014; Kovich 1994), it is evident that somatics provides what Kampe (2014) describes as "emancipatory potential" in a pedagogical environment such as the university and that it can provide a "technology of the self" as Sylvie Fortin, Adriane Vieira, and Martyne Tremblay (2009) attest. The latter notion (drawn from Michel Foucault) is employed by Fortin, Vieira, and Tremblay (2009: 48) to describe a means for the individual to navigate the dominant discourses in dance training through "the marginal somatic discourse."

Dancers need to be highly versatile in this current age. The diversity of choreographic signatures and range of movement investigations that circulate throughout the dance sector require practitioners/dancers to possess a strong foundational technique alongside the ability to incorporate a range of approaches, not least more instinctive reactions in improvisatory moments. For example, when discussing her piece *Scan* (2000), choreographer Rosemary Butcher outlined her intention to engage with a type of expertise that is less discernible than the usual technical prowess of the dancer; she said that "the piece was still dominated by the skills of the professional dancer. ... I was trying to decrease those skills while using them" (Butcher, Melrose 2005: 153). This need to balance high-level skills with more instinctive, creative responses adds to the complexity of designing an appropriate training program so that technical training does not limit creativity and, equally, creative expression does not undermine adaptability to the standards of the professional environment. Although still employed in many training institutions, canonical modern dance and ballet techniques are now less prevalent as a means of training, maintaining, and recalibrating the embodied practices of dancers. Melanie Bales and Rebecca Nettl-Fiol (2008) outline that "eclectic" approaches to training are the norm in the post-Judson dance landscape and somatics plays an important role in this.

I propose that contemporary dancers should develop a moving identity throughout a career path, "which incorporates past dance experience, anatomical structures, and conditioned human movement as a self-in-process" (Roche 2015). I believe that the somatic approach is critical for dancers in establishing this sense of self in movement alongside the versatility to incorporate the various choreographic signatures encountered in professional practice.

The development of autonomy within the learning process connects to the core theme of my research in which I propose that the independent contemporary dancer is capable of being many expressive bodies in one by incorporating a multiplicity of choreographic signatures that will, over time, accumulatively establish an idiosyncratic moving identity. The idea of the moving identity redirects focus from the abstracted ideal dancing body, which is never fully achievable, back to the individual and could be described as the dancer's signature way of moving. The accumulation of past movement experiences over time becomes "sedimented" into movement pathways as the moving identity is constructed through a specific life path and range of experiences that make it particular to that person. Richard Shusterman explains that the "preferred repertoire of neural pathways" forms "the precise makeup of an individual's nervous system," thus highlighting the individuality that is implied in human embodiment (2006: 4). When contemplating the variety of movement signatures and creative processes that a dancer may encounter as part of their career, it seems clear that there needs to be a sense of being grounded in an identity from which the dance artist/performer can encounter difference and negotiate change.

The value of established dance techniques should not be underestimated, and there are many arguments for the distinctive skills that intensive training in a single movement style can impart (Claid 2006). Traditionally, however, institutional training objectifies the dancer, further causing self-objectification, and can have a negative impact on performance through a split focus and attention, so that the subject may be both acting and simultaneously "watching the self acting on the environment" (Quinn, Twenge, Fredrickson 2006: 60). There is an intrinsic tradition of objectification in dance training, which is applied in order to galvanize students for a career of observation. It can be argued that there is value in this tradition or that at least students seek the skills in order to be able to endure this experience in the wider world. Therein lies the challenge of bringing somatic approaches into an educational environment, an environment that seeks to prepare students for engaging with the real employment pressures they will face in diverse professional contexts.

One of the issues I face in my teaching is how to elicit an experience of the first-person perspective of embodiment, or "soma" as defined by Thomas Hanna (1986/1995), within a traditionally structured dance class. The somatic perspective contrasts with the Cartesian "object body" in that the dancer may have a mechanical experience of the body from which they are somewhat removed as an agent. When aspiring to bring the student into an experience of mind/body integration, I find that there needs to be a balance in my approach; it is the space that I create for them, and the qualities of my awareness allow them to explore other ways of being embodied. The main areas I focus on pedagogically are incorporating improvised movement explorations at the beginning of a class to connect students to the "soma," before channeling this into more structured dance phrases. I integrate adapted lessons from Hanna Somatics as part of the warm up and pay attention to scanning the soma at the beginning of each class.

Further developments include giving students the opportunity to choreographically develop class phrases alone or in partners in order to re-embody the movement from other perspectives. More recently, I have focused on eliciting connection to the sensate body, inspired by my explorations into Peter Levine's (1997) trauma therapy: Somatic Experiencing. Adapting some of the principles from this therapeutic form, I mainly focus on awareness of sensation as a means for dancers to repossess and re-inhabit their bodies as an antidote to the objectifying processes outlined above. Interestingly, Carrie Noland equates awareness of sensation or proprioception to "individuation" (2009: 4), which I believe fits well within an educational context.

On an individual basis, the approaches outlined above may not seem groundbreaking in themselves, but it is through the daily challenge of amalgamating and applying these ideas within the context of exam-assessed technique classes that unexpected discoveries are made and innovations in pedagogical practice emerge. Rather than establishing a defined system, it is the way in which teachers integrate these principles from somatic resources to encourage conscious engagement by their students within the studio that shapes the learning process and determines the effectiveness of the somatic approach.

SOMATIC ACQUAINTANCESHIP

Libby Farr and Jacob Storer

Upon receiving a request to submit an article on the topic "How might somatically oriented teaching and learning practices support the development of competencies young dancers need in the contemporary dance landscape?", we rapidly engaged in a dialogue about our personal interests in the topic from the divergent viewpoints of teacher and student. In doing so, we discovered our mutual perception of the integration of somatic practices and ballet. In today's pedagogy of codified forms, a majority of instructors personally engage in somatic research, which informs their approach and is already implicitly interwoven into their translation of knowledge.

Our research, reading, and discourse has led us into a process of somatic research between the two points of view, observing how it is filtered into daily classes. Our impulses encouraged others to enter into their own process of investigation and to further their dialectic research. As a result of our experience, we believe it is important for these processes to be present between the active body and the subconscious self, between students and teachers, and between practitioners and researchers.

We feel it is imperative that somatic practice is included in conservatory training. As time management is always an issue in conservatories, however, we want to make it clear that somatic work develops over a period of time, inside and outside of the studio. This must be taken into account. Somatic work encourages more self-awareness and, within a conservatory setting, self-regulation is crucial. The body is always changing, developing, growing, existing, surviving, and decaying. A somatically oriented practice supports and allows for the curiosity to seek out a daily reacquainting with the self in order to establish a foundation for ongoing growth and creativity.

Excerpts from the dialogue on somatic acquaintanceship

Libby: I had not really thought about it before, but looking back to where I became acquainted with somatic work, I realized it was in my training in Texas. A teacher of mine worked with kinesiology, which affected my approach to ballet. This became more important to me as I got older and even more so when I started teaching. … I wanted to figure out a way to make ballet easier, more efficient, and less stressful in terms of learning how to work with abstract movement vocabulary. Essentially to find a way to "humanize" ballet.

Through my dancing, I tried different forms such as Pilates and various floor barre exercises, which helped at the time. But as my body changed, I had to search for a practice that worked for me and supported these changes. So, I brought in Alexander Technique, which opened up a whole new perception—initiating movement from the bones rather than the image. This allows the movement to happen, rather than fixing or forcing it, and it allows one to find "the stack of the skeleton" in order to discover a neutral starting point. This integration also made me much more aware of the words I choose when teaching, for instance, so phrases like "lifting up," "shoulders back and down," and "hold" were thrown out the window.

Being an observer for more than thirty years and having taught in many places, it is interesting to see how people simply walk in to take a class—how they arrive and go to the same place at the barre every day, take the class in the same way, and try to replicate it in the same way. When a human is interested and focused on their own process, they are interested in their body as it is in that moment, whether it be ballet, contemporary, choreography, or improvisation. An artist tries not to replicate.

Furthermore, from my perspective as a teacher, Alexander Technique has made me aware of how important it is to stay in your practice as you teach, because if the role of an outside eye is dominant, teachers can quickly fall into wanting to help by intruding into a student's personal process as the student is trying to figure it out on their own. By staying in one's own practice, in the role of an observing eye, the one who observes allows the information to actually flow to them, which will assist in their delivery of the information.

This led to my practice of Gyrokinesis, which changed my outlook entirely in regard to the center/core of the body (the spine). I came to realize that there are many centers that can act as a transmitter to feed information to the rest of the body. This method literally creates space/volume in the body, which helps functionality naturally and, moreover, rehabilitation. With students, I have seen how it changes the way they carry their bodies, by not just being "on" the legs but "up and over" the legs. The combination of Alexander Technique and Gyrokinesis has become the backbone of my work, which is still in progress.

Ok, Jacob, I have a question for you. How have somatic practices influenced your daily practice and approach in class?

Jacob: First off, when I started to do somatic work, it changed my physicality and mentality in relation to technique. I started ballet at eighteen so, of course, the first thing

I did was mimicry. There was a lot of stress. Thoughts like "I'm not good enough" appeared, but when you start to practice somatic work, you begin to take responsibility for your body. As opposed to obeying the "rules," it became about listening to my body and its functionality in relation to what was being proposed and to reevaluate the unnecessary patterns that blocked my progress.

Somatic work gave me permission to be me, not a slave to a form. On the other side of the coin, I feel that I have started to fall into overprocessing with somatic work. I don't follow the framework of the class as much as I could because I am so concerned with the functionality and really being "aware"—it can become over-awareness somehow. Now I want to find the balance between the two—between the process and the product, if we think in that way.

L.: Yes, and I have seen this happen! The important thing is not to become overly fixated on any one way of working. Bodies change daily; it is inevitable. The somatic approach returns the practitioner to the body as it is in the moment. The fear of losing something that has been recently discovered can make a young dancer grab and hold on, which is actually against what we are trying to achieve. You are in practice, always, so finding balance is the key. Synthesis. This applies not only in and out of the studio, but also when performing. Were you able to use a somatic approach in the last student performance?

J.: Absolutely. There were certain moments, for example, when I was thinking about the relation between the heel of my hand and the tip of my scapula, which is what I was thinking about while I was moving. That helped to put me somewhere else mentally, and then the next movement came and I followed. That is how I learned the material—and how I did the material in rehearsal—so why would it be different when I was performing?

L.: Exactly. Basically, the movement is itself performative. You don't have to add anything else. You meet your appointments. There is no striving to prove oneself to an audience. It's just doing the work through a somatic approach. No extra tension, just doing what you need to do, when you need to do it.

J.: Somatics is a process, not an aesthetic. I was exploring something inside my body, and because I was exploring it, I invited the audience into the material. It is about what you want to be busy with and what you want to share with people.

L.: For me, there is a difference between performing the process and letting the process be performative. It is also about redefining for oneself what performing means. It is just being. As simple as doing the material and being aware that other people are in the room watching you. In somatics, you are viewing yourself and observing your real self. By observing others you are able to somehow get it into your body. Eyes are connected to the nervous system, which is activated by watching.

J.: This is how humans learn.

L.: It's not about trying to replicate the same feeling. Repetition is important, but it is how you repeat.

J.: And then it is about where you repeat. Waiting for the bus, cooking dinner—our bodies are our instrument.

L.: The instrument is part of you; it's with you everywhere, always. It is not separate. You need to tune an instrument all the time. And when you tune in you are listening deeply. You need to know the mechanics. A mechanic knows their vehicle, and sometimes you need to change the oil.

J.: Attentive and aware. You need to be your own teacher, observer.

L.: And somatic approaches support that awareness.

J.: Realization, understanding, grasp, appreciation. The sensibility to reacquaint yourself with your self.

L.: Acquaintance! Yes! You have to meet yourself every day!

7. SYNAESTHETIC SEEING:

PERSPECTIVES ON THE BODY IN DANCE

Jürgen van Buer

& EXPERIENCING DIFFERENCE:

PRACTICES OF ATTENTION AND REPETITION IN DANCE *Nina Patricia Hänel*

SYNAESTHETIC SEEING:
PERSPECTIVES ON THE BODY IN DANCE

Just as pre-formed perceptions and attitudes influence how things are seen or, of course, overlooked, we can arrive at stigmatizing stereotypes or find the freedom to see these things in a new light.
(Schürmann 2008: 151)

The world only emerges through each individual's sight. Strategies for visual perception allow us to obtain a differentiated view of the world around us from varied perspectives. In this regard, visual perception is a symbiosis of an individual's developing worldview and the physiological process of seeing (Schürmann 2008: 156). Visual perception can be considered an activity, and the process of seeing can be considered an action that engages the entire body. In this way, perceptions of the world are interdependent with practices inscribed in the body. These practices result in layers of conditioning that influence our beliefs and worldviews and, in turn, are perpetuated in bodily practices (Bredekamp, Krois 2011). According to Eva Schürmann, seeing can be understood as a practice that gives rise to subjective viewpoints, which are classified as "figurative forms of mediation between the self and the world" (2008: 151).

This essay aims to reflect upon the practice of seeing in the context of contemporary dance practice and somatic methods in dance education. In the first part of this essay, I will focus on the acquisition of dance techniques and their conscious or subliminal influence on our aesthetically conditioned view of the body.

The second section focuses on how we direct our vision inward, within the body. This method, primarily used in somatic practices, will be illustrated in detail through examples from the Feldenkrais Method. By gazing "into" rather than "upon" the body, we emphasize a viewing practice in which introspective experience is prioritized before perspectives on the body emerge. This approach conceives of vision as a synaesthetic process that draws upon the perceptions of other senses, such as kinaesthesia.

In practice, there is great diversity in how somatic practices are integrated into dance techniques and choreographic methods through the way they are researched and taught (see chapter 2). In particular, teaching and learning situations for dance training, during which contributions are actively sought from all participants, raise another question, which I will explore in the third section of this essay: How does a perspective of the body shaped by aesthetic idealization interact with a somatic visual practice shaped by viewing the body from within? Moreover, to what extent is the resulting restriction of visual practices taken into account? Is it possible to negotiate both aspects with all participants in the learning process?

How contemporary dance practices view "seeing"

As we learn dance techniques, a broad range of divergent methods, practices, and task-oriented choreographic approaches strongly influence how we view our bodies. These perspectives on the body are continuously reproduced, whether deliberately or not. As opposed to the manifestation of a single, specific dancing body and its ongoing reproduction, the focus is placed on its continuous re-creation and re-negotiation. This gives rise to a multitude of aesthetic views and viewing practices regarding the body, "oscillating constantly between the dimensions of outer dictation and conscious determination from within" (Schürmann 2008: 151).

Susan Leigh Foster distinguished three concepts of the body: the "perceived body," the "aesthetically ideal body," and the "demonstrative body." She conceives of the perceived body and the aesthetically ideal body as subject to continuous re-creation by way of the demonstrative body (Foster 1986: 237). Movements are registered by imitation, and not only through the demonstrative body as witnessed by the instructor. Collectively shared views of the aesthetically ideal body are also created by an "outer view" of the body in dance by replaying digital media, for instance, or by repeatedly observing the choreographer's signatures. Choreographic methods that generate movement material primarily through task-oriented approaches, such as GAGA movement language or Improvisation Technologies, actually impede the acquisition of movements through immediate and intuitive imitation. Nevertheless, both methods are recognizable by their familiar movement styles. This begs the question of the degree to which the performance of such a style arises out of these sorts of movement-making tasks, as opposed to arising out of consciously imitating movement in awareness of that style, which can then be remembered in practice.

During the learning process, specific corrections are possible only if other views of the body are taken out of context and temporarily suspended. However, multiperspectivity plays a unique role in the continuous transformation of views of the body, enabling us to "read" and enact the body in ever new and different ways.

From this standpoint, the practice of seeing walks a fine line between inviting "stigmatizing stereotypes" and encouraging "the freedom to see things in a new light" (Schürmann 2008: 151). For this reason, everyone involved in the learning process needs to be open to a critical, reflective approach to the various types of visual practice and views of the body.

How somatic practices view "seeing"

As outlined above, somatic practices interpret visual perception not as an isolated sensory impression, but as merely one element interwoven with a variety of other sensations, therefore making it "synaesthetic" (Hassa 2015: 14; Sieben 2003: 28-33). As is the case with embryonic and early childhood development, visual perception is learned in close association with the development of the vestibular (balance) and kinaesthetic (deliberate movement) senses. In her article "*Sechs Sinne*" ("Six senses"), Irene Sieben describes the development of eye function, which initially activates in conjunction with the closely related sense of movement in vestibular perception (2003: 28-32). At a later stage, our eyes are almost exclusively associated with their visual function. The eyes' initial close relationship to the spine's management of movement and the perception of movement is often completely ignored.

In the group technique Awareness through Movement (see chapter 2) in the Feldenkrais Method, the act of seeing is practiced in equal measure from the viewpoint of the person moving and from that of the observer. By following verbal instructions for movement, the moving person's introspective view intersects with their self-reflection on their movement, leading to an awareness of new, emergent movement concepts. As an observer, the instructor strives to adopt an inner attitude of questioning in order to remain open to the ways in which the practitioner is implementing their own experiences of movement as described above. The instructor must try not to influence these movements by demanding certain actions based on their own body concepts.

This manner of seeing can be illustrated by the Functional Integration (FI) technique (see chapter 2) used in the Feldenkrais Method, which focuses on tactile interaction between two individuals. In this exercise, one person is moved by the touch of the other person's hands, which are simultaneously guided by the movements of the first person, turning the experience into a "tactile and visual" experience for both. Consequently, the verbal instructions in the Awareness through Movement group technique can be enhanced by the tactile and visual experiences gained through the Functional Integration method in individual work. In this regard, verbal instructions are closely linked to the kinaesthetic, proprioceptive, vestibular, and tactile dimensions of movement. Ideally the instructor will encourage the practitioner not to follow preexisting conceptions of movement, but to explore and introspectively feel the various possibilities for movement during their actual enactment. In this way, the person moving can no longer rely on copying the movements, but learns them by exploration with the aid of verbal instructions and by carefully observing their own decisions. Unlike other somatic practices, such as Ideokinesis or the Franklin Method, this approach is not based on imagining movement (Hassa 2015) Those methods tend to use images such as "balance your pelvis on your femur," which trains the imagination skills so important in dance (Bernard, Stricker, Steinmüller 2003: 131). Although such an approach also entails an inward shift of awareness, the images derived from that awareness can also lead to idealizing a specific understanding, for instance with regard to alignment.

The Feldenkrais Method encourages the visualization of movement that can be adapted to each situation. Rooted in personal experiences and explorations, the person moving develops an inner image of simple and complex movements. These can vary widely and are governed less by preset norms. In this way, new views on the body can be created continuously depending on what makes most sense at the time. Rather than producing an arbitrary view of the body, this helps to illustrate its unique diversity, making barely visible variations seem strikingly distinct. In this context, the body is perceived, both outwardly and inwardly, as an entity in constant flux.

Interweaving aesthetically idealized and somatic viewing practices

The preceding sections have shown that, in dance practice, we must distinguish between somatic, introspective, and explorative viewing methods—such as the Feldenkrais Method—on the one hand, and perspectives grounded in a specific context that subscribe to a specific aesthetic idealization on the other.

As a teacher of contemporary dance and a Feldenkrais practitioner, I often ask myself to what extent the two approaches' viewing practices can be negotiated on equal footing among all participants within the learning process. Choreographic and artistic approaches have already explored a wide variety of methods for visualizing and "reading" the body, and there is no shortage of scientific material on the subject. Somatic and introspective vision, and visualization, however, are still considered barely articulable, as they fall within the practitioner's subjective experience.

An array of research is already investigating how somatic practices interweave with methods from contemporary dance practice. I am therefore particularly interested in finding out how the different forms of seeing derived from somatic processes are reflected upon, discussed in depth, and conveyed between instructors and students.

An open, critically constructive negotiation of both views in dance practice, involving all individuals partaking in the process, is therefore invaluable. It could help individuals understand their patterns of perception, perhaps even their potential limitations. This could pave the way for a new learning situation that is free of expectations, yet equally specific. It would take into account the complexity of realization possibilities for movement's creation and adaption and could permit—or even demand—the "freedom to gain other viewpoints" (Schürmann 2008: 151). Whenever there is an open negotiation over the aesthetically idealized and introspective views of the body, as well as over the correspondingly diverse options for enacting them, all participants in the learning process are invited to take greater personal responsibility and maintain a consistent awareness of how they each are individually situated in the learning process.

EXPERIENCING DIFFERENCE:
PRACTICES OF ATTENTION AND REPETITION IN DANCE

Perhaps the highest object of art is to bring into play simultaneously all these repetitions, with their differences in kind and rhythm, their respective displacements and disguises, their divergences and decenterings; to embed them in one another and to envelop one or the other in illusions the "effect" of which varies in each case.
(Deleuze 1994: 365)

Simply following instructions is a far cry from learning through awareness of one's own actions. According to Jon Kabat-Zinn, the prerequisites for genuine learning are an open and alert state of mind and the will to truly perceive (2003: 45). The author is referring to the capacity for autonomous action that is necessary for the learning process, which is contemplated many times in this handbook. This essay will explore individual potentialities for action, defined as autonomous decision-making within the often copious repetitions of movement sequences in dance. From a sensorimotor perspective, in particular when dancers redirect their attention while repeating a sequence, they are able to pick up on the subtlest differences in movement.

Differentiation through repetition

Copious repetition is a component of daily practice in dance training and is required in order to develop or train automatic behaviors in regard to specific movement sequences and patterns (see chapter 6, section 2.4). These automatic behaviors are embedded patterns associated with individual habits and interests or aesthetic preferences (Clarke, Cramer, Müller 2011: 212). In order for dancers truly to have the space to be open to new possibilities, specific movement sequences need to happen as if by themselves, without deliberation (Clarke, Cramer, Müller 2011: 212).

If we take the performance of movement, beyond pure reproduction, to be situational and contextually specific, we can understand movement as something perpetually recreated. In this view, automatic behaviors are necessary for the dancers' desire and ability to interrogate movement afresh each time. The awareness of such potentialities for action and possibilities for differentiation can help dance students penetrate movement's complexity and treat it as individually shapeable.

Dancers' self-redirection of attention as a scoring practice

The broadening of the concept of choreography is due in no small part to the influence of "scoring" practices and collaborative working structures (see chapter 6, section 2.4). The term "choreography" encompasses a multiplicity of procedures for "structuring or analyzing movements" (Hardt, Stern 2011: 15). The boundaries between the settings of improvisation, real-time composition, and choreography are often blurry in practice. Thus choreographic procedures form complex frameworks within which dancers follow external requirements, while exploring the scope of their individual flexibility for action.

The expanded definition of choreography has made it necessary also to employ task-oriented and problem-solving procedures during the process of imparting the tools of dance technique in order to elicit action from dancers that is based on individual sensorimotor decisions within set frameworks. Settings in which dancers compose movements in real time, while perpetually directing their own attention, pose them major kinaesthetic and proprioceptive challenges (Noland, quoted in Batson, Wilson 2014: 37). This is especially true of structures that are improvised or composed in real time where individual action is always based on sets of rules.

If the movement material is preset, however, this calls upon dancers to be aware of the scope of flexibility for autonomous decision-making, which in settings of improvisation and real-time composition may only seem more direct and obvious due to their open-ended structures. Because preset movement material is predictable and repeatable in its sequence, the steady and autonomous direction of one's own attention causes each movement to be renegotiated each time and allows dancers to explore the subtlest opportunities for differentiation. Constant re-interrogation makes it possible to identify and appropriate the specificities implicit in the movement material. These specificities vary widely and span proprioceptive, kinaesthetic, aesthetic, discursive, analytical, emotional, intuitive, imaginative, and associative traits (Clarke, Cramer, Müller 2011: 227). In this light, action both in structures of improvisation or real-time composition and in preset movement material requires a state of being-in-the-moment that is situational, intuitive, alert, and synaesthetically perceptive. This demands an ability to reflect, which, as Donald Schön explains in his concept of "reflection-in-action" (1983; 1987), is directly embedded in one's own actions and cannot be distanced from them. Because reflection-in-action always questions one's own assumptions—a practice termed "knowing-in-action"—he considers the skill of reflection to be the critical, constructive interrogation of one's own actions. Reflection-in-action enables spontaneous experimentation and thinking ahead with direct implications for individual, situational action (Schön 1987; chapter 2). The interplay of constant interrogation, intuitive decision-making, and spontaneous action can be described as "ongoing sensing/thinking" ("*mitlaufendes Spüren-Denken*"), which processes complex, high-density information primarily through associative concepts, images, and sense impressions (Böhle, Porschen 2011: 60). From a sensorimotor perspective, this constant decision-making is experienced and negotiated in both "feedforward" and "feedback" loops. Feedforward refers to conscious intentionality of decisions; feedback spontaneously reflects upon what has just occurred (Batson, Wilson 2014: 132). Mihaly Csikszentmihalyi describes how harnessing the autonomous direction of attention can trigger an experience of "flow." When individually and voluntarily directed focus is aimed at an object so that sensorimotor-driven action exploits individual abilities and skills up to their limits, problem-solving in challenging contexts is perceived as admirable and rewarding (Csikszentmihalyi 1990: 3).

Understanding movement through its underlying principles

The more insight dancers glean about the specific attributes of movement, the greater the range of decisions they have at their disposal in order to accomplish a differentiated treatment of movement. Knowledge about the functions and principles underlying each movement comes into play especially in methods of bodily perception, such as Bartenieff Fundamentals, the Feldenkrais Method, the Alexander Technique, and Body-Mind Centering®. These techniques include exercises that reflect on the functions of primitive reflexes, righting reactions, and equilibrium responses in the prenatal and early childhood stages of development, as well as their complex interrelationships. It is particularly in view of the heterogeneity of contemporary dance, which has no unified and binding movement vocabulary, that these methods are of fundamental importance. The Feldenkrais Method, for example, uses the term "primary image lessons" to encompass conceptions that are helpful in differentiating key elements within the extraordinary complexity of movement organization.[1] Knowledge of these conceptions, and of their deliberate sensorimotor visualization, can help dancers to grow aware of aspects of their basal movement functions (Smyth 2007), which they can then harness as part of complex movement material.

Conclusion

I have demonstrated that repetition in dance education does not mean stereotypically "playing back" movement. Rather, practices of repetition involve an autonomous direction of attention that equates to insights and knowledge acquisition about specific attributes of motion, and the principles and concepts underlying them. This opens up individual decision-making options that allow the dancer to cultivate a differentiated, case-specific treatment of movement. Throughout numerous repetitions of movement sequences, dancers have recourse to tools for constantly exploring their personal range of options afresh. As movement is imbued with complexity and many-layered details, potentialities for action emerge and the numerous repetitions with "their differences in kind and rhythm, their respective displacements and disguises, their divergences and decenterings"—in Deleuze's words—are viewed as extraordinarily specific and perpetually mutable (1994: 365).

1 Cliff Smyth has published more detailed explanations of these conceptions in the context of "primary image lessons," which are available online at http://www.feldenkraissf.com.

8. REFLECTIONS OF CHOREOGRAPHERS

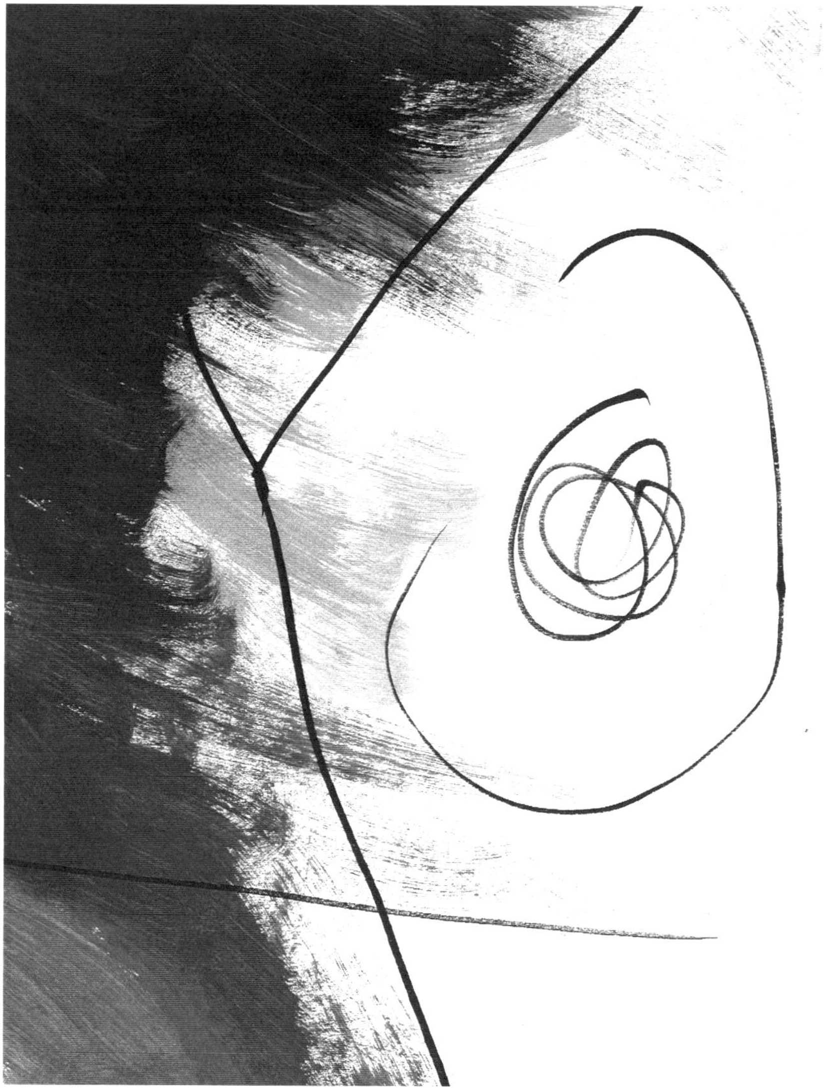
Tina Warmuth

THE ECHO OF A MOVEMENT

An interview with Shumpei Nemoto

Jenny Coogan: You work as a choreographer, teacher, and dancer. Could you speak briefly about the characteristics that define your work?

Shumpei Nemoto: My practice as a teacher is mainly based upon experiments or experience that I developed in sessions of research and reflection during my practice as a dancer. Teaching is more about movement, in general, while, as a choreographer, the situation is different. As a choreographer, I am more concerned with compositional questions. My interest is not specifically about the movement itself; it is rather about composing movements.

J.: What is your particular interest in composition and composing? And how do you see the interrelationship between composing, constructing, choreographing, and creating?

S.: My main concern is to understand the compositional aspects of choreography. This does not mean that I don't work with movement quality, but I generally need a specific subject, which could, for example, come from a book. I take things, and then I try to polish them until I have the impression that "It's really it." Rather than saying, "This piece is about such and such," I also aim to create a space for the observer's individual interpretation.

J.: You work in different environments and cultures, and with professionals and students alike. Do your processes change accordingly?

S.: I try not to change everything in different situations, but different environments especially affect how I communicate with the dancers. When working with students, for example, I sometimes need to approach them from the viewpoint of a teacher, which is not the case with a professional company. However, as dynamics and cultural backgrounds differ notably from place to place, the information being exchanged is also recognized differently.

J.: As a choreographer working in the field of contemporary dance both in educational and professional contexts, what competencies do you believe young dancers need in order to navigate the world of professional performance in dance today?

S.: My observation is that those dancers who are good at one style are the ones who are best able to deal with the diversity of the dancing field today. A curiosity for different forms of physicality supports that. In my experience, the curiosity and exposure I had with other styles of dance definitely informed and enabled me to approach movement and choreography in different ways. It can also be a very joyful experience trying to figure out or learn something by yourself, something that a single-minded education cannot provide. For example, I know street dancers (urban dancers) who, only after reaching the top of their careers, started taking ballet classes as they felt the need to look somewhere else for more information. Movement styles and approaches do change from one context to another. It is essential that dancers are open to approaching movement vocabularies or ideas with which they might not be familiar or understand immediately. At the same time, they should not be excessively judgmental, as that attitude can block their development and creative process. Young dancers need what I call an "analytical mind," a skill for understanding their own bodies and those of others. When dealing with new material, dancers need to be able to understand what it is about—they need skills to analyze tiny differences in order to transfer information to their own bodies.

I have the idea that if you are able to articulate any place in your body, you have the ability to apply it to any kind of dance style. As dancers, we need articulation to create networks and connections. Determination is a competency that is essential. If a choreographer sets tasks, the dancer needs to be focused and just keep working rather than waiting for feedback. Some of my students mention that this approach can be particularly difficult when working with improvisation. In order to maintain concentration in rehearsal, the mental processes need to be as well trained as the physical processes. I call this "stamina of the mental process." A comprehensive knowledge of performing arts today is very important. Knowing what is going on out there in the circus, in the theater, and in other performing arts is important in order to build a relationship with an interdisciplinary understanding of dance. And, last but not least, the competencies (as asked in the question) also correspond to developing a sense of a "methodological language." Each choreographer has a specific method of verbal articulation when it comes to sharing ideas and approaching the phenomenon of dance, just as the dancers have to find their own approach to embody such ideas and approaches.

J.: Now, can you speak about your pedagogical and creative processes in their relation to the often tension-filled quest for young dancers to access agency alongside developing artistic identity and the physical skills necessary to work within diverse choreographic signatures?

S.: As I cannot change students' way of thinking, I focus my energy on sharing knowledge with students. They have to change themselves. In order to develop further as a student, it is essential to learn through experience, to have "aha!" moments. It's not enough to have an understanding in the mind, the dancer needs physical understanding to be able to dive into experience. Otherwise the dancing becomes mere mimicry in shaping a form, and this is definitely not my intention. I want to mention the concept of "echoing a movement." By this I mean that the movement starts before it starts and ends after it ends. In other words, dancers don't just act, rather they are aware that after each action an echo of the movement remains. It is their choice to either cut the echo and move on or to let the movement echo further. Following this idea, movement should not be automatic. When I move my arm it is about the intention, how I follow the sensation within my body in order to penetrate the movement. I would say that starting the movement before I even move my hand and letting it end after finishing the movement is the interplay between intention, motivation, and the actual movement.

J.: What a lovely metaphor. Is the combination of the idea of "echoing the movement" and physical competency something that may be already present in students/young dancers, or does this need time to develop through professional experience?

S.: I think it is more about how one articulates the motivation or the energy through one's own body. I saw students and even professionals struggling with themselves and getting angry and frustrated because of their failure when trying out movement. This energy blocks the sensory awareness in the body. But by going through that period of not being able to fulfill a task, which probably comes after trying again and again, afterward the dancer can come to a place of posing questions, such as "What am I doing?", "Why does that work?", "How can I make it better?", or "If I try this, what will happen?" and so on. Especially when learning particular material, dancers need to be able to distance themselves from it and navigate their energy. I believe you need a specific kind of mindset, which might include a somatic approach, to achieve something—as well as being aware of how the body reacts in certain situations or in certain ways.

In my opinion, it is more beneficial to learn how the body deals with the movement in order to really apply that knowledge to every single step to be performed. It is my aim to teach students how to use the body and to determine what helps in accomplishing specific steps—information that the dancer can then apply to many different things. In this sense, ballet is not so different from hip-hop, and hip-hop is not so different from jazz dance. Perhaps the outcome might look different, but the source, the articulations of how one approaches the body, may in fact be the same.

J.: The ability to dive into the complexity of individual experience and connect to the echoes of your movements—imaginative and reflective—has given me food for thought. I thank you for this inspiring conversation.

HOW THE PURSUIT OF ACCESSING THE INDIVIDUAL LED ME TO STREAM-FLOW

An interview with Heidi Vierthaler

Jenny Coogan: Can you offer insights into the characteristics that make up your artistic signature?

Heidi Vierthaler: Yes, there are a lot of different things actually. As an artist it's important for me to bring in the individual. I love to have time to get to know the person. As we work together, I certainly do set tasks that create aesthetics that are pleasing to me. As I start to feel what's effective, most of the time I can access dancers rather quickly in order to bring them into my ideas. I tried for many years to have dancers mimic me in the manner of my own repertoire. Although very useful at times, I have found it much more advantageous if they are able to bring themselves into the work. I want them to feel empowered to make choices and to share their ideas.

I always collaborate with dancers in building the material. We then take a look at it, shape it, and then reshape it, bringing in new dynamics or situations. I always incorporate a wide range of sensations or perhaps some of the "efforts" from the Laban system.

J.: Is this the manner in which you engage with students and professionals alike?

H.: Yes. I truly enjoy working in so many different contexts. I work internationally with professional dance companies and university students. When working with students, I love to have an intensive work period. In 2014, I made a new creation for the students in the graduating class of the BA program at Palucca University. The students were quite diverse, so the extended rehearsal time gave everyone the opportunity to find the best way to interpret their own personal ideas and movement phrases. It ended up being a very rewarding experience for all of us.

J.: What competencies do you believe young dancers need to possess in order to navigate the world of professional performance in dance today?

H.: I think that dancers definitely need the ability to create movement in different contexts, explore it, and adapt to different movement styles and situations. For example, cross-discipline collaborations seem to be building a new sense of community among dancers and other artists. And to keep the process alive, I tap into the things a dancer needs to help them to shift their ideas, become more aware of their habits, and be open to change. Aside from that, dancers simply benefit from an open and curious mind. Your body becomes more intelligent, and you become more accessible to those with whom you work. It's helpful to possess the ability to adapt to unfavorable situations and to find ways of being creative while working with choreographers in those situations. If the students can develop a strong sense of self and mindfulness, their ability to adapt to different personalities can boost their creativity. To venture out into the freelance market, they really have to be clever in how they manage themselves. This includes good networking skills, a driven and motivated approach, and an inquisitive nature. Basically, dancers need the ability to submerge themselves in the ideas of others while being aware of what is important to them. I encourage them to share their ideas and opinions. When I'm in the studio, I strive to be open, curious, and a good communicator.

It's ideal to find a good balance between maintaining a technical level and somatic approaches, and to recognize how one can affect the other.

J.: You talked a lot about the skills needed to work within collaborative processes. I notice that you spoke of "technique" last of all.

H.: I know. It can be beautiful if you have a strong ballet technique but, for me, it's all about how you approach it. I spent so many years trying to lose my technique in order to embrace new ideas. I remember working with Bill Forsythe. When he hired me, he mentioned that he did not want to work with any ballerinas who are afraid of losing technique. It's like, "Well, you can't lose it." You just keep adding to it or deliberately taking things away.

During my education, there was little focus on the importance of breath, release work, softening, or using less energy to execute a movement. For example, knowledge of Gyrotonics, or floorwork, helped me balance out my body and truly enjoy endless possibilities.

Therefore, I am really invested in endowing my ballet classes with a somatic approach. This means incorporating the ideas of my own Stream-Flow method. Stream-Flow is the base for all my creations and is effective in bringing heightened awareness to each section of the body.

J.: How would you describe your "Stream-Flow" method?

H.: My Stream-Flow method is triggered by a clear visual and physical meditation that journeys through each section of the body. First, we connect to the way we stand with a lot of softening in the knees, so that we are ready to shift in any direction. I place a big emphasis on the abdominal and rib connection, in order to risk more with the movement pathways or stay with one's self. As a certified Gyrotonics trainer, I reference some ideas from this method. Its principles continuously add layers to my movement and breath awareness.

Then I guide the dancers through a visual exercise exploring each part of the body. We start with the image of a small ball rolling between the eyes or gently pushing the inside of the eye in different directions. The eye leads the head, which leads the neck, which then shifts the shoulders and so on. We try to follow through with an initiation that comes solely from the eyes' space and then see if softening anywhere else in the body deepens the pathway.

Next we go to the ears and to the space in between the ears, searching for all the possibilities and pathways traveling from ear to ear. People are always quite surprised to find that it is possible to access the ear space by imagining that they are "seeing" the space with their ears. We then travel to the neck space, where the image of a warmer and softer ball can assist in softening, before continuing to the shoulder space. We visualize the collarbone and upper back melting away. We then move our arms from the shoulder space.

We explore from shoulder to elbow and from elbow to wrist. The wrist initiates hand movement, and from there we go on to the endless initiations in all of the joints of the fingers. I like to call this whole upper part of the body the "upper octopus" because you start to feel like you have so many limbs. And the relationship between the pelvis, upper legs, knees, lower legs, ankles, and feet, I call the "lower octopus."

Next I might give a phrase along the lines of "Tilt your shoulder space to the left, release your left thigh, lift and rotate your right upper arm from underneath, and extend the lower arm from your little finger." This is a functional way of moving and building material. As soon as the dancer can approach each movement as something precious, a quality emerges where they are in the moment. This is when the movement quality becomes truly rich.

The second phase would include a more tactile exercise with a partner in which all the sections of the body are triggered from the surface. It's great to see how outer awareness is heightened after an inner awareness has been stimulated and explored.

Sometimes I give a Stream-Flow warm-up and then teach a ballet class. I am finding that I require much less effort to do things now because I know and feel where the students are coming from. It's been years and years of searching for the things that are most effective.

J.: Your somatic way of directing attention and specifying a particular sensation seems to not require a dancer to have experience with a particular kind of training.

H.: That is what is so great about it. I will describe an experience I once had. When I was giving a Stream-Flow workshop for dancers in Seoul, South Korea, a local theater director asked me if his actors could join in as well. The result with the actors and the director himself was surprising. Unlike many of the dancers, the actors did not have to undo layers of training, they could just be in the moment. During the showings of the actors' solos, some of the dancers could not believe they had never danced before. So the absence of any technical dance training did not seem to hinder their ability to create and access movement initiating from within the body.

I started ballet at a very young age, and it's wonderful to have this rich information in your body. I wonder what I would be like now if I had not had all the other technical training and replaced that with the amount of awareness I have now.

J.: To close the interview, can you speak a bit about the skills needed to realize the physically expressive directives or choreographic signatures of those with whom dancers are working?

H.: It is about the ability to bridge different forms of dance, incorporating ideas like Stream-Flow. In my Stream-Flow workshops for professional ballet companies, the qualities of softening and experiencing different sensations were initially not very present. It took me quite some time and rigor until I managed to inspire a group of less open-minded dancers. To them, it felt a bit like breaking the rules and stepping outside of their comfort zones. Stream-Flow is a lot about bridging, breaking habits, and creating an atmosphere where you can allow yourself to make mistakes—all of which can be pivotal moments of change.

For example, in a ballet class there can be a lot of emphasis on achieving high legs, multiple turns, and the like. In Stream-Flow, the emphasis is placed on "how" to arrive at these places, as well as the quality and the pathways. I realized that there are a million ways to lift my arm, so it is the pathway that adds quality—if you are really in the moment of what you are doing, it can be so beautiful.

J.: This quality of presence resonates with me! I thank you for sharing your method with me.

THE VIRTUOSITY OF BEING

An interview with Yuval Pick

Jenny Coogan: As a choreographer and teacher, could you speak briefly about the characteristics that define your work?

Yuval Pick: Transmission. I am creating through transmission. I can say that the fundamental qualities, the mental things, that I am interested in working with, and that the dancers possess, are the sensorial body and the "traversed body." This is a body in a state of creation—a body in a state of relation to the ground, in the sense of weight and muscles that have the quality of being solicited. My vocabulary is very much about the flesh, about the body's mass and the way it travels—the body being explored and transmitted into space. I don't know how to say it differently. I am forming my dancers in this way because this view is so particular to my work. There is something very materialistic, in the sense of materia, the body as materia, about what we are and what the body contains. There is something spiritual about it for me because it is something about the body and the soul. For me, it is all intertwined. While working on muscle, on flesh, one is, at the same time, working on the mechanics of the soul. So it is very important that the dancer is a very attuned to their masa—to their weight, the floor, gravity, and how they expand from it. I call it expansion, not extension. My way of transmitting or teaching material is developing. Sometimes I work with a tennis ball or with an imaginary object, which allows me to construct a precise trajectory from the center to the periphery. At other times, the dance happens through imagination, through instructions, and through exercises the dancers know. So my process moves through different levels.

J.: When working with the graduating class at Palucca University last spring, you directed the students through a rigorous movement exploration of a singular principle, without paying attention to what the movement looked like.

Y.: Yes, exactly. I think how you present your body is how you are "being" with your body, how you are engaging with intention or with the choreographic tasks or choreographic structures at hand. And there is a big difference between being and demonstrating—being is not demonstrating. To present or to demonstrate is a part of teaching, a part of learning; there is something of it in the mirror, and there is something of it on stage. The torso, the chin, and breathing are very, very important. If you put yourself in the mirror, it is not only your gaze that can become fixed but also your breath, your sternum, and your spine.

There is something about the way we study as dancers. We want to arrive at a high level of skill in the body and, to achieve this, we engage in certain kinds of demonstrations. This is a very complex situation because when you study, there is emphasis on demonstration because you need to achieve something, so you demonstrate what you achieved, demonstrate your competencies. These learning processes are concerned more with the achievement of skills. But there are other factors that are important, about how to deal with all that you have achieved and how to *be* with all your achievements. This area is huge.

> ***J.: As a choreographer, you work in the field of contemporary dance both in educational and professional contexts. What competencies do you believe young dancers need to possess in order to navigate the world of professional performance in dance today?***

Y.: Competencies are not always measured in the movement vocabulary exercised in a body that is demonstrating material. I think "execution" is a good term as it implies that you need to move into action. I live in France and the schooling there is quite traditional, in the sense that the bodies are conditioned in one way. In France, students train primarily in either a contemporary/modern or classical style of dance. What the dancers need today is an opening up of the body. This is something that, for instance, I see in America. What I have experienced at Palucca, and understand as the vision of the school, is already a mixture of training idioms. Though the school has a strong classical orientation, the dancers are learning ballet, modern, and contemporary dance styles, and engaging with improvisation. This mix is in itself an effective way to open the body up and to strive to exceed personal boundaries. Tradition is, for me, wonderful if it stays as a technique, as a functional practice, a technical practice without a stylistic bodily inscription. If you want to maintain a tradition, it should be for the style. I think there is a way to teach the past without being bound to its forms.

I think we need to start opening educational programs to different practices earlier—the parallel streams of achievement of technical skill and presence need to be intertwined. This might not be necessary at the beginning of one's dance education, but it is very important for the dancer today. The dancers need to be present, to know how to walk, how to be. I think dance is a way to be. This is so much about the inner trajectory.

I mean, it is not about what the dancers learn but how they engage with their learning processes. It is not about presentation from the outside, but rather about finding inner trajectories. And finding inner connections is difficult.

In addition, urgency is important. I love dancers that have the urgency to engage in dialogue with their bodies in order to dance. They need this dialogue in order to feel that they are dancing. This is a need to be in a state of creation with your imaginary, inventing, dancing body. It is not cerebral. I am relating to this imaginary body, and when I feel it, I have no problems afterward in transforming this quality into representations of the dancer's body: the gaze, the way they walk, the way they are, whether they are connected to their imaginary body. This need of the dancers, this need that I feel, is what I can work with. It is what inspires me.

> ***J.: Can you speak about the tension-filled quest dancers embark upon to access agency? And how does this exist alongside developing artistic identity and the physical skills necessary to work within diverse choreographic signatures?***

Y.: So in teaching you have to put the dancers in action subconsciously, without them knowing it. You lead them to actions. If the dancers connect to tasks, to what they are doing, then they can bring in the imagination, and then they are in the state of dance. Then they are "being" with the dance without even knowing it. It could be walking tasks or looking tasks; it can evolve from there. What they have to understand, and I think it is very important to use the word virtuosity here, is that all this is a skill: to be is a skill. Virtuosity is not only the ability to do ten pirouettes, it is also taking risks and evoking interest in yourself while doing an action or task. This is virtuosity.

Sometimes dancers don't treat virtuosity in this way because they aren't set challenges like "You have to do to ten pirouettes," or "You have to lift the leg so high," or "You have to look like this." These skills are not trained because we are a goal-oriented society. We do not train according to models but to achieve goals. So the word virtousity is very important because you have to be virtousic everywhere—evoking interest in a task and evoking the imagination is being virtuosic. You have to practice it, work on it, find it, research it—you have to recognize it.

> ***J.: I think that's it—commitment to oneself and the idea that all skills can be virtuosic.***

Y.: Yes, exactly. I mean that everything is virtuosic, since in simply being you have to apply the same vocabulary as you do for pirouettes. There should not be contradictions, such as when one says "I am good in classical dance or good in class, but when I have to improvise I get stuck." To achieve the fullness of the artistic communicative gesture, one should not have a binary approach to teaching and learning. One should not think, "This is one thing, and then that is another thing."

J.: If you relate this idea to a Mobius band, as you look at it and turn it around, you see that everything is part of the same spiral.

Y.: For teaching it is important to articulate and have compartments, but it is also important to have a full image of yourself. You have to set this in order to see yourself.

In order to create people who are "alive," you need to nourish them without boundaries and to give them nonhierarchical, democratic information concerning the things they need to do—like goals and achievement. This is contemporary dance for me, and it is what I am aiming for. There is always a hierarchy. It has to do with roles—one is the choreographer, the director, the administrator, the dancer, and the secretary. There is verticality, but you have to work horizontally, to emphasize the horizontal.

J.: Hierarchy is built into life.

Y.: Yes, but it is also built into the roles. This is how it is. I think it's best when the information is given horizontally, by which I mean in a reciprocal way. Technique classes should be regarded in the same way as improvisation classes, in addition to tasks and compositions. In this way, everyone advances with their own style. You know that we, as choreographers and teachers, cannot demand that everybody is the same everywhere.

I like to speak about this because I think this is a great idea and not a lot of people are dealing with it. It is very refreshing for me to see—it's incredible to see in fact—what a dancing body is.

J.: You have spoken about many fundamental issues for dance artists, such as commitment, achievement, residing in oneself, and the meaning of virtuosity. Thank you for this stimulating conversation.

VISIONS OF PHYSICALITY

An essay by Georg Reischl

As I see it, my greatest task as both a choreographer and a higher educator is inviting young dancers to embody their visions of dance. From a contemporary perspective, this requires them first to question all externally influenced ideals in order to give their own physicality a chance. Each and every dancer is interesting and important to me as a person: their technical capabilities and acquired habits give me a range of areas to work with. Fun and sweat, success and failure go hand in hand to strengthen the love affair between "authentic being-oneself" and dance. I say love affair because, for me, trust and feeling are meaningful in the body's decision-making processes. According to Heidegger, "authentic being-oneself" signifies withdrawal from heteronomy into a genuine form of individual being (Figal 2000: 129). And therein lies the task of a contemporary dancer: to strive for the unique.

As a choreographer, I try to find a verbal language that clearly conveys my ideas and goals. Each generation is drawn to its own themes and develops its own communication patterns, both of which influence our interests and our language. For example, by virtue of growing up with the Internet, "digital natives" have values and select themes quite different from those of "digital immigrants" (Bund 2014: 17). I belong to the latter group, and did not grow up with the Internet as the "natives" did. Use of the Internet is changing us and the way we communicate. Sherry Turkle demonstrates this compellingly and critically in her books *The Second Self* and *Alone Together*. She writes in *The Second Self* that "technology catalyzes changes not only in what we do but in how we think" (2005: 18). Such changes are palpable in everyday interactions with dancers. Only a language that truly communicates can hit the mark and have a motivating impact.

That is why I am interested in building connections to dancers' lived experiences in order to encourage them individually. I try to overcome hierarchy in my exchanges with dancers so as to bolster flexibility, responsibility, and self-direction—very much along the lines of a somatic approach. Exercising social competency, discussing things verbally as part of training sessions, making high-quality decisions in performance, withdrawing from familiar movement patterns and habits, responding positively to the body's limitations, and practicing economy of movement—in other words, the methodical, efficient deployment of strength—are all aspects that I involve in my classes, value as a choreographer, and expect from dancers.

Commitment and decision-making skills

The process of choosing movements first gains depth and clarity through the dancer's own decision-making skills and commitment, which cultivate a convincing bodily language. Movement becomes accessible not only by the form of our bodies' decisions, but by the way we reach them; this also gives the audience a stake in them. Intentional sequences of movement emerge from an inner tension. In this kind of movement, the body is able to bring to light a complexity that cannot be choreographed or reconstructed by mere muscle strength. A body that understands how to eliminate inefficient patterns and habits of action, one that succeeds in dancing choreographic handwriting through movement differentiation, is poised to keep on crossing boundaries.

My point of departure for achieving the desired choreographic result is always, first and foremost, feeling. But out of the feeling, the form emerges. This notion, often cited in the dance world, comes from David Howards. He strongly influences my work as a choreographer today and enabled me at a young age to experience classical ballet as a contemporary art form. Later that served me well in my work with William Forsythe. In those years, I had the time and the right environment to seek and find this same ideal inside myself by taking a kind of kinaesthetic approach that focuses on the dancer's experiences and perceptions of their own movement while exploring their body's possibilities. Somatic practices of many kinds have often led me in the right direction during this quest as a dancer and choreographer. The emotions and feelings that movement sparks are always paramount. I have the American dancer and choreographer Anna Halprin to thank for the insight that a person cannot move without giving rise to a feeling or emotion. I consider recognizing and experiencing the connection between movement and feeling to be essential.

Joy in movement

There is no such thing as perfection in conveying steps. The clarity of movement sequences comes from the ability to translate subjective movement patterns into a language the dancer understands. In this process, I steadfastly concentrate on each individual's unique needs in order to make sure I'm understood. I work at getting my dancers to recognize and control complex and dynamic movement sequences by relaxing their bodies. Only through conscious relaxation can dynamic impulses discharge into organic movement sequences. What's interesting to me as a choreographer is watching dancers make decisions, dancers who know their bodies very well, who connect with a given situation and behave accordingly. Instead of focusing on the result—the form—I try to recognize how each person approaches movement. The more clearly they make decisions, the more articulate their body language becomes.

In the studio, I create situations for my dancers to make self-directed decisions playfully in order to strengthen the power of their decision-making on stage. Dancers who are able to confront technical challenges playfully are ideally placed to meet the requirements of contemporary dance. This playful attitude is of enormous importance to me.

The Dutch cultural anthropologist Johan Huizinga defined "play" as "a voluntary activity or occupation executed within certain fixed limits of time and place, according to rules freely accepted but absolutely binding, having its aim in itself and accompanied by a feeling of tension, joy and the consciousness that it is 'different' from 'ordinary life'" (Huizinga 1998). Thus play manifests itself in intrinsically motivated, intentional movement sequences within a fixed context which follow fixed rules that require tension and joy in order for dancers to find their reality in unfamiliar worlds and throw themselves into each moment.

Play is an age-old word, derived from the Old English word plega, meaning "brisk movement," and related to the Middle Dutch pleien, "leap for joy, dance." This reminds me of what, for me, dance ultimately means: joy in movement. And so, "play" describes my requirements for myself as a dancer—and for the dancers I work with as a choreographer.

Tina Warmuth

9. APPLIED FELDENKRAIS IN CONTEMPORARY DANCE PRACTICE: THREE EXAMPLES

Jenny Coogan and Nina Patricia Hänel

Introduction

This chapter offers readers contexts for movement exploration in which the inherently synergistic relationship between the Feldenkrais Method and contemporary dance practice can be experienced. Three different movement scores are proposed that can be investigated either individually, in pairs, or in groups. The aim is for students and teachers alike to experiment with these examples in their own movement practice, whether in choreographic processes, dance improvisation, or more conventional forms of dance instruction. All three scores are task-oriented explorations that give precedence to the self-image in action and are guided by directing attention to one's own sensations and kinaesthetic feedback. Individually, they address the following themes: novelty in repetition experienced through a method of self-questioning; the fashioning of a constraint as a strategy for choreographic invention; and the interplay between proximal- and distal-joint initiations to enhance mobilization.

Both the practice of contemporary dance and the Feldenkrais Method are process-oriented forms of learning, propelled by individual questioning that seeks to discover the inseparability of the cognitive and physical components of any action. Therefore, each example in this chapter underscores a different aspect of the concept "reflection in action," which is an oscillation between the doing of and conscious reflection on any given action (see chapter 2). Feldenkrais described this as thinking while acting and acting while thinking, a condition that he believed would always lead to new action (1981).

Discovering novelty in the "repetition" of a swing motion

POINT OF FASCINATION:
The deceptive simplicity of repeating a familiar movement can reveal a range of kinaesthetic variation that supports the disruption of routine.

BACKGROUND:
Learning to dance requires practice, and practice involves repetition. It might be challenging to revisit movement patterns on a daily basis in a way that circumvents the onset of mechanical routine. However, this exploration is guided by a form of self-questioning aimed at stimulating and encouraging the dancer to experience repetition as a process of discovery. A non-locomotive and familiar dance movement was selected in order to eliminate possible coordinative challenges. By using functional, observational, and suggestive language, imaginative, and somewhat paradoxical, questions are posed that direct the practitioners' attention to three different time-space parameters of a swing movement: unified awareness that gives precedence to breath and the unity of the action; postural awareness that emphasizes grounding and the homologous movement pattern; and awareness of variation created through differentiating between the movement's points of initiation.

FUNCTION:
The conscious direction of attention can enable refined discernment of kinaesthetic feedback and create subtle neuromuscular variations.

OUTCOME:
An enhanced proprioceptive body image. Internally perceived differences can be recognized in the movement's external representation and thus can effect a greater range of choice for artistic expression.

HOW TO PRACTICE:
Work in pairs or groups, with one person verbally guiding the movers through the score. While repeating a swing motion in loop-like fashion, the dancers simultaneously hear and kinaesthetically visualize the verbally posed questions.

START:
Stand in a parallel position distributing your weight equally between both legs; elongate your arms above your shoulders. Create a swinging motion by releasing the weight of the spine and torso forward through the sagittal plane in an arc-like shape, allowing the arms to move along a peripheral pathway. Recover to a vertical posture by successionally unfolding the spine. The pelvis and joints of the legs sink and rise, flexing and extending in the vertical axis.

It is recommended that you progress through a single category of the questions below before beginning with another. For a more advanced practice, one can alternate between the three categories. **Allow time to assimilate the questions. Take time to rest.**

UNIFIED AWARENESS

What happens when you bring your attention to your breath?

When do you breathe in and when do you breathe out while swinging?

Do you notice a change?

How much time do you take for the inhalation, and for the exhalation?

Pay attention to how your breath can move freely through your whole torso.

When do you hold your breath?

Notice the upward and downward movement of breath as you release and recover back to the vertical.

Imagine swinging in the middle of a cloud.

How do you feel the air circulating around you as you move?

How long is the movement of your breath?

Can you begin the swing allowing all parts of yourself to move at once?

Watch all parts of yourself simultaneously fold in as you swing.

Allow all parts of yourself to unfold in the same amount of time as you swing.

Follow the movement of your arms and legs to the summit of their elongation.

When do you arrive at the deepest place of the motion?

Is the path down the same as the path up?

GROUNDING, HOMOLOG[1]

Follow the sinking and rising of your pelvis when you swing.

Can you sense a buoyant pulsation in your pelvis both downward and upward when you swing?

Does the amount of pressure of the soles of your feet on the floor change when you swing?

Can you allow your ankle and knees to participate in the pulsation of the movement?

Watch the distance between your sitting bones and your heels when in motion.

Does this distance remain constant?

Imagine the back of the knees softly moving forward and the soles of the feet yielding downward while you swing.

Pay attention to the directional movement of the knees as the soles of the feet push away from the floor.

Can you watch the curving of the front of your spine and the folding of the back of your spine at the same time?

While you swing, can you notice the shape of your spine and the distance between your head and tail?

How do you feel the space on your right side and on your left side while you swing?

What shapes do your arms make in response?

Pay attention to the spatial pathway between your two ears and your two shoulders while you swing.

Follow the movement of your ears and shoulders, and spread your attention at the same time to include your two trochanters.

Can you include your right and left ankle joints in your attention, as well as your ears, shoulders, and trochanters?

Measure the distance between your head and feet and your two shoulders while you swing.

MOVEMENT INITIATION

Allow the weight of the head to initiate the swing, and listen to how the spine, arms, pelvis, and legs respond.

Let the weight of the pelvis initiate the movement and listen to how the head, spine, arms, and legs respond.

Begin the swing from the place where you feel the first movement of your exhalation.

Direct the first movement of your exhalation to another part of yourself. Begin the swing from this place.

Begin the swing from releasing the back side of your head.

Can you initiate the swing by softening the chest?

Curve out from the tip of the nose to begin the swing.

Imagine the forehead dropping as you start the swing motion.

Is it possible for you to round the whole torso as you begin to swing?

Begin the return to the vertical by opening out from the center of yourself.

Do you use the pressure of your feet on the ground to propel you back to the vertical?

Do all parts of your arms fall into gravity at once?

Follow the release of your arms from your elbow joints.

Can you initiate the release of your arms from your shoulder joints?

Outline an arch with the tips of your fingers in space as you swing forward and return to the vertical.

Caress
the air with the
underside of your
arms as you initiate
the swing.

Follow
the sequence
of your body parts
releasing and recovering
into space when you
swing.

REFLECTION:

To what do you habitually pay attention when you do a familiar movement? In what directions does your attention shift when you allow it free rein? Revisit what was interesting for you. Create your own questions.

---

1 One of the fundamental patterns of full-body organization is the homologous movement pattern. Through the simultaneous, and usually symmetrical, flexion and extension of both arms and/or both legs, and by utilizing the sagittal plane, one learns to differentiate between the upper and lower half of the body, which are connected through the center (Cohen 1993: 103).

A structural constraint as a creative catalyst

POINT OF FASCINATION:
The creative potential of a structural constraint for generating choreographic material; and to illuminate the inseparability of physical and emotional responses in the movement exploration.

BACKGROUND:
The Feldenkrais Method uses constraints as a strategy for creative self-reorganization. Constraints are fashioned by restricting movement in a part or parts of the body. Working within these self-constructed situations can elicit novel forms of behavior for stimulating invention in movement. Unusual corporeal and spatial relationships can be formed that inhibit movement from progressing along habitually organized routes.

FUNCTION:
The constraint induces spatial and physical alterations, variations, and permutations in the learning context that challenge the dancer to discover novel solutions that will lead in new and unexpected directions.

OUTCOME:
The development of choreographic material that focuses on the interrelation of bodily sensations and their emotional responses. Thus the dancer may experience the constraint as a catalyst for creativity.

HOW DO YOU PRACTICE:
The movement exploration is non-locomotive. After an initial phase of individual investigation, the dancers are asked to reflect on their attitude toward the task through writing or drawing. Therefore, you will need paper and a writing utensil. Next, the dancers are asked to compose their own movement score and to join with a partner in sharing their scores through observation and verbal exchange. **You will need at least 45-60 minutes for this exploration.**

START:

Choose a place in the space where you feel most comfortable. Although you will not be traveling through the space, check to make sure that you have enough room to fully expand into your kinaesphere.

Lie on your back, and allow your arms to rest comfortably on the floor along your sides. Bend one knee and stand on that foot; the front part of the standing foot (the point between the big and second toe) should remain firmly attached to the floor at all times. The heel and arch of this foot have the freedom to move, turn, swivel, and leave the ground. Your other leg is your gesture leg. It has an unlimited range of motion, as long as a large or small surface area of this leg and/or foot remains in contact with the floor at all times. In this way, your exploration does not move through the space, but allows for a 360-degree radius of movement within your kinaesphere.

Imagine the floor underneath you and the ground around you as a giant map or landscape. Begin to explore this landscape with your "gesture," or traveling leg and foot, in a way that allows for movement in all different directions. Remember to keep your standing foot in place and to maintain contact between a part or parts of your exploring leg and foot and the floor at all times. Can you travel to the right and left sides of yourself, to places downward and upward? Move your traveling leg and foot with varying degrees of pressure along the floor. Allow different parts of your gesture leg to dance along the floor. Try it out with different amounts of its surface area.

Consider how you shift your weight, change your spatial orientation, use your arms for support, or reorganize your trunk in relation to your legs as you investigate the possibilities of movement within this constraint.

Take a rest on your back—attend to kinaesthetic feedback.

Return to the starting posture and continue to explore your floor landscape with **only** the **inside** surface of your leg and foot. After a time, switch to the **outside** surface.

How does the inward and outward rotation alter the relationship of the leg to the hip joint? How do you organize your torso? What changes do you notice in the quality or range of movement?

Try this out with only a part or parts of the **front** side of your leg and foot, and then finally with only the **back** side. Alternate between all four sides. Watch how the possibilities for movement are related to which parts of your leg and foot surfaces come into contact with the floor. Consider the range, ease, and flow.

What kinetic considerations emerge when you experiment with the 360-degree radius of the movement possibilities for your leg and foot?

Allow your exploration to bring you into different spatial orientations, sitting, standing, positioned on your belly, upside down, in quadrupedal stance, or changing levels.

How might you need to (re)organize parts of your body in order to accommodate changes in spatial orientations?

Roll over to one side to come to a standing position. Begin to walk through the space. How do you sense your verticality? What differences can you appreciate in your right and left sides?

Return to your place and reestablish the constraint in the spatial orientation of your choice. Continue to explore, while paying particular attention to recurring movement motives. Can you identify your preferences?

Watch how you reach out into your kinaesphere and come back toward your center. Do you prefer movements that are more expansive or more constrained? How do you feel about this task? How does it impact upon you?

Follow the energetic and shape qualities that emerge.[2]

Allow your preferences to take precedence. Let go of all that does not surface repeatedly. Create a movement score based on the preferences you have identified. Dive into the dance of your score.

Rest and consider your inner attitude toward this constraint. How does this attitude relate to the movement choices you have made?

Take a moment to note your thoughts in words or images.

When you are ready, reestablish the constraint and resume your movement score.

What do you notice about your movement personality and the patterns that are appearing? Did the self-reflective act of writing endow your exploration with greater clarity?

Share your score with a partner—one person dances, the other observes. Change roles.

What changes when you share this self-directed exploration with another person?

Enter into a verbal exchange with your partner and note your reflections in words or images.

VARIATION:
Create another of your own scores by finding contrasting alternatives to your own preferences in regard to the use of the kinaesphere, spatial orientations, dynamics, and shaping.

How does the new score alter your emotional responses to the constraint?

REFLECTION:
How might your inner attitude toward the constraint have contributed to the dynamic structure of your score? What changed when self-observed and self-directed processes were witnessed by and exchanged with another person? Form your own constraint. What parameters could you construct that would lead to the generation of choreographic material?

2 In Laban Movement Analysis, "shaping" is understood as the modes of changing one's shape in relation to one's environment (or not); "dynamics" are the interactive ever-present energetic qualities of flow, weight, space, and time.

Mobilization of both proximal and distal parts of joints

POINT OF FASCINATION:
The conscious mobilization of joints, from either their distal or proximal parts, can lead to a more comprehensive understanding and sense of the entire joint's potential for movement.

BACKGROUND:
The human body is made up of 143 joint connections. Joint mobilization is a complex process; it consists of both a proximal part, which is located closer to the center of the body, and a distal part, which is more distant from the center of the body. The participation of multiple joints is present in nearly every movement. We tend to have more thoroughly internalized distal initiations of joint movement.[3] Executing the same movement from the proximal part of the same joint often requires the rethinking of one's own kinaesthetic sense.

FUNCTION:
The consciousness and ability needed to enact a balanced relationship between proximal- and distal-joint mobilization enhances the spectrum of movement.

OUTCOME:
The differentiation of movement initiations from proximal and distal parts of joints can lead to more efficient movement organization within the entire joint.

HOW TO PRACTICE:
This movement exploration has three parts:

- Body scanning in the form of a "tuning in" process, which prepares and conditions the body to direct attention to the joint's connections
- Introduction to the concept and initial explorations involving individual joints
- Expanded implementation of the concept; establishing and maintaining a continuous flow of movement, while simultaneously shifting attention to different joints in the body

START:

Find a place in the room for this movement exploration and assume either a lying down, sitting, or standing position. This exploration does not include any prescribed movement patterns. Allow at least **30 to 45 minutes** for this entire exercise.

BODY SCANNING AND "TUNING IN"

Take a moment to focus your attention internally and to visualize your skeleton, both its bones and its joints.

Are there parts of your skeleton that you can perceive with your inner eye more clearly? Which joints can you visualize? Which bones can you visualize?

Start to move, visualizing the movement initiating from your joints. In your imagination, gradually begin to visualize how you can move from different joints. Give yourself enough time for this exploration.

How does it feel when you imagine yourself moving solely from your joints? Are there joints from which you can move with greater ease? When do you move from a single joint, from two joints, or from multiple joints at the same time?

INTRODUCTION OF THE CONCEPT

Choose a starting place, either in a lying down or sitting position, in which it is possible to place the palm of your right or left hand and the respective lower arm on the floor.

How have you organized yourself to do this?

Direct your attention to the wrist of the hand that is in contact with the floor. Lift your hand from the floor and bring it back down to the floor again. As you lift your hand, the lower arm remains on the floor. Repeat this movement several times.

How do you perceive the movement in the wrist?

Now, find other ways to move your wrist. As a possibility, lift the lower arm from the floor while keeping the hand in contact with the floor. In order to accomplish this, you might have to change the position of your body. Repeat this movement until it becomes very familiar and comfortable.

Has the perception of movement in the wrist changed? What might be different?

Both of these wrist movements are made possible by different parts of the joint. When the lower arm lifts from the floor and the palm of the hand remains on the floor, the wrist is moved proximally; when the lower arm remains in contact with the floor and the palm of the hand lifts off the floor, the wrist is moved from a distal place of initiation.

Now bring your attention to your elbow joint.

What possibilities for movement from the **distal part** of your elbow joint emerge when the **upper arm** remains in contact with the floor?

How can the elbow joint be moved from its proximal part?

Is it easier for you to use a surface to support your lower arm so that it remains in contact with the floor?

Pause, take a rest.

How do you perceive the joints of your arms? Has something changed in your perception of your hand and elbow joints?

Find a position from which you can use this same principle to explore the proximal and distal movement possibilities of your shoulder joint.

EXPANDED EXPLORATION

Begin to move in a moderate tempo on the floor. Find a continuity of flow in your movement. Allow your entire body to participate. As a result of the flow, your attention can wander between different, flexible joint connections. Give yourself enough time to find both the movement flow and the movement organization.

Can your attention stay with one joint as you move through the space with your whole body?

Direct your attention to one joint and observe whether the proximal or distal part of this joint in involved in the movement. Stay with this intention without disrupting the flow of movement throughout your entire body.

Now draw your attention to another joint and notice how its distal or proximal part mobilizes the movement.

How long can your attention remain with the same joint?
Are there joints to which your attention repeatedly wanders?

Allow your attention to shift from one joint and, with time, to another joint.

How do you orient yourself in the space as you simultaneously direct attention to joint mobilization and to your position in the space?

Find a playful approach to your exploration, in the knowledge that it is impossible to perceive simultaneously the proximal and distal initiations of multiple joint movements.

Remain in "flow" and begin to move, varying your spatial levels by alternating between the floor, middle, and standing stages.

Is it easier for you to differentiate between proximal and distal initiations of joint mobilization the longer you engage in this movement exploration?

Give yourself time to find an end to this movement exploration—standing, sitting, or lying down—and take a moment to become sensitive to your kinaesthetic feedback.

What might have changed in your perception of the relationship between and within joints during the course of this exploration? Are there joints that are exceptionally clear in your perception? How might you carry this consciousness over into your daily life?

REFLECTION:

Do you know of any everyday movements that are initiated from the distal part of the joint? Do any dance movements spring to mind that are moved from the distal part of the joint? What dance movements use the same joint in motion from its proximal part?

Observe others as they dance on the floor in full body movement. What joints are involved in the movement? Which of these joints use proximal participation and which involve distal participation.

3 There are a number of examples in dance where the hip joint is moved from its distal parts, including tendu, jeté, grand battement (articulation of the limbs in relation to the center of the body). In comparison, when the weight of the upper body and head hangs forward toward the floor from a standing position—in which the weight is equally divided between the two legs (so that the head is directed toward the floor and the sitting bones toward the ceiling)—the hip joints are proximally articulated. When rolling through the spine to recover to a vertical position, the hip joints move from their proximal parts.

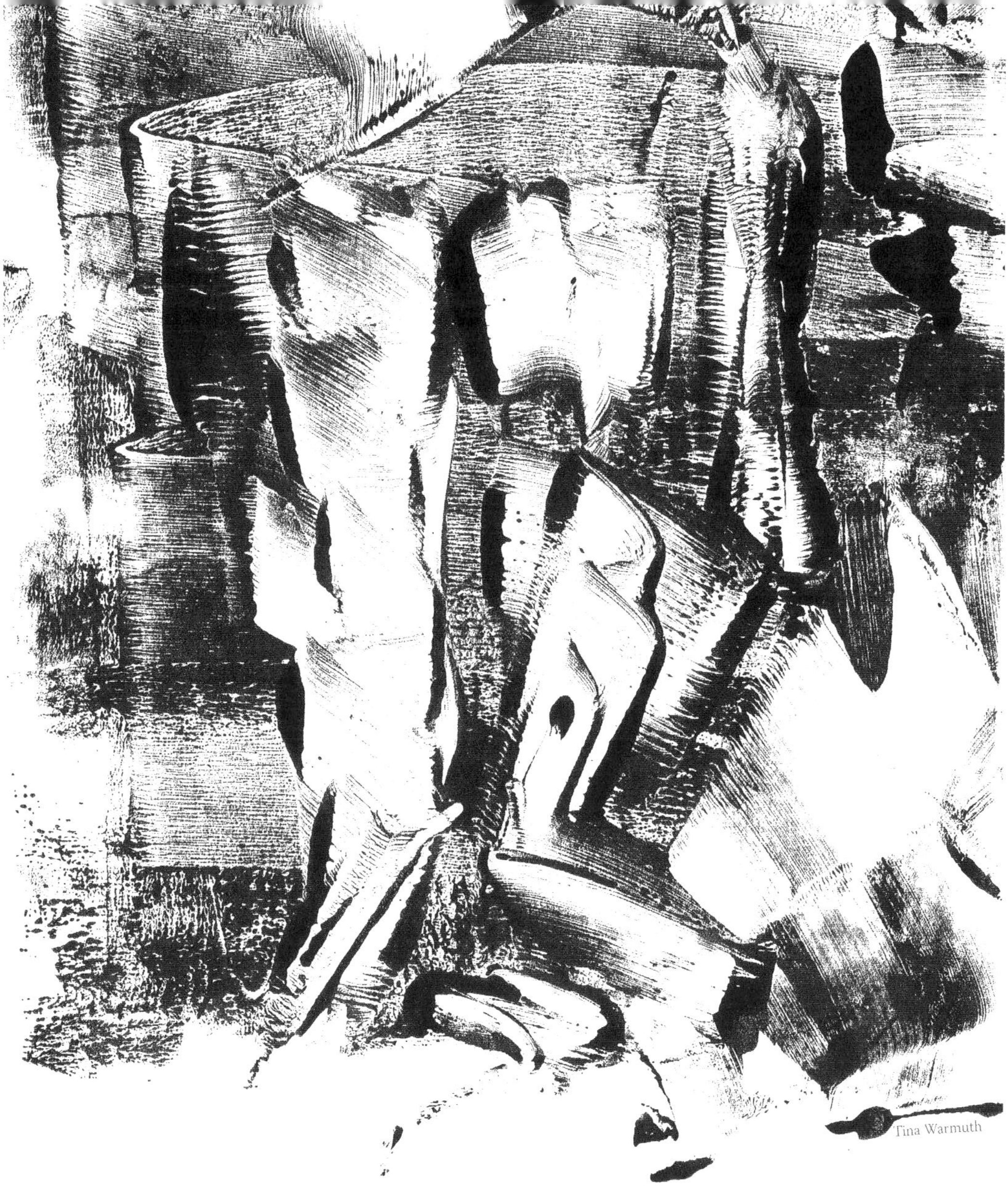

10. STATEMENTS OF PROGRAM DIRECTORS

DANCE SOMATICS AS RADICAL PEDAGOGY:

REFLECTIONS ON SOMATIC PRACTICE WITHIN UK HIGHER EDUCATION AND TRAINING IN DANCE

Sara Reed

In this essay I draw on my experience, over many years, as a dancer, dance pedagogue, and director of dance and performing arts higher education departments in the UK and, currently, as Head of the Department for Performing Arts at Coventry University. In addition, I draw on my research, including the experiences of my contemporaries from the mid-1970s onwards. This time frame forms part of the postmodern period attributed to dance in the UK, which affected dance training, pedagogy, and higher-education practices.

The discussion ranges over a number of topics relating to the professional profile of a dancer performing in the hybrid field of contemporary dance today. In addition, I discuss what it is that may enable a dancer to deal with the demands of the professional dance world within the context that they choose to work.

To begin, the field of contemporary dance today is, indeed, a hybrid, and the demands are both great and at times even contradictory. In the past, clearly, many dancers have endangered their own health and fitness by overtraining in a way that is detrimental to their futures by causing permanent damage to their joints. Darcey Bussell is the latest to confirm that she has hip problems due to an over-suppleness in her joints, which she was "happy to push" (2015). This is something that all dancers and teachers need to be aware of.

A broader dance education, which promotes in-depth awareness of the body as well as highly developed dance technique, is, I believe, absolutely essential as an integral part of all professional dancers' initial training.

What qualities and concepts of self do today's dancers need to possess? I think the list would include, though not exclusively: technical ability; somatic understanding and sensibility; curiosity; adaptability (in being a teacher, performer, maker, collaborator, administrator, and more); creativity; resilience; hunger for learning and doing; energy; expressivity; emotional intelligence; performance presence; fitness (another question here would be: "What is fitness for the twenty-first century dancer?"); and health. I could go on, but these are some of the most important attributes. The complexity of such requirements demands a multiplicity of forms of training, which are largely different now than they were some thirty, twenty, or even ten years ago. For a start, we live in a digital age, and this has had an effect on performance contexts and practices.

How then do we, and should we, articulate and defend twenty-first century methods of training to the young dancer? In order to fully appreciate the context within which the shifting landscape of dance education/training has been situated during the latter part of the twentieth and the beginning of the twenty-first centuries, it is useful to look at work that is being performed in the professional world and to then ask what is needed to prepare dance students for this world. It is therefore absolutely essential to understand the needs of the professional dance world.

In UK universities, the majority of dance students will not become full-time professional dancers, though most will progress into careers in a wide variety of dance or arts contexts other than, or as well as, performance and choreography. Although the dance conservatories in the UK, for example Trinity Laban Conservatoire of Music and Dance and the Conservatoire for Dance and Drama, give full-time professional training to dance students to prepare them for the professional dance world, many of these students will also go on to work in the wider dance or performing arts industries as teachers, managers, somatic practitioners, and arts/dance administrators. Therefore, we also need to ask what concepts of self dancers must possess to enable them to meet the demands of the hybrid practices of performance today. Currently, professional dance work spans a wide range of areas, including: classical and contemporary dance companies; film; dance theater; site-specific work outdoors and in galleries, museums, and public spaces; community contexts and workshops; and this list is not exhaustive. Such a breadth of work testifies to the state and eclecticism of the dance profession today and highlights the need, within dance conservatories and university departments, for training and education to equip students for a diversity of careers.

Wayne McGregor's work, for example, is well known for its use of visual and sound technologies, as well as the technical virtuosity of the dancers he uses. McGregor's preference is to work with highly technically trained dancers, who often have a ballet background. Jonathan Burrows, whose style of dancing and choreography is very different to McGregor's, also has a strong connection to ballet and traditional dance technique. Burrows suggests that the principles of ballet grant extraordinary physical sense and that there are few physical systems in the world as complex as ballet, as it requires the coordination of mind, eyes, arms, legs, head, gravity, and anti-gravity (Burrows, cited in Perazzo Domm 2007: 15).

Rosemary Butcher, in contrast, whose work is very different again from both McGregor's and Burrows', suggests that dance training is not producing the dancers she is looking for. Butcher, a recipient of the 2015 Bonnie Bird Lifetime Contribution to Choreography Award, always chooses highly technically trained dancers, but she also wants them to have a particular sensibility, and way of thinking and working in the studio. What she is looking for is informed by certain philosophies, and she has a great sympathy for the somatic approach. A dance-somatics approach brings, in her words, "an understanding of the body and a sense of democracy and ownership" (2009). This approach is now the more prevalent one within UK independent contemporary dance practice today.

Dance technique alone is not enough. Something more is needed from today's dancers, something that comes from a broad understanding of culture and the arts, and a deep sensory awareness. Indeed, many of these values and qualities are those that have grown through the development and practice of somatic-based dance education and training. Nevertheless, some argue that a somatic-dance curriculum is not fit for purpose within the dominant discourse of dance training in a conservatory context and, indeed, somatic practice has been highly criticized by the likes of the international, UK-based, contemporary dance choreographers Lloyd Newson, Akrahm Kahn, and Hofesh Shecter (Jennings 2015). The power relations that traditionally exist within dance put the democratic and holistic nature of somatic practice at odds with this dominant discourse (Fortin 2008; 2009).

Without a doubt, developing a strand of somatic practice alongside dance technique can be, and often is, problematic. However, it is important to keep dance students dancing, and Kirsty Alexander maintains that "dance needs to reassert itself as a practice," to be authentic and include a duty of care (2015). This reflects more recent developments in contemporary dance education/training. That said, some conservatories are, of course, specifically preparing young dancers for commercial settings, such as musical theater or contemporary dance and ballet companies, and they have, therefore, a responsibility to prepare students for the rigors of auditions and demanding daily schedules. As Emilyn Claid recently asked, "Can ethical uncertainty and technical fixing exist together? Is there too much yielding and not enough push?" (2015).

Students who have been learning dance from a young age, whether through ballet, modern, and/or postmodern techniques, may have to let go of old patterns of moving and move beyond purely physical skills in order to embrace the relationship between technical, somatic-based, and creative practice. Alexander states that "the traditional boundaries between technical performance and choreographic approaches [are] becoming blurred through the influence of somatic practices" (2015). This transgression of boundaries is a major influence on how dancers need to develop today and on what we teach students within the four walls of the conservatory, dance school, or university.

The recent backlash by some male choreographers in the UK, as mentioned above, suggests, I believe, a misunderstanding of embodiment and somatic practice as being somehow only related to a therapeutic context and not related to a broad and valuable dance training and education for the twenty-first century. A dance-somatics training/education may include the dominant elements from postmodern dance that emerged through the 1960s and 1970s and yet, arguably, may be seen to have run their course in their current form and are therefore in need of review. It is through the key concepts of dance-somatics, namely increased sensory awareness, body-mind functional integration, and efficiency of movement, that postmodern dance can be seen to have made its greatest contribution to twenty-first century dance-somatics pedagogy. In addition, a dance-somatics approach can encourage a very different pedagogical style of teaching, one not based on the dominant paradigm of external modeling. The integration of somatics can have a profound influence on the safe learning of dance technique through enhanced sensory awareness, care of oneself and of others. The use of language, attitude of the teacher, and a more inclusive and supportive pedagogical style all have the potential to empower dance students.

A dancer's health and fitness will also benefit from learning in and through somatic practices, such as the Alexander Technique and Feldenkrais Method, as additions to technical training. An important aspect of teaching somatic practices as well as, not instead of, dance technique is that they enable dancers to dance better, for longer, and with greater strength and awareness of their physicality. The Feldenkrais Method, for example, through subtle stimulation of the senses that results in complete body (re)organization, allows dancers to make changes that will affect their overall performance and ability to avoid and/or deal with injury (Batson 2007).

Within the context of somatics-informed dance training/education, we need to look at how we can:

- introduce somatic practices to dance students within a safe and caring environment;
- nurture understanding of dance-somatic practice;
- support students through their (possible) perception of the loss of previously learned dance skills and knowledge, and therefore sense of self;
- prevent "loss of heart" and help students celebrate new ways of knowing (Varela, Thompson, Rosch 1991);
- help dance students understand the relational and intertwining aspects of old and new practices; and
- foster a sense of cooperation, care of self and others within a dance-somatics creative learning environment.

We might do this in a number of ways, including helping students to develop their conscious awareness, which is the inevitable result of involvement with somatic practice and a constant thread running through somatic work. Moshé Feldenkrais' concern was that people will stop learning as soon as they develop enough skills to just "get by," and that this "limiting ability" enables them to function within a minimal potential zone (my words). This is a good starting point for me to encourage and allow students to move beyond their limiting ability and to fulfill their potential beyond that zone. Providing the opportunity to experience a more radical dance pedagogy, underpinned by a dance-somatic based dance curriculum, encourages students to understand their development as dancers from a first-person perspective—thus developing their own authority or empowered embodiment. Better-educated, trained, and informed dance graduates can only be of benefit to the dance profession in all career areas—whether it be performance, choreography, pedagogy, community dance, dancers' health, or elsewhere.

The question of what is now needed for dance graduates to flourish in the twenty-first century remains. Ideally, somatic practices need to be taught alongside dance techniques, but not subsumed within them. Through somatic practices, students gain a deep knowledge of the bodymind from an experiential understanding of function, anatomy, physiology, and biomechanics. A dance-somatics education is one that allows the development of a thinking dancer, a dancer who is able to bring all aspects of their education and training together creatively in a variety of contexts and with a range of outcomes. It is an education that will fully prepare them for the professional dance world and their future success and health.

DANCING FROM THE INSIDE OUT:

RESEARCHING THE INTEGRATION OF SOMATIC PRACTICES IN DANCE TRAINING

Jason Beechey

Dance is probably one of the most fragile art forms. As one that exists only "in the fleeting moment," we all know that every performance is different and can never be exactly reproduced. Nor would this be in the interest of our art form; who would want to see a photocopy and not the original? With our bodies as our instruments, we also know how different they can feel from not only one day to the next, but from one moment to the next. The moment a dancer steps in front of an audience, they are completely exposed. Their thoughts and movements can be seen by all and are open to scrutiny and critique, as well as to the perception that they are vessels to provide enlightenment.

Today, probably more than ever, the barriers between "dance styles" are being challenged. What current ballet company doesn't do contemporary work? Many contemporary companies and independent artists train with ballet, but of course this is not "ballet" from a hundred years ago, nor are we working with the knowledge and bodies from that time period either. From breaking out from behind the proscenium arch to interact, all the way up to the virtual world, borders are constantly being challenged and reinvented. But when our body is our instrument, where does this leave us? How do we ultimately enable ourselves to discover new realms and means of expression from inside our bodies and imaginations without being overwhelmed by the barrage of outside information available to us today? Do we start a day with meditation, yoga, by going to the gym, or jogging? Then do we carry on with Pilates, Gyrotonics, or Feldenkrais? After that, we have ballet and contemporary, followed by rehearsals and creative processes. There has never before been such a plethora of techniques and methods through which we can discover our potential but, at the same time, there are also such intense time pressures to always be at the top of the game and to constantly be "new and innovative."

Dancers today, who continue to inspire me, are no longer identifiable as "ballet" dancers or "contemporary" dancers, but as "dancers." Dance artists have transcended such barriers and labels. In a contemporary world, the range of repertoires is vast, and I see more and more of these hybrid dancers—in whom, ultimately, I appreciate more and more their abilities as thinking, autonomous individuals who are unafraid to explore both the world inside themselves and their surroundings, regardless of which technique or style they are exploring. Take Sylvie Guillem, for example, who comes from the Paris Opera, has danced with an incredible range throughout her whole career, and is revered for her ability to explore and challenge such conventional labels.

Take for example a company such as our own Semperoper Ballett, where the versatility of the dancers is such that the same dancers are cast for Marius Petipa and George Balanchine, as well as Ohad Naharin and William Forsythe. Traits such as musicality, coordination, awareness of space, and focus have far surpassed gender barriers, the traditional assignment of roles, and/or stereotypes. Some dancers are tall, some are small—but they all have drive, passion, and the ability to dance in common.

Now, how can we foster such versatile minds in education? We have the incredible opportunity here at Palucca that most dancers come to us aged ten as a blank sheet, having never danced before. To give them the chance to explore their own ideas and creativity over nine years provides an ideal time frame. By working to develop a common mentality, and through exploring contemporary dance, ballet, and improvisation, assigning them all equal importance, I hope that our team will inspire our students to discover who they are and what they can do with their instruments through learning these three intertwined techniques. No one can be a "jack of all trades," but when the approach is built upon common traits and skills, it can be a wonderfully inspiring journey. This is where the true core of education lies, in the individuals who take part. To see them grow and discover new things, challenge themselves, and develop a sense of accomplishment and awareness is incredibly rewarding. Ultimately, it is only when the inner journey has been taken that we can see the accomplishments on the outside.

The curriculum has been completely restructured since 2006 with the introduction of body-awareness classes, a full-time body-awareness coach, and the inclusion of classes in Pilates, Feldenkrais, and a long-term project with GAGA, developed by Ohad Naharin, which is having an immense impact. The dancers who graduate are more self-aware, calm, and mature, and have come much farther on their inner journey.

The goal of *InnoLernenTanz* (ILT) in 2012 was to create an opportunity for research to be undertaken to see how somatic practices can be fostered and play a role first in contemporary dance classes and then, hopefully, be transferred to other dance techniques. Ultimately, regardless of what technique is being taught, the same minds and bodies are present in the classes. Students can only benefit by making connections. The graduates from Palucca go on to a variety of companies, a fact that we are proud of, while we also encourage them to look around for different opportunities. Our wish is that they discover for themselves the various avenues they can pursue to explore dance further and play an active role in our profession. I hope the research carried out in the ILT project will provide some food for thought and the keys to help them unlock other such explorations and processes in dance education.

Conducting a research project, in itself, was a first for our university and a challenge in its own right. To institute such changes within the education system is much easier said than done. One has to deal with set parameters, tight budgets, and personnel limitations, in addition to making decisions to allow the slow introduction of additional somatics training, which had to be done at the expense of reducing or eliminating other techniques and with careful consideration of a multitude of factors. We have been fortunate to receive additional funds for ILT and new positions and, over the past ten years, we have completely redefined the profile of Palucca. This was only made possible through years of discussion and teamwork, which also involved new collaborations with the Semperoper Ballett, The Forsythe Company, and the Festspielhaus Hellerau. To have such opportunities is rare.

I have the good fortune that I am able to travel and visit many dance-education institutions and companies. I do see that, especially in Anglophone countries, the fields of dance research are much further developed than in the continental EU. But, at the same time, the dance profession in many non-EU countries has truly become an art form where only the elite and rich can afford to participate. There are pros and cons, but I see a dominant trend toward using the knowledge from the dance and sport sciences, in combination with somatic practices, to create a much healthier and long-term dancing life for professionals.

The professional dance world today requires dancers to be more alert, versatile, and accomplished than ever before. When I created the D.A.N.C.E. program in 2005, I will never forget how William Forsythe commented that the most important thing is that we develop a "curriculum with no curriculum." The biggest problem he encountered with young dancers was that they were so attuned to following a set, rigid schedule that they couldn't adapt to working in a company where a director/choreographer comes in and has new ideas, for which they have to be ready, willing, and able to jump on board and dive in. It is about having a mind-set where one can both tune in to oneself, while remaining in touch with one's surroundings.

One can argue whether all these body techniques actually help develop creativity and artistry or merely turn dance into a sport. In response to this, however, I believe that a healthy mind and body are the foundational elements necessary for creating inspiring art. I don't agree that, as one of my former teachers told me, you have to suffer to be great. Yes, it is hard work, but when you are living out your passion, what greater opportunity can one have?

I hope the research undertaken by ILT will provide insights, ideas, and tools to help propel the evolution of dance education and inspire generations to come.

Tina Warmuth

11. A LOOK INTO THE FUTURE

DARING TO CREATE GAPS

Gabriele Wittmann

I remember my first Feldenkrais lessons well. After many years of rigorous ballet training, I was now listening to a friendly voice telling me: "Perceive what is happening." My kinaesthetic sense spoke up: "The shoulder joint won't rotate any further." My mind replied: "I won't accept that. Should I rotate or not?" I was undecided. Unfettered, I was alone with what everybody seems to want: freedom. What a shock! Now what? The voice gently advised me: "Feel your limitations."

It is from here, at the limit, that future decisions evolve. On a small scale, it may mean enhancing the perception of one's pelvic region, on a bigger scale it might encompass the widening of political discussions for a new a district project—life will always pave the way for new options. Somatic education helps people make authentic decisions, because by sensing a temporary limitation deeply, we allow space for heightened consciousness. And it is here that new impressions and possibilities can enter. These give rise to new resources, which in turn can pave the way for different types of decisions. Choreographer and activist Anna Halprin refers to this process as "creative evolution" (quoted in Wiltmann 2011).

Somatically oriented pedagogical approaches such as the Feldenkrais Method, Body-Mind Centering®, or the Life/Art Process have inspired me for years, as I apply these techniques in the creation of curricula for writing different text types around the issue of perception. I have come to call this method "Scoring Writing." For this, I often follow the scores of Anna Halprin's Life/Art Process (Wittmann 2012). Her method is based on the RSVP cycle[1]—a technique that makes creative processes visible, individually or in groups of more than one hundred citizens. The participants, in unison, define their resources, create scores, perform them, and subject them to a "valuaction"[2] before moving on to the next cycle. The process of valuaction is generally oriented toward positivity. Rather than learning through criticism, the participants augment their range of perception by becoming more and more aware of their own actions and those of others. They give each other feedback, not through the predominant method of commenting on each other's texts, but mostly by "becoming" the other text—being another person's text, using the other person's words, dancing the other person's text. These shifts create gaps, which in turn open up the possibility for new combinations and interpretations of understanding in the other person. The interconnectivity between the medium of writing, movement, and speaking is equally as important as the shifts between solo, duet, and group work. This process gives rise to continually growing perception of the effects of dance and language and, intrinsically, a gradual awareness of differences, which ultimately leads to more precision.

The core of all somatic approaches is opening the space up to allow for the growth of consciousness. Referred to as "Theory U," these ideas have also reached the world of economics. Alongside colleagues from the Massachusetts Institute of Technology (MIT), Otto Scharmer (2011) developed "presencing" as a social technique, which can be used to moderate change-management processes within companies in a thorough and sustainable way. Some of the key words resemble the terminology used in somatic methods: beginning with "emerging" and "pausing," "sensing" into the situation, "letting go," and "connecting" with the source. Then, at the turning point of the consciousness curve, "'letting inner knowledge emerge from the stillness," compressing it, bringing it forth, and personifying it. The crucial point is always presencing, in other words the deeper, contextually integrated "becoming present" (Scharmer 2011: 66), which emerges when thinking, feeling, and the act of willing have been opened up. Since the turn of the millennium, the authors Peter M. Senge, Joseph Jaworski, and Betty Sue Flowers have been advocating for a paradigm shift. After hierarchical and auto-poetic systems, such as those coined by Niklas Luhmann, the new approach is about solving questions "from a holistic and integrative perspective across all fields ... and interdependencies" (Scharmer 2011: 362). The authors want to promote processes for social change, where guidance and learning arise from the "developing future," which is "sensed" by everyone involved in the process, regardless of their positions in the participating workforces.

Is individual somatic consciousness already political? The fact is that self-awareness, at its core, automatically leads to more sustainable external behavior. Working with somatic methods in training processes helps the individual to expand consciousness of inner thought patterns, develop empathy and patience, and accept responsibility for their own decisions, with all the consequences that entails. The result of this personally induced and enacted process is self-efficacy. The individuals experience the consequences of their actions and see the impact they have on their environment. The experience of self-efficacy is regarded as a crucial factor for resilience today and plays a major role in the prevention of burnout and salutogenesis, namely the active process of staying healthy.

These factors are invaluable in democratic societies that are facing increasing immigration and the demand for more "direct democracy." A growing number of people consider the times of representation to be obsolete—not just on stage but also in the political organization of citizens. What comes next? In order to promote peaceful change, it is important to treat oneself and one's fellow citizens with care and sensitivity. The ability to say "I" or "myself" is at the core of these self-organized processes, regardless of whether we are dealing with an institution, a project group, or a lengthy democratic process. The choreographer Anna Halprin is using the Life/Art Process to make sure that all members of a group are "present," not only in the body but as sensing and feeling individuals. They are encouraged to express their sensations and remain perceptive of the expressions of others. The constant alteration between impression and expression leads to communication. This requires the ability to continually sense one's limitations, to constantly balance them out, and also to accept them.

Somatic techniques such as the Feldenkrais Method teach exactly that: the perception of limitations. Accept them lovingly. By becoming aware, one can create new opportunities. Limitations can soften and make space for subsequent decisions, when the time is ripe for change.

---

1 For a detailed explanation of Halprin's RSVP cycle, see Halprin, Kaplan 1995: 46ff.

2 "Valuaction" is a term coined by Lawrence and Anna Halprin. It merges "value" and "action," and means giving value to an action or activity. For further details on the Halprins' principles of creative processes, see Schorn 2015.

3 A groundbreaking production in the field of dance was Project by Xavier Le Roy (2003). Back then, the choreographer was already criticizing "representation" as a means of parliamentary democracy and confronted the audience with a complex dramaturgy, in which the viewer's perception constantly shifted between seeing representative actions and ad-hoc decisions in a ball game (Xavier Le Roy 2004; in interview with the author).

CLOSING WORDS

Jenny Coogan and Jürgen van Buer

This volume began with a question that dancers often pose to one another at the Palucca University, namely "Who made you a dancer?" As outlined in the introduction, this particular question led to a number of follow-up ones that are underscored in this book: "How are the parameters that are crucial to the understanding of contemporary dance, such as personal agency, embodied?"; "How does the German educational system in dance foster such parameters?"; and "How could we more effectively encourage young dancers to experience their education from a first-person perspective of empowered, embodied, and somatic authority?" All these questions point to the ways in which somatic approaches, philosophies, concepts, and practices within dance education can support students in attending to their own development with enhanced self-reliance, self-reflection, social consciousness, and acceptance of the multifarious perspectives experience, knowledge, and understanding bring. The contributions of dance artists, educators, and academics presented in this volume have addressed all these questions. Their vantage points are varied, and the arguments and empirical evidence presented invite critical reflection on the variety of approaches that prepare dancers to meet the ever-changing challenges of professional performing careers.

Research in dance education demonstrates that new and unfamiliar training practices, which are often connected with somatic approaches, can be challenging for students, as they are asked to (re)consider their learning strategies, to encounter the "new" with curiosity and commitment, to accept uncertainty as positive and constructive, and to move forward with courageous willingness for simply trying things out. Less familiar methods and materials for practice can be met with limited acceptance and emotional resistance from students. Individual responses flow into the group processes and influence implicitly and/or explicitly the planning, procedures, and assessment of the situation. Resolution requires time. The empirical findings reported here support the idea that working somatically requires a long breath, perseverance, and patience from both the students and teachers/facilitators alike. Students are called upon to reconcile the developmental potential of the "new" with their own intentions and aspirations, and the role of the teacher/facilitator is to recognize and support these individual needs.

Studies in education indicate that innovative pedagogical concepts, as well as curricular constructs, cannot be added into teaching programs in a "patchwork" manner, for example in accordance with their singularly verified effectiveness or by theoretical argumentation that seeks to justify the expected effects. Such a patchwork approach increases the risk that innovation may disappear entirely out of daily practice or that it may be reconfigured beyond all recognition. The viewpoints expressed in this volume affirm the potential for somatic approaches in dance teaching and learning to be a curricular and didactic motor of integration, an alternative to a patchwork arrangement.

Certainly, implementing such an integrative approach demands a hefty dose of collaboration between all the institutional actors involved. As trivial as this statement may sound, this is a highly relevant factor when considering the sustainability of curricular as well as didactic innovation in programs of study. Practice-based studies in education point to this conclusion, as the quality of pedagogy and curricular coherency attained at any one time have to be continually (re)mastered in institutional everyday life.

Therefore, our cautiously optimistic look into the future draws attention to the challenges faced by dance education institutions in Germany for organizing and implementing curricular programs. These programs need to integrate the diversity of pedagogical approaches available in ways that encourage students to embrace the value and relevance of multiple perspectives and methods as a synergetic whole for facilitating personal development and dance artistry. This leads to the question of when and in what contexts teaching and learning with a somatically oriented approach should begin. This is a question that reaches beyond the microcosm of professional dance education in performance to larger cultural and political contexts. Whatever the educational context, the decisive factor lies with each participant, and asks for both their active engagement in co-creating the teaching and learning situations, and for their curiosity, courage, resilience and ,especially, their continual willingness to pursue individual measures for self-education.

REFERENCES

Achtenhagen, F. (2006) *'Lehr-Lern-Forschung'*, in: Arnold, R., Lipsmeier, A. (Eds.) *Handbuch der Berufsbildung,* Wiesbaden: VS Verlag für Sozialwissenschaften, 586-609

Alexander, K. (2003) 'Unravelling the dance: an exploration of dance's under-developed relationship with its kinaesthetic nature, with particular reference to Skinner releasing technique', in: Hargreaves, M. (Ed.) *New connectivity: Somatics and creative practices in dance education. Papers from Laban Research Conference,* London: Laban Centre, 19-22

Ibid. (2015) *Independent Dance HE Round Table,* 'Artist or Instrument? Changing notions of techniques and creative practice', London

Allemann-Ghionda, C., Stanat, P. (Eds.) (2010) *Migration, Identität, Sprache und Bildungserfolg,* 55. Beiheft der Zeitschrift für Pädagogik, Weinheim: Beltz

Autorengruppe Bildungsberichtserstattung (2014) *Bildung in Deutschland 2014. Ein indikatorengestützter Bericht mit einer Analyse zur Bildung von Menschen mit Behinderungen,* Bielefeld: Bertelsmann

Baacke, D. (1973) *Kommunikation und Kompetenz. Grundlegung zu einer Didaktik der Kommunikation und ihrer Medien,* München: Juventa

Bales, M., Nettl-Fiol, R. (Eds.) (2008) *The Body Eclectic: Evolving Practices in Dance Training,* Urbana: University of Illinois Press

Bandura, A. (1977) 'Self-efficacy: Toward a unifying theory of behavioral change', in: *Psychological Review,* 84 (2), 191

Batson, G. (2007) 'Revisiting overuse injuries in dance in view of motor learning and somatic models of distributed practice', in: *Journal of Dance Medicine & Science,* 11(3), 70-75

Batson, G., Schwartz, R. (2007) 'Revisiting the Value of Somatic Education in Dance Training Through an Inquiry into Practice Schedules', in: *Journal of Dance Education,* 7(2), 47-56

Batson, G., Wilson, M. (2014) *Body and Mind in Motion, dance and neuroscience in conversation,* Bristol: intellect books

Baumert, J., Bos, W., Lehmann, R. (Eds.) (2000) *TIMSS/III. Dritte Internationale Mathematik- und Naturwissenschaftsstudie – Mathematische und naturwissenschaftliche Bildung am Ende der Schullaufbahn,* Band 1: Mathematische und naturwissenschaftliche Grundbildung am Ende der Pflichtschulzeit, Opladen: Leske + Budrich

Beavers, W. (2008) 'Relocating Technique', in: Bales, M., Nettl-Fiol, R. (Eds.) *The Body Eclectic: Evolving Practices in Dance Training,* Urbana-Champaign: University of Illinois Press, 126-133

Behnke, E.A. (1990) 'Moving into a Somatic Future', in: *Somatics Magazine-Journal of the Bodily Arts and Sciences,* 8(1), 48-52

Bellack, A. A., Kliebard, H. M., Hyman, R. T., Smith, Jr., F. L. (1966) *The Language of the Classroom,* New York: Teachers College

Berger, J., Karabenick, S. (2011) 'Motivation and students' use of learning strategies: Evidence of unidirectional effects in mathematics classrooms', in: *Learning and Instruction,* 21, 416-428

Beringer, E. (1997) 'Feldenkrais', in *Groundworks: Narratives of Embodiment,* Johnson, D.H. (Ed.) Berkeley: North Atlantic Books, 81-100

Ibid. (2001) 'Self-imaging', in: *The Feldenkrais Journal 13,* 33-38

Bernard A., Stricker, U., Steinmüller, W. (2003) *Ideokinese: Ein kreativer Weg zu Bewegung und Körperhaltung,* Bern: Hans Huber

Bernstein, B. (1971) 'Elaborierter und restringierter Kode: eine Skizze', in: Klein, W., Wunderlich D. (Eds.) *Aspekte der Soziolinguistik,* Frankfurt a. M: Athenäum, 15-23

Bernstein, N. (1996) 'On Dexterity and its Development', in: Latash, M., Turvey T., Mahwah, M. (Eds.), *Dexterity and its Development,* New Jersey: Lawrence Erlbaum Associates, 171-207

Biber, D. (2006) *University Language: A Corpus-based Study of Spoken and Written Registers,* Amsterdam: John Benjamin

Bishop, S., Lau, M., Shapiro, S., Carlson, L., Anderson, N., Carmody, J., Devins, G. (2004) 'Mindfulness: A proposed operational definition', in: *Clinical Psychology: Science and Practice,* 11, 230-241

Bjork, R., Dunlosky, J., Kornell, N. (2013) 'Self-regulated learning: Beliefs, techniques, and illusions', in: *Annual Review of Psychology* 64, 417-444

Boekaerts, M., Pintrich, P., Zeidner, M. (2005) *Handbook of Self-Regulation,* New York: Elsevier

Böhle, F., Porschen S. (2011) 'Körperwissen und leibliche Erkenntnis' in: Keller, R., Meuser, M. (Eds.) *Körperwissen,* Wiesbaden: Springer Fachmedien

Bredekamp, H., Krois, J. (Eds.) (2012) *Sehen und Handeln,* Berlin: De Gruyter

Brodie, J., Lobel, E. (2007) 'Integrating fundamental principles underlying somatic practices into the dance technique class', in: *Journal of Dance Education,* 4(3), 80-87

Ibid. (2012) *Dance and Somatics. Mind-Body Principles of Teaching and Performance,* Jefferson, North Carolina: Mcfarland & Co Inc

Bromme, R., Prenzel, M., Jäger, M. (2014) 'Empirische Bildungsforschung und evidenzbasierte Bildungspolitik. Eine Analyse von Anforderungen an die Darstellung, Interpretation und Rezeption empirischer Befunde', in: *Zeitschrift für Erziehungswissenschaft,* 17 (4), 3-54

Brown, K., Ryan, R. (2003) 'The benefits of being present: Mindfulness and its role in psychological well-being', in: *Journal of Personality and Social Psychology,* 84, 822-848

Brügelmann, H. (2014) *'Gilt nach Hattie: Je häufiger, desto besser? Zur Bedeutung von "Evidenzbasierung" für pädagogisches Handeln vor Ort',* in: Terhart, E. (Ed.) Die Hattie-Studie in der Diskussion. Probleme sichtbar machen, Seelze: Kallmeyer in Verbindung mit Klett, 38-50

Buckroyd, J. (2000) *The student dancer,* London: Dance Books

Buer, J. van, Niederhaus, C. (2010) 'Kommunikation und Interaktion in pädagogischen Kontexten – berufs- und wirtschaftspädagogische Perspektiven', in: Nickolaus, R. (Ed.) *Handbuch Berufs- und Wirtschaftspädagogik,* Stuttgart: UTB, 101-111

Bund, K. (2014) *Glück schlägt Geld. Generation Y: Was wir wirklich wollen,* Hamburg: Murmann Publishers GmbH

Burnidge, A. (2012) 'Somatics in the Dance Studio: Embodying Feminist/Democratic Pedagogy', in: *Journal of Dance Education,* 12(2), 37-47

Burns, S. (2007) *Mapping Dance: Entrepreneurship and Professional Practice in Dance Higher Education,* Palatine: The Higher Education Subject Centre for Dance, Drama and Music

Butcher, R., Melrose, S. (Eds.) (2005) *Rosemary Butcher: Choreography, Collisions and Collaborations,* Middlesex: Middlesex University Press

Caldwell, K., Adams, M., Quin, R., Harrison, M., Greeson, J. (2013) 'Pilates, mindfulness and somatic education', in: *Journal of Dance and Somatic Practices,* 5 (2), 141-153

Claid, E. (2006) *Yes? No! Maybe ... Seductive Ambiguity in Dance,* London: Routledge

Ibid. (2015) Keynote address at the *Ethics and Repair: Continuing Dialogues Within Somatic Informed Practice and Philosophy,* Coventry University Centre for Dance Research (author's notes)

Clarke, G., Cramer, F. , Müller, G. (2011) 'Minding motion', in: Diehl, I. , Lampert, F. (Eds.) *Dance Techniques 2010,* Leipzig: Henschel Verlag, 199-229

Cohen, B.B. (1993, 2008) *Sensing, feeling, action,* Northhampton: Contact Editions

Corbin, J., Strauss, A. (2015) *Basics of Qualitative Research: Theory and Procedures for Developing Grounded Theory,* Thousand Oaks: Sage Publications

Creswell, J. (1998) *Qualitative Inquiry and Research Design: Choosing among five traditions,* Thousand Oaks: Sage Publications

Csikszentmihalyi, M. (1990) *flow: The psychology of optimal experience,* New York: HarperCollins

Czetczok. H.E. (1995) *Die Feldenkrais-Methode,* Stuttgart: Bibliothek der Feldenkrais-Gilde e.V., Nr. 8

Damasio, A. (1994) *Descartes Error: Emotion, Reason and the Human Brain,* New York: HarperCollins

Deci, E., Ryan, R. (2000) 'The "what" and "why" of goal pursuits: Human needs and the self-determination of behavior', in: *Psychological Inquiry,* 11, 227-268

Deese, J. (1966) *The structure of Association in Language and Thought,* Baltimore: The Johns Hopkins University Press

DeLahunta, S., Hoerster, E. (2007) 'Rethinking Tools: based on interviews collected during MODE05' in: DeLahunta, S., Hoerster, E. (Eds.) *Reverse Engineering Education: In dance, choreography and the performing arts.* MODE05, Berlin: b_books verlag, 88-95

Deleuze, G. (1994) *Difference and Repetition,* London: The Athlone Press

Denzin, N., Lincoln, Y. (2013) *Collecting and Interpreting Qualitative Materials,* Thousand Oaks: Sage Publications

Dewey, J. (1997) *Experience and Education,* New York: Touchstone

Ibid. (2008) *Art as Experience,* New York: Perigree

Dobrick, M. (1985) '(Miß-)Verstehen im Unterricht, ein verstehens-psychologischer Erklärungsansatz für einige soziale Phänomene im pädagogischen Kontext', in: *Bildung und Erziehung,* 38 (4), 429-440

Doidge, N. (2015) *The Brain's Way of Healing, Stories of Remarkable Recoveries and Discoveries,* London: Allen Lane

Dragon, D. (2015) 'Creating Cultures of Teaching and Learning, Conveying Dance and Somatic Education Pedagogy', in: *Journal of Dance Education,* 15, 25-32

Dubs, R. (2007) 'Kognitive Kompetenzen', in Euler, D., Pätzold, G., Walzik, S. (Ed.), ‚Kooperatives Lernen in der beruflichen Bildung', in: *Zeitschrift für Berufs- und Wirtschaftspädagogik,* Beiheft 21, Stuttgart: Franz Steiner 147-164

Dunlosky, J., Rawson, K., Marsh, E., Nathan, M., & Willingham, D. (2013) 'Improving students' learning with effective learning techniques promising directions from cognitive and educational psychology', in: *Psychological Science in the Public Interest,* 14, 4-58

Eberth, J., Sedlmeier, P. (2012) 'The effects of mindfulness meditation: A meta-analysis', in: *Mindfulness,* 3, 174-189

Eddy, M. (2009) 'A brief history of somatic practices and dance: historical development of the field of somatic education and its relationship in dance', in: *Journal of Dance and Somatic Practices,* 1(1), 5-27

Ibid. (2015) 'Early Trends', in: Whatley, S., Garrett-Brown, N., Alexander, K. (Eds.) *Attending to Movement, Somatic Perspectives on Living in this World,* Axminster: Triarchy Press, 285-297

Eddy, M., Williamson A., Weber, R. (2014) 'Reflections on the Spiritual Dimensions of Somatic Movement Dance Education', in: Williamson, A., Batson, G., Whatley, S., Weber, R. (Eds.) *Dance, Somatics and Spiritualities: Contemporary Sacred Narratives,* Bristol: intellect books, 159-194

Enghauser, R. (2003) 'Motor learning and the dance technique class: Science, tradition, and pedagogy', in: *Journal of Dance Education,* 3, 87-95

Feldenkrais, M. (1949, 1988) *Body and Mature Behavior: A Study of Anxiety, Sex, Gravitation and Learning,* Madison: International Universities Press

Ibid. (1972) *Awareness Through Movement,* New York: Harper & Row

Ibid. (1980) *Learn to Learn,* San Diego: Feldenkrais Resources

Ibid. (1981) *The Elusive Obvious,* Cupertino: Meta Publications

Ibid. (1984) *The Master Moves.*,Cupertino: Meta Publications

Ibid. (1985) *The Potent Self: A Study of Spontaneity and Compulsion,* San Francisco: Harper & Row

Ibid. (2010) *Embodied Wisdom, The Collected Papers of Moshé Feldenkrais,* Beringer, E. (Ed.), Berkeley: North Atlantic Books

Ibid. *Professional Training Program,* June, 1975. 3. Feldenkrais, M. Unpublished autobiography, undated

Fernandez, M., Wegerif, R., Mercer, N., Rojas-Drummond, S. (2001) 'Reconceptualising "scaffolding" and the Zone of Proximal Development in the context of symmetrical collaborative learning', in: *Journal of Classroom Interaction,* 36 (3), 54-63

Figal, G. (2000) *Martin Heidegger. Phänomenologie der Freiheit.* Weinheim: Beltz Athenäum Verlag

Foster, S. (1986) *Reading Dancing: Bodies and Subjects in Contemporary American Dance,* Berkeley: University of California Press

Ibid. (1997) 'Dancing Bodies', in: Desmond, J. (Ed.) *Meaning in Motion,* Durham: Duke University Press

Ibid. (2010) *Choreographing Empathy: Kinesthesia in Performance,* London/ New York: Routledge

Fortin, S. (1993) 'When Dance Science and Somatics Enter the Dance Technique Class', in: *Kinesiology and Medicine for Dance,* 15(2), 88-108

Ibid. (2003) 'Dancing on the Mobius Band', in: Hargreaves, M. (Ed.) *New connectivity: Somatics and creative practices in dance education. Papers from Laban Research Conference,* London: Laban Centre, 3-10

Fortin, S., Girard, W., Lord, M. (2002) 'Three Voices: Researching How Somatic Education Informs Contemporary Dance Technique Classes', in: *Research in Dance Education,* 3(4), 155-179

Fortin, S., Vieira, A., Tremblay, M. (2009) 'The experience of discourse in dance and somatics'. in: *Journal of Dance and Somatic Practices,* (1), 47-64

Fraleigh, S. (2014) 'Permission and the Making of Consciousness', in: Williamson, A., Batson, G., Whatley, S., Weber, R. (Eds.) *Dance, Somatics and Spiritualities: Contemporary Sacred Narratives,* Bristol: intellect books, 239-262

Gallagher, S. (2005) *How the body shapes the mind,* Oxford: Oxford University Press

Galloway, Ch. (1976) *Silent language in the classroom,* Bloomington: Phi Delta Kappa Educational Foundation

Gershkoff-Stowe, L., Thelen, E. (2004) 'U-shaped changes in behavior: A dynamic systems perspective', in: *Journal of Cognition and Development,* 5(1), 11-36

Giguere, M. (2015) 'Dance education action research: a twin study', in: *Research in Dance Education,* 16(1), 16-32

Ginot, I. (2010) 'From Shusterman's Somaesthetics to A Radical Epistemology of Somatics' in: *Dance Research Journal,* 42(1), 12-29

Ibid. (2011) 'Body Schema and Body Image. At the Crossroads of Somatics and Social Work', in: *Journal of Dance and Somatic Practices,* 3 (1&2), 151-165

Ginsberg, C. (1988) 'Communication and Learning, the roots of Functional Integration', in: *Feldenkrais Journal*(4), North American Feldenkrais Guild 13-20

von Glasersfeld, E. (1995) *Radical Constructivism. A Way of Knowing and Learning,* New York: Routledge

Gläser-Zikuda M., Hascher, T. (Eds.) (2007) *Lernprozesse dokumentieren, reflektieren und beurteilen: Lerntagebuch und Portfolio in Bildungsforschung und Bildungspraxis,* Bad Heilbrunn: Julius Klinkhardt

Green, J., Stinston, S. W (1999) 'Post-positivist Research in Dance', in: Fraleigh, S., Hanstein, P. (Eds.) *Researching Dance: Evolving modes of inquiry,* Pittsburgh: University of Pittsburg Press, 91-123

Green, J. (2000) 'Social Somatic Theory, Practice and Research: An Inclusive Approach in Higher Education Dance', in: Willis, J., LaPointe-Crump, J., Dance Critics Association (U.S.), Society of Dance History Scholars (U.S.), National Dance Association (Eds.) *Conference Proceedings. Dancing in the Millennium: an International Conference,* Washington DC: Dancing in the Millennium, 213-217

Ibid. (2001) 'Socially Constructed Bodies in American Dance Classrooms', in: *Research in Dance Education,* 2(2), 155-173

Ibid. (2002a) 'Somatic knowledge: The body as content and methodology in dance education', in: *Journal of Dance Education,* 2(4), 114-118

Ibid. (2002b) 'Somatics a Growing and Changing Field', in: *Journal of Dance Education,* 2(4), 113

Ibid. (2015) 'Moving in, out, through, and beyond the tensions between experience and social construction in somatic theory', in: *Journal of Dance & Somatic Practices,* 7(1), 7-19

Gudjons, H. (2001) *Handlungsorientiert lehren und lernen. Schüleraktivierung – Selbsttätigkeit – Projektarbeit,* Bad Heilbrunn/Obb: Julius Klinkhardt

Hackney, P. (1998) *Making Connections: Total body integration through Bartenieff fundamentals,* Amsterdam: Gordon and Breach

Hanna, T. (1976) 'The Field of Somatics', in: *Somatics,* 1(1), 30-34

Ibid. (1979) *The Body of Life,* New York: Knopf

Ibid. (1986) 'What is Somatics', in: Johnson, D. H. (Ed.) (1995) *Bone, Breath and Gesture. Practices of Embodiment,* Berkeley: North Atlantic Books, 341-353

Hardt, Y., Stern, M. (2011) *Choreographie und Institution: Zeitgenössischer Tanz zwischen Ästhetik, Produktion und Vermittlung,* Bielefeld: transcript

Hassa, T. (2015) 'Bewegung ohne Bewegung? Bewegungsvorstellung in Feldenkrais und in der Neurowissenschaft', in: *Feldenkraisforum,* 91 (4), 12-16

Hattie, J. (2009) *Visible learning: A synthesis of 800+ meta-analyses on achievement,* London: Routledge

Ibid. (2015) *Lernen sichtbar machen,* Hohengehren: Schneider

Helmke, A. (2003) *Unterrichtsqualität erfassen – bewerten – verbessern,* Opladen: Westdeutscher Verlag

Higgins, St., Hall, E., Baumfield, V., Moseley, D. (2005) *A meta-analysis of the impact of the implementation of thinking skills approaches on pupils,* London: University of London

Holdaway, G., Kovich Z., Simmonds, J. (2002) *Somdance Manuel,* Sydney: University of Western Sydney Press

Horak, F. (2006) 'Postural Orientation and Equilibrium: what do we need to know about neutral control of balance to prevent falls?', in: *Age aging,* 35 (2), ii7-ii11

Huizinga, J. (1998) *Homo Ludens: A Study of the Play-Element in Culture,* London: Routledge

Hüther, G. (2006) *The Compassionate Brain: A Revolutionary Guide to Developing your Intelligence to its Fullest Potential: How Empathy Creates Intelligence,* Boston: Trumpter Books

Ihde, D. (2002) *Bodies in Technology,* Minneapolis: University of Minnesota Press

Ingenkamp, K. (1971) *Die Fragwürdigkeit der Zensurengebung,* Weinheim: Beltz

Johnson, D.H. (1994) *Body, Spirit and Democracy,* Berkeley: North Atlantic Books

Ibid. (Ed.) (1995) *Bone, Breath and Gesture: Practices of Embodiment,* Berkeley: North Atlantic Books

Joly, Y. (2004) 'The experience of being embodied: Qualitative Research and Somatic education- A Perspective Based on the Feldenkrais Method', in: *The IFF Feldenkrais Research Journal,* 1, 10-23

Kabat-Zinn, J. (2003) *Full Catastrophe Living: Using the Wisdom of Your Body and Mind to Face Stress, Pain, and Illness,* New York: Bantam

Kampe, T. (2014) 'Moving after Auschwitz: the Feldenkrais Method as a soma-critique', in: *The Journal for the Anthropological Study of Human Movement,* 33 (6), 237-258

Ibid. (2015) 'Eros and inquiry: The Feldenkrais Method® as a complex resource', in: *Theatre, Dance and Performance Training,* 6 (2), 200-218

König, St., Stibbe, G. (Eds.) (2016) *Facetten eines Erziehenden Sportunterrichts: Theoretische Ansätze, empirische Studien und praktische Konzepte,* Berlin: Logos

Kovich, Z. (1994) 'Somatic education and the dancer', in: *Dance and the Child International Conference,* Macquarie University, Sydney

Krasnow, D., Wilmerding, M. (2015) *Motor Learning and Control for Dance: Principles and Practices for Performers and Teachers,* Champaign: Human Kinetics

Labov, W. (1971) Die Logik des Nonstandard Englisch (Auszug), in Klein, W., Wunderlich, D (Eds.) *Aspekte der Soziolinguistik,* Frankfurt a.M.: Athenäum, 80-97

Langer, E. (1997) *The Power of Mindful Learning,* New York: Addison-Wesley Publishing

Ledergerber, C. (2015) *Unterrichtskommunikation und motivational-emotionale Aspekte des Lernens. Eine videobasierte Analyse im Mathematikunterricht,* Münster: Waxmann

Lehmann, R. H., Peek, Gänsfuß, R., Lutkat, S., Mücke, St., Barth, I. (2000) *QuaSUM. Qualitätsuntersuchung an Schulen zum Unterricht in Mathematik, Ergebnisse einer repräsentativen Untersuchung im Land Brandenburg,* Potsdam: Ministerium für Bildung, Jugend und Sport des Landes Brandenburg

Leri, D (1993) 'Learning how to learn,' in: *Gnosis Magazine,* Fall 1993, 49-53

Levine, P. (1997) *Waking the Tiger: Healing Trauma, The Innate Capacity to Transform Overwhelming Experiences,* Berkely: North Atlantic Books

Long, W. (2002) *Sensing Difference: Student and Teacher Perception on the Integration of the Feldenkrais Method of Somatic Education and Contemporary Dance Technique,* Unpublished MA thesis, University of Otago, Dunedin, NZ

Louppe, L. (1997) *The Poetics of Contemporary Dance,* Brussels: Contredanse

Luhmann, N. (1995) *Social System,* Stanford: Stanford University Press

van Manen M. (2007) 'Phenonomelogy of Practice,' in: *Phenonomology and Practice,* 1(1), 11-30

Mangione, M. (1993) *The origins and evolution of somatics: interviews with five significant contributors to the field,* Columbus: Ohio State University

Marcovitch, S., Lewkowicz, D. (2004) 'U-shaped functions: Artifact or hallmark of development?,' in: *Journal of Cognition and Development,* 5(1), 113-118

Marossek, D. (2016) *Kommst du Bahnhof oder hast du Auto?: Warum wir reden, wie wir neuerdings reden,* Berlin: Hanser

Maturana, H., Varela, F. (1980) *Autopoiesis and Cognition,* Dordrecht: D. Reidel Publishing Company

McCloskey, D. (1982) 'Signals of proprioception in man,' in: *Proprioception, Posture and Emotion,* Garlick, D. (Ed.) Kensington: University of New South Wales

Meyer, H. (2004) Praxisbuch: *Was ist guter Unterricht? Mit didaktischer Landkarte,* Berlin: Cornelsen Scriptor

Ibid. (2014) 'Auf den Unterricht kommt es an! Hatties Daten deuten lernen,' in: Terhart, E. (Ed.) *Die Hattie-Studie in der Diskussion. Probleme sichtbar machen,* Berlin: Kallmeyer in Verbindung mit Klett, 117-133

Mollenhauer, K. (1972) *Theorien zum Erziehungsprozeß,* München: Juventa

Möller, J., Schiefele, U. (2004) 'Motivationale Grundlage der Lesekompetenz' in: Schiefele, U., Artelt, C., Schneider, W., Stanat, P. (Eds.) *Struktur, Entwicklung und Förderung von Lesekompetenz. Vertiefende Analysen im Rahmen von PISA 2000,* Wiesbaden: VS Verlag für Sozialwissenschaften, 101-124

Müller, H. (2013) *Jugendsprache im Wandel,* München: GRIN Verlag

Myers, M. (1983) 'Body Therapies: and the Modern Dancer,' in: *Dance Magazine,* 57 (August), 1-24

Noë, A. (2004) *Action in Perception,* Cambridge: MIT Press

Noland, C. (2009) *Agency and Embodiment: Performing Gestures/Producing Culture,* Cambridge: Harvard University Press

OECD (2016) *Low-Performing Students. Why they fall behind and how to help them succeed,* Paris: OECD Publishing

Oomen-Welke, I. (2004) 'Körpersprachen und Extrasprachliches verschiedener Kulturen in Welt, Schule und Unterricht' in: Rosenbusch, H. D., Schober, O. (Eds.) *Körpersprache und Pädagogik,* Hohengehren: Schneider Verlag, 68-98

Pant, H. (2014) 'Visible Evidence? Eine methodisch orientierte Auseinandersetzung mit John Hatties Meta-Metaanalysen', in: Terhart, E. (Ed.) *Die Hattie-Studie in der Diskussion. Probleme sichtbar machen,* Seelze: Kallmeyer in Verbindung mit Klett, 134-146

Parviainen, J. (2002) 'bodily knowledge: epistemological reflections on dance', in: *Dance Research Journal,* 34 (1), 11-23

Ibid. (2003) 'Dance techne: Kinetic bodily logos and thinking in movement', in: *The Nordic Journal of Aesthetics,* 159-175

Pauli, St. (2011) *"EyAlter, du bist voll der Wort-Checker!": Jugendsprache: Eine empirische Untersuchung von Jugendlichen und Erwachsenen,* Hamburg: tredition

Pauls, F., Macha, T., Petermann, F. (2013) 'U-shaped development: An old but unsolved problem', in: *Frontiers in Psychology,* 4, 301

Perazzo Domm, D. (2007) *Dancing Poetry: Jonathan Burrows Reconfiguration of Choreography,* unpublished doctoral thesis, University of Surrey, Guildford

Pertersen, St., Cotter, M. (Eds.) (2015) *Challenging interdisziplinary Science Experiments. Volume 2: Tasks of the European Union Science Olympiads 2008-2012,* Münster: Waxmann

Peters, A., Sieben, I. (2009) *Das große Feldenkrais-Buch,* München: Heinrich Hugendubel Verlag

Piaget, J. (1971) *Biology and Knowledge,* Chicago: University of Chicago Press

Pintrich, P. (2004) 'A conceptual framework for assessing motivation and self-regulated learning in college students', in: *Educational Psychology Review,* 16(4), 385-407

PISA-Konsortium (2008) (Ed.) *PISA 2006 in Deutschland: Die Kompetenzen der Jugendlichen im dritten Ländervergleich,* Münster: Waxmann

Porsch, R. (2016) *Einführung in die Allgemeine Didaktik: Ein Lehr- und Arbeitsbuch für Lehramtsstudierende,* Stuttgart: UTB

Praetorius, A., Lenske, G., Helmke, A. (2012) 'Observer ratings of instructional quality: Do they fulfill what they promise?', in: *Learning and Instruction,* 22(6), 387-400

Pribram, K. (1971) *Languages of the Brain: Experimental Paradoxes and Pronciples in Neuropsychology,* New York: Brandon House

Quinn, D., Twenge, J., Fredrickson, B. (2006) 'The disruptive effect of self-objectification on performance', in: *Psychology of Women Quarterly,* (30), 59-64

Reed, S. (2015) 'Attending to movement', in: Whatley, S., Brown, N. G., Alexander, K. (Eds.) *Attending to Movement: Somatic Perspectives on Living in This World,* Axminster: Triarchy Press, 207-218

Reese, M. (1985) 'Foreword', in: *The Potent Self: A Study of Spontaneity and Compulsion,* San Francisco: Harper & Row, ix-xxxiv

Retter, H. (2002) *Studienbuch Pädagogische Kommunikation,* Bad Heilbrunn/Obb: Klinkhardt

Robson, C. (2011) *Real World Research,* Chichester: John Wiley & Son Ltd

Roche, J. (2015) *Multiplicity, Embodiment and the Contemporary Dancer: Moving Identities,* Basingstoke, Hampshire: Palgrave Macmillan

Roche, J., Huddy, A. (2015) 'Creative adaptations: Integrating Feldenkrais principles in contemporary dance technique to facilitate the transition into tertiary dance education', in: *Theatre, Dance and Performance Training 6 (2),* 145-158

Rolff, H.-G. (2014) 'Sind schulische Strukturfaktoren wirklich nicht so wichtig?', in: Terhart, E. (Ed.) *Die Hattie-Studie in der Diskussion. Probleme sichtbar machen,* Seelze: Kallmeyer in Verbindung mit Klett, 67-77

Rosenbusch, H. D., Schober, O. (Eds.) (2000) *Körpersprache und Pädagogik,* Hohengehren: Schneider Verlag

Rosenbusch, H. S. (2004) 'Nonverbale Kommunikation im Unterricht – Die stille Sprache im Klassenzimmer' in: Rosenbusch, H. D., Schober, O. (Eds.) *Körpersprache und Pädagogik,* Hohengehren: Schneider Verlag, 138-176

Rouhiainen, L. (2008) 'Somatic dance as a means of cultivating ethically embodied subjects', in: *Research in Dance Education,* 9 (3), 241-256

Ruge, U. (2002) 'Sprache und Körper bei Martin Buber und Moshé Feldenkrais', in: *feldenrais zeit, Journal für somatisches Lernen* (3) 39-46

Rywerant, Y. (1983) *The Feldenkrais Method, Teaching by Handling,* San Francisco: Harper & Row

Schäfer, K.-H. (1971a) 'Didaktik zwischen Autorität und Emanzipation', in: Schäfer, K.-H., Schaller, K. (Eds.) *Kritische Erziehungswissenschaft und kommunikative Didaktik,* Heidelberg: Quelle & Meyer, 96-132

Ibid. (1971b) 'Emanzipatorische und kommunikative Didaktik', in: Schäfer, K.-H., Schaller, K. (Eds.) *Kritische Erziehungswissenschaft und kommunikative Didaktik,* Heidelberg: Quelle & Meyer, 133-166

Schaller, K. (1971) 'Pädagogik der Kommunikation' in: Schäfer, K.-H., Schaller, K. (Eds.) *Kritische Erziehungswissenschaft und kommunikative Didaktik,* Heidelberg: Quelle & Meyer, 63-95

Scharmer, O. C. (2011) *Theorie U – von der Zukunft her führen. Presencing als soziale Technik,* Heidelberg: Auer

Schmidt, R., Wrisberg, C. (2001) *Motor Learning and Performance,* Champaign: Human Kinetics

Schön, D (1983) *The Reflective Practitioner: How Professionals Think in Action,* New York: Basic Books

Ibid. (1987) *Educating the Reflective Practitioner: Toward a New Design for Teaching and Learning in the Professions,* San Francisco: Jossey-Bass Publishers

Schorn, U. (2015), *The healing encounter of dance,* Gestalt, and art based on Anna Halprin's Life/Art Process', in: *British Gestalt Journal,* 24(2), 14-20

Schulz von Thun, F. (1981) *Miteinander reden I – Störungen und Klärungen. Allgemeine Psychologie der Kommunikation,* Reinbek: Rowohlt

Schunk, D. H., Meece, J., Pintrich, P. (2012) *Motivation in Education: Theory, Research, and Applications,* New York: Pearson Higher Education

Schürmann, E. (2008) *Sehen als Praxis – Ethisch-ästhetische Studien zum Verhältnis von Sicht und Einsicht,* Frankfurt am Main: suhrkamp wissenschaft

Schwandt, T. (1994) 'Constructivist, interpretivist approaches to human inquiry', in: Denzin, N. Lincoln, S. (Eds.) *Handbook of Qualitative Research,* London: Sage Publication, 118-137

Senge, P., Scharmer, C. , Jarowski, J., Flowers, B.S. (2004) *Presence. Exploring Profound Change in People, Organizations and Society,* New York: Crown

Shapiro, S. (Ed.) (1998) *Dance Power and Difference: Critical and Feminist Perspectives on Dance Education,* Leeds: Human Kinetics

Sheets-Johnstone, M. (1979) 'The Work of Dr. Moshé Feldenkrais', A New applied kinesiology and a Radical Questioning of Training and Technique, in: *Contact Quarterly,* Fall, 24-29

Ibid. (2016) 'Foundational Dynamics of Animate Nature', in: Eberlein, U. (Ed.) *Intercorporeity, Movement and Tacit Knowledge,* Bielefeld: transcript, 51-69

Shusterman, R. (2004) 'Somesthetics and Education: Exploring the Terrain' in: Bresler, L. (Ed.) *Knowing Bodies, Moving Minds,* Boston: Kluwer, 51-61

Ibid. (2006) 'Thinking through the Body, Educating for the Humanities: A Plea for Somaesthetics', in: *The Journal of Aesthetic Education,* 40 (1), 121

Ibid. (2007) 'Expeditions to the Inner Teacher: How the Pioneers of Movement Studies Inspire Dance', in: Gehm, S., Huseman, P., von Wilke, K. (Eds.) *Knowledge in Motion, Perspectives of Artistic and Scientific Research in Dance,* Bielefeld: transcript, 137-147

Ibid. (2008) *Body Consciousness, a Philosophy of Mindfulness and Somaesthetics,* New York: Cambridge University Press

Sieben, I. (2003) 'Sechs Sinne: Ohne Bewegung gibt es keine Wahrnehmung – Warum Tanz am Anfang aller Künste steht' in: *ballettanz,* 28-33

Ibid. (2011) 'Working Somatically, Supporting Techniques for Contemporary Dance', in: Diehl, I., Lampert, F. (Eds.) *Tanztechniken 2010,* Leipzig: Henschel Verlag, 136-145

Simmel, L. (2014) *Dance Medicine in Practice. Anatomy, injury prevention, training,* New York: Routledge

Smith, R. (2011) 'The Sixth Sense: Towards a History of Muscular Sensation', in: *Genaerus,* 68 (1) 218-271

Spatz, B. (2015) *What a body can do, Technique as knowledge, Practice as Research,* New York: Routledge

Stavy, R. (Ed.) (2012) *U-shaped behavioral growth,* New York: Elsevier

Steinmüller, W. Schaefer, K. Fortwängler, M. (2001) *Gesundheit – Lernen – Kreativität,* Bern: Hans Huber Verlag

Stinson, S. (2000) 'Choreographing a life: reflections on curriculum design, consciousness, and possibility', in: *Journal of Dance Education,* 1(1), 26-33

Ibid. (2004) 'My Body/Myself: Lessons from Dance Education', in: Bresler, L. (Ed.) *Knowing bodies, moving minds: towards embodied teaching and learning,* London: Kluwer, 153-169

Sweigard, L. (1974) *Human Movement Potential, Its Ideokinetic Facilitation,* New York: Harper & Row Publishers

Switalla, B. (1982) *Sprachliches Handeln im Unterricht. Verständigungsschwierigkeiten zwischen Lehrern und Schülern,* München: Urban und Fischer

Terhart, E. (2014) 'Vorwort', in: Terhart, E. (Ed.) *Die Hattie-Studie in der Diskussion, Probleme sichtbar machen,* Seelze: Kallmeyer in Verbindung mit Klett, 6-9

Turkle, S. (1984, 2005) *The Second Self: Computers and the Human Spirit,* Cambridge: MIT Press

Vago, D., Silbersweig, D. (2012) 'Self-awareness, self-regulation, and self-transcendence (S-ART): A framework for understanding the neurobiological mechanisms of mindfulness', in: *Frontiers in Human Neuroscience,* 6, 296

Varela, F.J., Thompson, E., Rosch, E. (1991) *The Embodied Mind: Cognitive Science and Human Experience,* Cambridge: MIT Press

Vlachopoulos, S., Michailidou, S. (2006) 'Development and initial validation of a measure of autonomy, competence, and relatedness in exercise: The Basic Psychological Needs in Exercise Scale', in: *Measurement in Physical Education and Exercise Science,* 10, 179-201

Walach, H., Buchheld, N., Buttenmüller, V., Kleinknecht, N., Schmidt, S. (2006) 'Measuring mindfulness—the Freiburg Mindfulness Inventory (FMI)', in: *Personality and Individual Differences,* 40, 1543-1555

Warburton, E. (2011) 'Of Meanings and Movements: Re-languaging embodiment in dance phenomenology and cognition', in: *Dance Research Journal,* 43(2), 65-83

Watzlawick, P., Beavin, J. H., Jackson, D. D. (2007) *Pragmatics of Human Communication: A Study of Interactional Patterns, Pathologies, and Paradoxies,* New York: Norton

Wenger, E. (1998) *Communities of Practice Learning, Meaning, and Identity,* Cambridge: Cambridge University Press

Whatley (2014) 'Part II: Reflections on the Intersections of Spiritualities and Pedagogy', in: Williamson, A., Batson, G., Whatley, S., Weber, R. (Eds.) *Dance, Somatics and Spiritualities: Contemporary Sacred Narratives,* Bristol: intellect books, 151-157

Wigfield, A., Eccles, J. (2000) 'Expectancy–value theory of achievement motivation', in: *Contemporary Educational Psychology,* 25(1), 68-81

Wilson, M. (2009) 'Dance Pedagogy case studies: A grounded theory approach to analyzing qualitative data', in: *Research in Dance Education,* 10(1), 3-16

Wirth, J., Leutner, D. (2008) Self-regulated learning as a competence. Implications of theoretical models for assessment methods, in: *Zeitschrift für Psychologie/ Journal of Psychology,* 216, 102-110

Wisker, G. (2001) *The Postgraduate Research Handbook,* New York: Palgrave Macmillan

Wittmann, G. (2012) 'Scoring Writing. A Tool for Collective Creative Analysis', in: Boxberger, E., Wittmann, G. (Eds.) *Partnering Documentation. Approaching Dance, Heritage, Culture,* München: Epodium, 28-33

Ibid. (2011) 'A Sensual Confrontation. Three key terms concerning nature and evolution from the work of Anna Halprin', in: Heun, W., Kruschkova, K., Mehanovic, L., Noeth, S. (Eds.) (2012) *Scores No.3 uneasy going,* Wien: Tanzquartier Wien, 72-77

Wittmann, G., Scheidl, S., Siegmund, G. (2011) 'Lance Gries – Release and Alignment oriented techniques', in: Diehl, I., Lampert, F. (Eds.) *Dance Techniques 2010: Tanzplan Germany,* Leipzig: Henschel, 264-294

Wuttke, E. (2005) *Unterrichtskommunikation und Wissenserwerb: Zum Einfluss von Kommunikation auf den Prozess der Wissensgenerierung,* Frankfurt a. M.: Peter Lang

Zeig, J. (1980) (Ed.) *A Teaching Seminar with Milton H. Erickson,* New York City: Brunner/Mazel Inc.

Ziemer, G. (2011) 'Situational Worlds: Complicity as a Model for Collaboration' in: Klein, G., Noeth, S. (Eds.), *Emerging Bodies. The Performance of Worldmaking in Dance and Choreography,* Bielefeld: transcript, 235-247

INTERNET SOURCES:

Bussell, D. (2015) 'Why at age 46 I love my hip', http://www.telegraph.co.uk/culture/11936621/Darcey-Bussell-Why-age-46-I-love-my-new-hip [accessed 24.10.2015]

European Commission (2016) *The Bologna Process and the Higher Education Area,* http://ec.europa.eu/education/policy/higher-education/bologna-process_en.htm [accessed 07.05.16]

Friedmann, J. (2013) 'Zurück zum Kerngeschäft' in: *Der Spiegel* [accessed 05.11.2016]

Jennings, L. (2015) ‚The Struggle for the Soul of British Dance', http://www.theguardian.com/stage/2015/jul/12/contemporary-dance-debate-shechter-kh [accessed 24.10.2015]

le Roy, X. (2004) an interview with Gabriele Wittmann: *Tele Tanz Journal 6*, Deutsches Tanzfilminstitut Bremen, ZDF/3Sat

Reese, M. (1984) 'Moshé Feldenkrais's Work with Movement – a parallel Approach to Milton Erickson's Hypnotherapy', http://www.achievingexcellence.com/Moshe-Feldenkrais-Work-with-Movement-A-Parallel-Approach-to-Milton-Ericksons-Hypnotherapy.html [accessed 26.06.2016]

Reese, M. (1994) 'The Feldenkrais Method and Dynamic System Principle', http://feldenkraislearning.com/html/dynamic_systems.html [accessed 23.03. 2016]

Smyth, C. (2007) 'The Idea of the Primary Image in the Feldenkrais Method', http://www.feldenkraissf.com/the-primary-image/ [accessed 5.11.2015]

PERSONAL NOTES (SARA REED):

Butcher, R. (2009) Private telephone conversation with Sara Reed (15/04/09)

Fortin, S. (2008) Conference held at John Moores University, Liverpool 'Somatic and Creative Practices' (Reed, S. notes from the conference and unpublished papers 9.02.08)

A SELECTION OF WEBSITES: THE FELDENKRAIS METHOD

The following lists significant websites both about the Feldenkrais Method and the other somatic movement practices discussed in this volume.

The International Feldenkrais Federation
Professional, part-time teacher training programs are offered throughout the world. These programs typically span a four year period and lead to certification as an accredited teacher of this method. The International Feldenkrais Federation (IFF) is the coordinating organization of Feldenkrais Guilds and Associations and other key Feldenkrais professional organizations worldwide.
http://feldenkrais-method.org/

Feldenkrais-Professional-Training-Programs worldwide:
Feldenkrais training programs in Europa und Israel:
http://www.eurotab.org
Feldenkrais training programs in Australia and Asia:
http://www.feldenkrais.org.au/training/training-programmes/
Feldenkrais training programs in Nord- und Südamerika:
http://www.feldenkrais.com/accredited-trainings

Feldenkrais Guilds and Associations worldwide:
Argentinia: ***http://www.feldenkrais.org.ar***
Australia: ***http://www.feldenkrais.org.au***
Austria: ***http://www.feldenkrais.at***
Belgium: ***http://www.feldenkraisbelgium.be***
France: ***http://www.feldenkrais-france.org***
Germany: ***https://www.feldenkrais.de***
Israel: ***http://www.feldenkrais-israel.org***
Italy: ***http://www.feldenkrais.it***
Mexico: ***http://www.feldenkraismexico.org***
New Zealand: ***http://www.feldenkrais.org.nz***
Niederlande: ***http://www.feldenkrais.nl***
North America: ***http://www.feldenkrais.com***
Norwegia: ***http://www.feldenkraismetoden.no***
Quebec: ***http://www.feldenkraisqc.info***

Spain: ***http://www.asociacionfeldenkrais.es***
Sweden: ***http://www.feldenkraismetoden.org***
Switzerland: ***http://www.feldenkrais.ch***
United Kingdom: ***http://www.feldenkrais.co.uk***

A LIST OF SOMATIC MOVEMENT PRACTICES THAT ARE REPRESENTED IN THIS VOLUME

http://www.labaninternational.org/c5
http://www.laban-eurolab.org
http://www.alexander-technik.org
http://www.alexandertechnique.com
http://hannasomatics.com
http://www.kleintechnique.com
https://www.gyrotonic.com
http://www.bodymindcentering.com
http://www.ideokinesis.com
http://heidivierthaler.com/streamflow-method
https://www.tamalpa.org

CONTRIBUTORS

JASON BEECHEY

has been the rector of the Palucca University of Dance Dresden in Germany since 2006. After training at Canada's National Ballet School, the Vaganova Ballet Academy in Saint Petersburg, and the School of American Ballet in New York City, he danced as a soloist for the London City Ballet, and then for fifteen years with Charleroi Danses in Belgium. Parallel to this, he was the pedagogical director for the National Choreographic Center of the French Community of Belgium, founded and ran his own studio, The Loft, and was the creator/coordinator of the D.A.N.C.E. Program under the artistic direction of Frédéric Flamand, William Forsythe, Wayne McGregor, and Angelin Preljocaj. Since joining the Prix de Lausanne as a member of the artistic committee in 2009, he continues his role there as an artistic advisor, and is also a regular jury member of the Youth America Grand Prix.

JÜRGEN VAN BUER

studied Romance Philology and Educational Science in Münster, Rome, and Göttingen. After receiving his doctorate from the University of Göttingen in 1980 and his habilitation from the Universität-Gesamthochschule Siegen in 1989, he was appointed chair in the Department of Business Education at the Humboldt University of Berlin in 1992. He held this position until his retirement in April 2016. Central to his work are research projects in the field of teaching and learning both in secondary school and university contexts, and the evaluative monitoring of pilot experiments and projects. This work has included conducting an evaluation at the Inter-University Centre for Dance in Berlin (HZT), expert monitoring of the BMBF-funded project, Diversity in Dialogue, at the University of the Arts in Berlin, and consultation for *InnoLernenTanz.* For his academic achievements, van Buer has been honored with numerous awards, including an honorary medal from Bessenyei University (Hungary), and an honorary doctorate from the University of National and World Economy in Sofia (Bulgaria). His photographic work has been exhibited internationally.

JAN BURKHARDT
is an independent dancer, choreographer, certified movement analyst, musician, and physiotherapist. His artistic and teaching practice focuses on the resonance of somatic exploration and how the communication of somatics unfolds in the dance space. Burkhardt cooperates internationally with diverse institutions and artists. Currently, he is an adjunct faculty member in university dance programs in Berlin, Stockholm, Copenhagen, and Cologne, and engages in artistic research with Laurent Chetouane, Sebastian Matthias, and Martin Nachbar.

JENNY COOGAN
is professor of contemporary dance at the Palucca University of Dance Dresden. After initial studies at Amherst College in Massachusetts (USA), she received a Bachelor of Fine Arts degree in dance from the Juilliard School in 1981. For the past thirty-five years, she has worked as a dance artist and educator, performing, choreographing, and teaching internationally. She was artistic director of the international touring ensemble, Coogan Dancers, from 1986 to 2000. Since 2010, she has directed the community dance ensemble, ArtRose. In 2001, she received certification as a teacher of the Feldenkrais Method, and is currently pursuing doctoral studies at Coventry University (UK). Her research interests are in somatics, the Feldenkrais Method, and intergenerational community dance practice.

LIBBY FARR
began her training in Texas and then continued her education at Ballet West and the School of American Ballet (both USA). She has performed in numerous companies, including the San Diego Ballet, Los Angeles Ballet, Dallas Ballet, Zurich Ballet, Deutsche Oper Berlin, Theater des Westens, and Tanz Theater Skoronel, as well as directing the dance department at Die Etage in Berlin. After working as a training director/dancer at the Deutsches Nationaltheater in Weimar for two years, she was the ballet mistress and assistant for Amanda Miller's company, Pretty Ugly. She is a regular guest teacher in P.A.R.T.S. in Belgium and the Salzburg Experimental Academy of Dance (SEAD) in Austria, and teaches companies throughout Europe. Farr is a certified Gyrokinesis teacher.

NINA PATRICIA HÄNEL

is a lecturer at the Center for Contemporary Dance at the University of Music and Dance in Cologne. From 2014 to 2016, she was a research associate in the domain of somatics within the *InnoLernenTanz* project. She holds a Diploma in dance from the Palucca University for Dance Dresden and a Master of Arts in Contemporary Dance Education *(Zeitgenössische Tanzpädagogik)* from the Frankfurt University of Music and Performing Arts. For more than 15 years, she has worked as a dancer, collaborating with a wide range of international choreographers. She is currently completing her training for certification as a Feldenkrais teacher, and is studying in the MA program in Dance Studies at the Free University of Berlin.

KARIN MUNTERS JAMESON

was educated at the University of Dance and Circus (DOCH) in Stockholm, Sweden, where she was awarded a Bachelor of Fine Arts degree in dance in 1984. She continued her dance studies in New York City, and in 1993 began studying the Klein Technique™ with Barbara Mahler and Susan Klein, receiving teacher certification in 2000. Jameson has been a freelance dance artist for more than 30 years, and since 2010 has been a senior lecturer in modern and contemporary dance at DOCH. She is a returning guest artist and coach at, among others, the Theater Academy of the University of the Arts in Helsinki, Cullberg Ballet in Stockholm, Ballet de Lorraine in Nancy, Danscentrum in Stockholm, and the Palucca University of Dance Dresden.

MATTHIAS MARKSTEIN

studied dance at the Palucca University of Dance Dresden. After graduating in 2001, he danced in a variety of companies in the works of Martin Stiefermann, Marguerite Donlon, Hans Henning Paar, Jiří Kilián, Rui Horta, Tero Saarinnen, and Constanza Macras, among others. He returned to the Palucca University, where he received a postgraduate degree in Dance Pedagogy, and was employed as an artistic associate at the same institution until the summer of 2016. Currently, he is working internationally as an independent dance artist and is enrolled in a certification program in Laban/Bartenieff Movement Studies.

KARIN MATKO

is a psychologist, yoga teacher, and researcher. She is currently pursuing her PhD in psychology, for which she is investigating differences between meditation techniques. In her research, she has been exploring measures that promote personal development with the help of creative, artistic, or spiritual processes. Dancing has been one of her favorite pastimes for almost ten years. For a year from October 2014, she was a research assistant in the *InnoLernenTanz* team, and was involved primarily in the case study. Matko lives and works in Dresden, where she regularly teaches yoga classes.

SUSANNE NARCISS

is a full professor and head of the research team Psychology of Learning and Instruction at the Dresden University of Technology (TU). This team is conducting theory-driven and design-based psychological research on issues related to lifelong learning and instruction with/within socio-technical systems. She received her PhD from Heidelberg University in 1993. From 1994 until March 2014, she worked at the TU in Dresden as an assistant and associate professor. From April 2014 until September 2015, she was a full professor of psychology at the University of Passau. Her current interests include research on promoting self-regulated learning, the role of motivation and metacognition in instructional contexts, and the conditions and effects of informative tutoring feedback. Her work on feedback strategies was considered cutting edge by the Association for Educational Communication and Technology (AECT), and was awarded the prestigious AECT Distinguished Development Award in 2007.

SHUMPEI NEMOTO

received his dance training in Japan and London, and danced professionally at the Royal Ballet, Deutsche Oper Am Rhein, and the Cullberg Ballet. He was awarded the Prix Jeune Espoir at the Prix de Lausanne in 1999, and second (2011) and third prize (2014) at the no ballet Choreography Competition in Ludwigshafen (Germany). Since 2010, he has worked internationally as a choreographer and teacher at, among others, SEAD (Austria), DOCH (Sweden), the Center for Contemporary Dance in Cologne (Germany), the National Conservatory Dance School in Lisbon, the Swedish Royal Ballet School, Norrdans (Sweden), the Cullberg Ballet's Carte Blanche, and the state theaters of Braunschweig and Kassel.

YUVAL PICK

is director of the Centre Chorégraphique National de Rillieux-la-Pape. He has had a long career as a choreographer, dancer, and teacher. He trained at the Bat-Dor Dance School in Tel Aviv, after which he joined the Batsheva Dance Company. He left to begin working with, among others, Tero Saarinen, Carolyn Carlson, and Russel Maliphant. In 1999, he joined the Lyon Opera Ballet, then founded his own company, The Guests. Since then, he has created a strong repertoire of works marked by their elaborate and layered movement vocabularies, which are accompanied by commissioned scores from renowned composers. In his work, the relationships between individuals and group(s) are often highlighted and challenged.

SARA REED

is currently head of performing arts at Coventry University in the United Kingdom. Following initial study at Trinity Laban and The Place (London), she worked as a freelance dance artist. Reed has an MA in Performing Arts from Middlesex University and a PhD from the University of Surrey. She has taught at Chichester University and the University of Surrey, where she led the professional dance practice. She has been director of dance at Dartington College of Arts, and acted as principal at the Northern School of Contemporary Dance in Leeds. Her research interests are in somatics, the Feldenkrais Method, physical literacy, the training/education of performers, and the development of creative practice. She continues to develop her experience and training within artistic, educational, health, and therapeutic contexts. Sara practices Scaravelli Yoga and is also a Feldenkrais practitioner.

GEORG REISCHL

began his dance training with Rosa Hartlieb in Salzburg and attended the Ballet School at the Vienna State Opera under the direction of Michael Birkmeyer. In 1993, he joined Liz King's ensemble in Heidelberg. Thereafter, Reischl danced for four years with the Scapino Ballet in Rotterdam. In 1999, Georg Reischl joined Ballet Frankfurt, where he experienced the repertoires and collaborative creative processes of William Forsythe. Since 2010, he works internationally as a choreographer and teacher.

JENNIFER ROCHE

is originally from Ireland, and is a lecturer in dance at Queensland University of Technology in Brisbane. Her research focuses on the creative practice of the contemporary dancer, and she explores and publishes on this subject from multiple perspectives, including philosophical, performative, and somatic. She has worked extensively as a dancer, was a founding member of the Fabulous Beast Dance Theater, and was artistic director of the Rex Levitates Dance Company in Ireland. She completed her PhD at Roehampton University in London in 2010. From 2007 to 2011, she was dance advisor to the Arts Council of Ireland. Palgrave Macmillan recently published her book, titled *Multiplicity, Embodiment, and the Contemporary Dancer: Moving Identities.*

JACOB STORER

trained at the University of Wisconsin–Stevens Point (USA) and at P.A.R.T.S. (Belgium). Storer is in a performance partnership with Theo Livesey under the name Amphigory, and has collaborated with Libby Farr by assisting in her classes and through their ongoing dialectic research on finding a more somatic approach to ballet and movement. Storer lives, creates, and performs in Brussels.

HEIDI VIELTHALER

is a dancer and has worked with some of the most prominent companies and choreographers throughout Europe and the USA, including the Gothenburg Opera Dance Company, Ballet Frankfurt, and The Forsythe Company. Currently, she teaches and creates works for companies, festivals, and universities worldwide. Her Stream-Flow method has been recognized as an effective somatic movement method that focuses on the individual, and her Amsterdam-based foundation Hato Projects ensures its constant growth. Hato's interdisciplinary collaborations across film and design attract a diverse audience, while simultaneously embracing a new community.

GABRIELE WITTMANN

writes about dance as a freelance journalist and critic for the German and Austrian public radio and television broadcaster ARD. She has been a guest lecturer at universities in Cologne, Salzburg, and Hamburg, as well as in China and India for the Goethe Institute/Max Mueller Bhavan. As a trainer, she teaches seminars on topics related to different forms of journalistic and poetic writing; as a researcher, she teaches dance history at the Frankfurt University of Music and Performing Arts, where she has also set up an international course that is situated between theory and practice called Creative Scientific Writing.

Kitchen-table talk participants

ALEXEI BERNARD
is from Australia. He completed his dance training at the Tanya Pearson Classical Coaching Academy, after which he continued his education at the Palucca University of Dance Dresden. In 2014, he was awarded the Esther Arnhold Seligmann scholarship, which enabled him to participate in the American Dance Festival as both a student and guest choreographer. In 2015, Bernard received a Bachelor of Arts in Dance and is currently working as a freelance dance artist in Germany with the JuWie Dance Company in Dresden, among others.

LUKE HAYWARD
is from Australia. He attended the Tanya Pearson Classical Coaching Academy and received a Bachelor of Arts in Dance, with honors, from the Palucca University of Dance Dresden in 2016. He was awarded the Ingrid Biederkopf Scholarship in 2016 for his choreographic piece *"Ich bin Fernweh."* Since September 2016, Luke dances with the Balet Moskva in Moscow, Russia.

VALERIA DANHAUSER
is from southern Germany. She attended the secondary school at the Palucca University of Dance Dresden, and continued her studies in the Bachelor of Arts Dance program at the same institution, from which she graduated in 2015. During her studies, she danced in the works of numerous guest choreographers, including Heidi Vielthaler and Ohad Naharin. Currently, Danhauser is studying German and Art History at the Dresden University of Technology.

NADJA GÜSEWELL
is from Stuttgart. In 2013, she began her pre-professional dance training at the Dance Academy of the Mannheim University of Music and Performing Arts. Güsewell is currently studying in the Bachelor of Arts program in Dance at the Palucca University of Dance Dresden, and will graduate in the summer of 2017.

SWANE KÜPPER
is from western Germany. She received her early dance training in the pre-professional dance program at Essen Werden High School. Currently, Swane is studying at the Palucca University of Dance Dresden, from where she will receive her Bachelor of Arts degree in Dance in 2017. In 2016, she was awarded the Esther Arnhold Seligmann scholarship, which enabled her to participate in the American Dance Festival as both a student and guest choreographer.

LARS REINSCHMIDT
was born in southern Germany. In 2008 he began his dance training at the San Jose Ballet School in California. In 2014, Lars graduated from the Palucca University of Dance Dresden with a Bachelor of Arts degree in Dance, where he danced in the works of choreographers such as Heidi Vielthaler and Ohad Naharin. He works internationally as an independent dance artist. Currently, Reinschmidt is teaching dance in Dresden at the TanzZentrum and the University of Technology.